THE KREISKY ERA IN AUSTRIA

ontemporary ustrian tudies

Sponsored by the University of New Orleans and Universität Innsbruck

Executive Editors
Erich Thöni, University of Innsbruck
Gordon H. Mueller, University of New Orleans

Editors
Anton Pelinka, University of Innsbruck
Günter Bischof, University of New Orleans, University of Munich

Assistant Editor
Irène Brameshuber

Production Editors
Robert L. Dupont
Gloria Alvarez

Copy Editor
Melanie McKay

Editorial Assistant
Ellen Palli

Designer
Allison D. Watling

Advisory Board

Felix Butschek
  Institute of Economic Research, Vienna
Wolfgang Danspeckgruber
  Princeton University
Peter Gerlich
  University of Vienna
David F. Good
  Director, Institute of Austrian Studies, University of Minnesota
Robert Jordan
  University of New Orleans
Robert H. Keyerslingk
  University of Ottawa
Radomir Luza
  Tulane University
Diemut Majer
  University of Berne
Andrei S. Markovits
  University of California, Santa Cruz

Sybil Milton
  United States Holocaust Memorial Council, Washington, D.C.
Hanspeter Neuhold
  University of Vienna and Director, Austrian Institute for International Politics, Laxenburg
Helga Nowotny
  University of Vienna
Michael Pollak (†)
  Institute of Contemporary History, National Center for Scientific Research, Paris
Peter Pulzer
  All Souls College, Oxford University
Rolf Steininger
  Director, Institute of Contemporary History, University of Innsbruck
Gerald Stourzh
  University of Vienna

Publication of this volume has been made possible through a generous grant from the Austrian Ministry of Foreign Affairs and the Austrian Cultural Institute in New York.
  Philip Lorio of Deutsch, Kerrigan & Stiles, the Austrian Honorary Consul of New Orleans, has also supported the publication.
  Konrad R. Müller has granted permission to publish his Kreisky portrait.

THE KREISKY ERA IN AUSTRIA

Contemporary Austrian Studies

Volume 2

Edited by
**Günter Bischof
Anton Pelinka**

Editorial Consultant
Oliver Rathkolb

Transaction Publishers
New Brunswick (U.S.A.) and London (U.K.)

Copyright © 1994 by Transaction Publishers, New Brunswick, New Jersey 08903.

All rights reserved under International and Pan-American Copyright Conventions. No part of this book may be reproduced or transmitted in any form or by any means, electronic or mechanical, including photocopy, recording, or any information storage and retrieval system, without prior permission in writing from the publisher. All inquiries should be addressed to Transaction Publishers, Rutgers—The State University, New Brunswick, New Jersey 08903.

Library of Congress Catalog Number: 93-22851
ISBN: 1-56000-705-2
Printed in the United States of America

Library of Congress Cataloging-in-Publication Data

The Kreisky era in Austria/edited by Günter Bischof, Anton Pelinka; editorial consultant, Oliver Rathkolb.
     p.   cm. (Contemporary Austrian studies: v. 2)
     Includes bibliographical references.
     ISBN 1-56000-705-2 (pbk.): $30.00
     1. Kreisky, Bruno. 2. Statesmen—Austria—Biography. 3. Austria—Politics and government 1945- I. Bischof, Günter, 1953- . II. Pelinka, Anton, 1941- . III. Series.
DB98.K7K74   1993
943.605—dc20   93-22851
                                                                             CIP

Table of Contents

Introduction by Günter Bischof ... 1

Topical Essays
Herbert Pierre Secher, *Kreisky and the Jews* ... 10
Otmar Höll, *The Foreign Policy of the Kreisky Era* ... 32
Peter Ulram, *Political Culture and Party System in the Kreisky Era* ... 78
Marina Fischer-Kowalski, *Social Change in the Kreisky Era* ... 96
Kurt W. Rothschild, *Austro-Keynesianism Reconsidered* ... 119
Oliver Rathkolb, *Bruno Kreisky: Perspectives of Top Level U.S. Foreign Policy Decision Makers, 1959-1983* ... 130

Non-Topical Essay
Susan Howell and Anton Pelinka, *Duke and Haider: Right Wing Politics in Comparison* ... 152

Forum
After the Central European Revolution of 1989: The Contemporary Meaning of Austrian Neutrality
Anton Pelinka, *Introduction* ... 172
Emil Brix, *The Position of Austria in the Architecture of Europe: The Quest for Identity* ... 175
Franz Cede, *The State Treaty and International Law* ... 183
Günter Nenning, *The 'Anschlußing' of Austria* ... 192
Josef Leidenfrost, *The State Treaty and Party Politics 1989-1992* ... 196

Review Essays
Peter Malina, *"Imagination Is More than Knowledge." Bruno Kreisky's Life as Biography* ... 205
John Haag, *Austrian Jews from Emancipation to Holocaust* ... 222

Book Reviews
Melanie Sully: Hans Dachs, Peter Gerlich et al., eds., *Handbuch des politischen Systems Österreichs* ... 238
Max Riedlsperger: Anton Pelinka and Fritz Plasser, eds., *The Austrian Party System* ... 241
Paul Luif: Thomas O. Schlesinger, *The United States and the European Neutrals* ... 245
Michael P. Steinberg: Gerald Stourzh, *Vom Reich zur Republik* ... 249

Annual Review of Austrian Politics
Rainer Nick and Sieghard Viertler, *Survey of Austrian Politics 1992* ... 252

Biographical Data of Bruno Kreisky ... 264

List of Authors ... 266

Bruno Kreisky
1911-1990

Introduction

Günter Bischof

I.

One day in the 1970s, while we were waiting for a roll call vote in the U.S. Senate, my longtime colleague Senator Edward Kennedy told me that the European leader who had most impressed him in recent years was Chancellor Bruno Kreisky of Austria. Since I was planning, as a member of the Senate Foreign Relations Committee, to lead a mission to Europe shortly, I asked for an appointment with Chancellor Kreisky on the basis of Senator Kennedy's appraisal.

The resulting conversation with Mr. Kreisky at his office in Vienna was no disappointment. I met with him on several subsequent visits to Austria, including two rather lengthy conversations at his home—the last visit taking place after he had completed his service as chancellor. I came to regard him as a counselor, an educator, an inspiration and a treasured friend. He had a combination of wisdom, experience, imagination, and historical perspective that is rare indeed among political leaders. He was the European statesman I most admired. He was also my source of tickets to the Salzburg music festival!

As the chairman of the Senate Subcommittee on the Middle East, I especially appreciated Kreisky's knowledge and insight relative to the Middle East. Although he was a Jew, he had the capacity to see the Arab-Israeli dispute with unusual objectivity. He believed that Israelis and Arabs could and should resolve their differences in practical negotiations that could result in a better life for all residents of the Middle East. He repeatedly attempted the role of moderator in encouraging such negotiations. He also lent his good offices to Arab-Israeli prisoner exchanges.

Kreisky combined realism with a strong sense of justice and compassion toward the people of the Middle East—especially the Palestinians. Vienna in the Kreisky era was a haven and transit point for Soviet Jews migrating to Israel. Kreisky shared their dreams of a life free of tyranny and discrimination. He also shared the special horror of Jews for Hitler's Holocaust. But he was capable of telling me one day in reference to an extremist Israeli politician that I should understand that "some Jews are fascists." The fact that they suffered terribly under Nazi rule has not immunized all Jews against the fascist virus, but some of them are hostile and indifferent to the Palestinians who also yearn for self-determination and an independent homeland.

Although his idealism gave him a special concern for the development needs of the Third World, detente and the necessity of East-West peace and cooperation, and the importance of economic and social justice for people around the world, Kreisky was also a political realist and pragmatist.

Mr. Kreisky and I also discussed the difference between American politics and the politics of the European democracies, especially the Social Democratic parties of Europe. He observed the blurred lines that separated Democrats from Republicans in the United States. He saw the essentially conservative or moderate guidelines which both of the major American parties followed—including their commitment to the "free market" and the dogmas of capitalism. He noted the virtual absence of a genuine political "left" in American politics as well as the rigid anti-communist, anti-Soviet postures of nearly all American politicians during the Cold War era.

Kreisky also shared my growing concern about the contemporary onslaught against American liberalism. Perhaps with the election of Bill Clinton as president in November 1992 the United States is entering a new era of liberal government.

George McGovern

George McGovern wrote this admiring cameo portrait of Bruno Kreisky's significance as Austrian and European statesman as an introduction to this volume. This description shows McGovern to be both a shrewd judge of men and a sound observer of statesmen. A historian by training, the Senator from the great American plains and 1972 presidential candidate has long been the Cold War liberal political and moral conscience of the U.S. Democratic Party. He succeeds in his brief sketch to outline some of the major themes of this collection of essays on Kreisky the man/statesman and his far-ranging cosmopolitan interests: 1) Kreisky's generally abiding passion for international affairs based on very high standards of justice and cooperation; 2) his particularly deep interest and wide experience in three of the great issues of the Cold War era—the Middle East, the Third World and East-West detente; 3) less explicitly, his ambivalent relationship with Israel and the Jews; 4) his realism and pragmatism in politics; 5) Kreisky's keen academic mind on most issues of political theory, comparative politics, and worries of his retirement years such as enlightened liberal welfare politics of a more prosperous era one day again coming under assault by anti-modern forces from the right.

Senator McGovern's trans-Atlantic perspective does not include observations on Austrian domestic politics, unless one takes his revelation of backchannels to Salzburg Festival tickets as a shrewd comment on how things work in Austria. Yet as these essays demonstrate, Kreisky's passions and interests ran similarly deep when it came to Austrian domestic politics. Like most successful politicians, Kreisky needed to be a pragmatist when it came to gaining and keeping power, which is not to say that he ever betrayed his socialist ideals. Kreisky's determination to elevate the poorer segments of Austrian society to middle-class comfort was proverbial. By furthering educational possibilities and expanding welfare state interference he succeeded in distributing wealth in Austria more equitably. In the process he also initiated a period of modernization in the Austrian economy and society comparable to the industrializing and modernizing spurt in World War II under the Nazi regime.

One of Kreisky's most lasting legacies may well have been his unbending determination to keep unemployment low, even at the price of high budget deficits and a ballooning national debt. Giving full employment such outstanding priority was surely based on a peculiar Austrian experience. Growing up in the depression-ridden 1930s with its high unemployment rates and deflationary politics, Kreisky (like the American Marshall planners) concluded that bad times and economic uncertainty open the flood gates for the popular appeal of political radicalism on either side of the political spectrum. In the final years of his life, Kreisky spent much of his energy on the study of international unemployment patterns. The insights of the final report of the International Kreisky Commission on Unemployment may well be more relevant today, when unemployment is growing around the world, than they were during the prosperous 1980s when the report was written.

II.

The individual essays in this volume try to suggest themes and a framework for a first solid scholarly assessment of Kreisky's life and times. They mainly cover the culmination of Kreisky's political career, the time of his chancellorship (1970-1983) which can be termed the "Kreisky era." The earlier chapters in his political career are only touched in passing.

Pierre Secher's essay tackles probably the most difficult and darkest chapter in any Kreisky biography—his ambivalent and often confrontational relationship with his own Jewishness, Jews and Israel. As a young man in his Swedish exile during World War II, Kreisky took care of Austrian POWs who were in the SS, but he showed no special interest at the time in the victims of the Holocaust, despite the fact that more than twenty members of his own family perished as victims themselves. As chancellor he was unapologetic about appointing four former "Nazis" (one Waffen-SS) to his first Cabinet of eleven ministers. He doggedly defended the leader of the "liberal" party, Friedrich Peter, who happened to serve in an SS extermination squad in the East during World War II, because the FPÖ balanced the Austrian party spectrum and might have served as a coalition partner (as it did for a Socialist government in the 1980s). While he protected Peter, he started an unsavory personal vendetta against the highly-respected Nazi-hunter Simon Wiesenthal, whose dogged research brought Peter's past to Kreisky's and the world's attention. Kreisky's verbal assaults on Menachem Begin created an international incident. Secher concludes: "Kreisky was truly a child of his time: the time of the alienated Jew who until the appearance of Hitler could no more than conceive of Auschwitz than of a state by Jews."

Secher also might have added that Kreisky's approach towards *Vergangenheitsbewältigung*—Austrians' role in World War II—was as strangely uncritical and superficial as that of his predecessors. Kreisky never publicly questioned the mythology of the "rape" of Austria in 1938 and Austria's "victim" ideology as enshrined in the Moscow Declaration of 1943. Socialist Chancellor Franz Vranitzky, in the wake of the international damage done to Austria during the extended Waldheim crisis, made a public statement in the Austrian parliament in July 1992 noting that Austrians were not only victims of Hitler's *Anschluß* but also perpetrators of war crimes in the Nazi killing machine. Such an admission had been long overdue—many Austrians did more than "their duty" in Hitler's *Wehrmacht*.

Otmar Höll presents a summary and analysis of possibly the most brilliant chapter in Kreisky's long and distinguished career—his long-standing involvement in Austrian foreign policy and Cold War international affairs. As undersecretary of state in the Austrian Foreign Office (1953-59), Kreisky was instrumental in securing the State Treaty in 1955 and subsequently in helping define Austrian neutrality. As foreign minister in ÖVP/SPÖ coalition governments he shaped *active* Austrian neutrality policy and relentlessly labored towards achieving East-West detente and an end to the nuclear arms race. Way ahead of time, he probed the possiblities of Austrian economic integration in the West by joining the EC. As Austrian chancellor (1979-83), he barnstormed through the world working toward solidifying East-West detente, introducing the Palestinians into the Middle East peace process with his controversial recognition of the PLO, and pushing the capitalist West to be more generous to the increasingly troubled Third World economies.

The changes in Austrian political culture alone may justify the term "Kreisky era" for the 1970s, as *Peter Ulram* shows. The rapid economic modernization, secularization and liberalization, along with improved economic opportunities and a decline in *Lagermentalität*, higher voter mobility and grass-roots political participation transformed the *mentalite* of Austrian politics. In the Kreisky era, Austrians increasingly expected state interventionism to guarantee their high standard of living, yet at the same time were highly critical when it came to responsiveness and moral behavior of their political elite. Quite paradoxically, Austrians managed to trust their politicians while charging the political class with ignoring people's needs. This period of "social-liberal consensus," as Ulram characterizes it, was replaced by a "political culture of malaise" in the 1980s.

Marina Fischer-Kowalski and *Kurt Rothschild* present the evidence for the significant changes Kreisky effected in the 1970s in the social and economic spheres. Fischer-Kowalski outlines how Kreisky's modernizing policies with regard to the family and labor were informed by massive social science research; more than that, Kreisky's keen mind actively solicited the input of what could be termed Austria's "best and brightest." In Kreisky's vision of an egalitarian middle-class society, marriages, children and women were actively supported; oddly enough, in the deeply Catholic Austria it was a Socialist chancellor who thus rang in the "golden age" of the family. Kreisky also made sure that expanding educational opportunities allowed more blue collar workers to move into middle-class white collar jobs. Kreisky's full employment policies were wildly successful; with 2 percent, Austria consistently figured at the low end of OECD unemployment averages. Rothschild characterizes "Austro-Keynesianism"—the economic instruments used to achieve high production and full employment. Austria was diving through recessions all around her by way of accepting budget deficits and high public debt. At the same time, shrewd exchange rate and income policies, along with stable wage and price controls steered by the uniquely Austro-corporatist model of the Social Partnership, kept inflation down and international competitiveness up. What does this modernizing spurt add up to in Fischer-Kowalski's conclusion? "Kreisky was the last emperor of good old modern society in Austria"!

Oliver Rathkolb deepens McGovern's assessment of Kreisky as widely-respected European statesman in the Cold War era frequently consulted by American statesmen. Kreisky personally knew the American presidents from Truman to Bush and had something to offer to each one of them. Kennedy, Nixon and Ford recognized Kreisky's personal efforts at building East-West detente and cooperation as well as furthering the Middle Eastern peace process by way of facilitating communications through Vienna and Salzburg summitry. Jimmy Carter was less enthusiastic about Kreisky's position on the Palestinians; Carter still utilized the neutral Vienna venue to sign the temporarily ill-fated SALT-II treaty with Breshnev. Reagan, on the other hand, clearly did not appreciate Kreisky's boldly reminding his administration of the inherent hypocrisy of busting unions at home while egging on the Polish Solidarity movement for Cold War reasons abroad. Whether the American leaders hated Kreisky or stood in awe of his independence of mind, they all respected him as an unusually brilliant statesman from a small country, as Rathkolb shows with rich new evidence from American archives and Kreisky's own personal papers.

The rest of this volume treats subject matters that Kreisky fully engaged in during his lifetime. As McGovern indicates above, Kreisky also worried about the decline of liberal politics and thus implicitly about the rise of the anti-modern politics of xenophobic fear and race. In this volume's non-topical, essay *Susan Howell* and *Anton Pelinka* utilize the long-standing and close cooperation between the political science departments of the University of New Orleans and the University of Innsbruck by marshalling the available empirical evidence on two continents for a remarkably tight argument on the differences and similarities of the two rabid populists David Duke in Louisiana and Jörg Haider in Austria. Both have appealed to the angry young men on the right of the political spectrum to gain power. While a mercurial Pat Buchanan snatched away the more disaffected conservatives from Duke in the 1992 presidential primaries, which may well have spelled the end to Duke's political career, the most recent development in Austria, not mentioned in the Howell-Pelinka essay, is the break-up of the FPÖ due to Haider's overreaching xenophopbia. In February the liberal wing under Heide Schmid broke away from Haider and formed the "liberal forum." Whether this bolting of the liberals from the FPÖ will spell the beginning of the end of "Haiderism" remains to be seen. It is hard to see how Haider will make political hay with the dying breed of old Nazis, blue-collar workers, skinheads and Austro-yuppies looking for a smashing young hero.

For the first time *CAS* presents a "forum" and hopes to make this a regular feature of informed contemporary political discourse in and on Austria. The question of the future of Austrian neutrality and the contemporary validity of the Austrian State Treaty of 1955 is a highly relevant one and has already been debated in volume I. The diplomats *Emil Brix* and *Franz Cede* review the pros and cons of the relative obsolescence of the State Treaty and neutrality from the perspective of the international environment and international law. The disappearance of the Soviet Union as one of the principal signatories to the State Treaty has widely affected the experts' interpretation of the State Treaty's relevance today. At the same time, the State Treaty and neutrality are still widely popular in Austria and have become psychologically important props to the Austrian identity. While neutrality may indeed be obsolete in the changed international environment, the State Treaty as an international legal instrument has to be cleaned of outdated provisions but cannot be cast away like an old pair of shoes. Among many other features, given the absence of an *Anschluß-Verbot* in the German 2+4 treaty, the prohibition of *Anschluß* in the State Treaty still has significance, namely to state unambiguously Austria's exclusion from Germany, as Brix points out. *Günter Nenning*, the grand old man of Austrian journalism, would probably agree with this conclusion. His essay, full of his characteristic ironic language, is an outcry against the foolishness of Austrian politicians and pundits, who in their rush toward Brussels and EC integration, are intent on casting Austrian neutrality aside like an old shirt; in the process they are oblivious to the real enemy, which in Nenning's mind lies waiting in Bonn/Berlin. *Josef Leidenfrost* rounds out the picture by casting Austria into the field of conflicting geostrategic gravitational pulls and outlining the domestic partisan debate on neutrality.

The two review essays by *Peter Malina* and *John Haag* are particularly interesting as future building blocks for an authoritative Kreisky biography. Malina's historiographical essay ably summarizes the already considerable body of Kreisky literature; Malina outlines the themes and a framework for future biographers. He surely is right in stressing how much

Kreisky's life is quintessentially tied to the ups and downs of Austrian politics since 1945. Any serious biography on Kreisky's "life and times" will also have to assess the Second Republic.

To figure out the deeper recesses of Kreisky's mind and the subtler layers of his subconsious, one needs to penetrate the uniquely rich history of Jewish Vienna, as Haag demonstrates so penetratingly in his review of the recent literature on this topic. The epochal modernizing departures of *fin-de-siècle* Jewish Vienna ring in the birth of both racialist anti-Semitism and Zionism. The travails of Jewish emancipation, assimilation and acculturation in the deeply divided Vienna Jewish community provide the background for Kreisky's life as well. The anti-Semitism of the interwar Social Democratic party and the fear of not being perceived as a *Judenschutztruppe*, of course, constitutes an intimate chapter in Kreisky's biography. A psycho-biographer would find a motherlode of interesting material in Kreisky's Jewish heritage and his self-denial of some of this past, as Secher indicates in his lead essay.

Some book reviews and the annual review of Austrian politics close out this volume.

III.

There can be little doubt: no Austrian political leader of the postwar era left such a strong personal impression on the times of his stewardship of the nation as did Kreisky. Certainly none of the chancellors of the Second Republic came close to building an international reputation of Kreisky's caliber. Due to the Near Eastern crises (Yom Kippur War), and Far Eastern Cold War entanglements (Vietnam, Cambodia), as well as the oil shocks, the beginning economic decline, and the domestic political and psychological crises due to Watergate, the 1970s have entered the American history books as an era of "malaise." This cannot be said of Austria, unless one takes the perspective of the political opposition who would like to see the malaise of the 1980s as a legacy of Kreisky's policies. Due to Kreisky's expansion of the welfare state at home and his active foreign policy abroad, many people are wont to remember the 1970s in Austria as "golden years."

Kreisky's ambitions at times may have outdistanced the more provincial minds in Austria. Many a cautious expert, political opponent and observer from abroad never forgave Kreisky for his consorting with Arafat and his stunning invitation of Ghadaffi. From the Arab perspective, however, this may well have made him one of the few Western statesmen who took them seriously by treating them as equals to the Israelis. The peace process initiated by Bush's Secretary of State, James Baker, seems to be predicated on such ideas of Arab and Palestinian equality on the round table. The current snail's pace of these Middle Eastern negotiations may well indicate that Kreisky's bold ideas will take further time before being acceptable. With his creative ideas Kreisky often was a man ahead of his times.

If this volume could spur on future research on Kreisky and his era, the editors would be more than pleased. Many topics await the careful researcher. If the current antiquated archival opening practices of the Austrian State Archives are an indicator, it will take years (or decades) before some of the final answers may be given. On the other hand, like American presidents, Kreisky is the only Austrian statesman who set up a foundation in his lifetime to house his and his associates' personal papers for future researchers. These personal records provide early insights into his policies, as Oliver Rathkolb suggests in his essays in this and *CAS*'s first volumes. Kreisky cared enough about his historical image and legacy to leave us two rich volumes of memoirs (unfortunately, he passed away before he could tackle the volumes(s) on the culmination of his political career—the crucial period of his chancellorship).

When we consider the stupendous biographical literature on Truman, Eisenhower, Kennedy, Johnson and Nixon, with some of America's best historians and biographers at work, it is astounding that none of Austria's postwar chancellors (Renner, Figl, Raab, Klaus) have found careful academic biographers. This may be due to a number of reasons: lack of personal records; Austria's backward archival opening practices; a neglect of the biographical approach in current Austrian historiography; or simply the gingerness (*Berührungsängste*) of historians to tackle figures involved in "Austro-fascism" or who personally suffered in Hitler's camps and in exile during World War II.

With Kreisky, Austria produced a figure of major historical significance. Together with his intimate friends Olof Palme of Sweden and Willy Brandt of Germany, Bruno Kreisky may well be considered one day a "wise man" among European leaders in the Cold War era, as I have suggested on other occasions. For this trio of Socialist statesmen tried to mediate and defuse the rigid tensions of the Cold War and the dangerous nuclear arms race more doggedly than most other Western leaders. If the George Kennans and Robert Lovetts are termed the "wise men" who defined America's position in the Cold War, Kreisky, Palme and Brandt surely will figure as the wise men of detente—of easing Cold War tensions. If nothing else, such a legacy of international cooperation, facilitated by small and middling powers, surely ought to be remembered in the post-Cold War world.

Munich, April 1993

Kreisky and the Jews

Herbert Pierre Secher

In April 1970 Dr. Bruno Kreisky was sworn in as chancellor of the republic of Austria. Kreisky had been chairman of the Socialist Party of Austria (*Sozialistische Partei Österreichs*, SPÖ) since 1967 and had fled Austria in 1938 to escape Nazi persecution as a Jew. It was the first time the Socialist Party governed alone, albeit as a minority government.

It was also the first time that a Jew governed a German-speaking country, and especially one reputed to have been an enthusiastic supporter of the Hitler regime. After the election of 1 March it had been assumed that the SPÖ would again turn to the other major party, the Austrian People's Party (*Österreichische Volkpartei*, ÖVP) to form the coalition that had governed Austria successfully for 20 years until 1966. But Kreisky, who had long since anticipated such a situation, temporized for several weeks until he could assure himself that the third and smallest party, the Austrian Freedom Party (*Freiheitliche Partei Österreichs*, FPÖ), would not join the other conservative party in a challenge to his minority government. Despite its economic liberalism, the chief support of the FPÖ came from right wing groups whose attachment to German nationalist, even Neo-Nazi programs and slogans, was well known.

Therefore, the chances of a Socialist party leader with widely publicized Jewish antecedents reaching out successfully to this party were generally discounted. But Dr. Kreisky, whose rise in the Socialist party hierarchy had run counter to a fairly well-known anti-Semitism within that party, had apparently achieved the impossible: when he presented his government to parliament, the FPÖ not only refrained from mounting the obvious challenge but received the Kreisky government with unrestrained enthusiasm. What had happened to make this political 'coup' possible?

Historically, there had always been a tripartite division of Austrian politics dating back to the monarchy: the Catholic conservative Right, the German-Nationalist Right and the Left Social Democracy.[1] During the monarchy, both Christian Socials and German Nationalists had shared in an all-pervasive anti-Semitism directed equally against the allegedly Jewish dominance in the world of finance and the perceived Jewish influence on the professional and cultural life of the nation. In the First Republic, only the German Nationalists continued this political anti-Semitism; for the Christian Socials the teachings of Catholic social theory outweighed any immediate benefits to be gained from an open advocacy of political anti-Semitism. The Social Democrats, steeped in Marxist rejection of religion and clericalism, nevertheless viewed anti-Semitism as the "socialism of simpletons," implying that scapegoating the Jews would not by itself get rid of the evils of capitalism. Politically conscious Jews mainly turned to the Social Democrats since such awareness normally also coincided with a loosening of ties with the religion of their fathers. Many such former Jews achieved positions of prominence in the party (SDAP, *Sozialdemokratische Arbeiter Partei*), but their 'Jewishness' became an issue only after the failure of the 1934 uprising in which an overly cautious leadership, many of them Jewish, did not live up to the revolutionary expectations of its rank and file following. While trying to avoid violence, this SDAP leadership was held responsible for heavy casualties among the party militants who resisted the onslaught by government troops with only inadequate mobilization of both human and material resources. It was after this doomed uprising in February 1934 that a deep, common hatred of the conservative Catholic regime began to unite Socialist and Nationalist forces, thereby paving the way for Hitler's annexation of Austria in 1938.[2]

During the years from 1934 to 1938 when both Socialists (Sozis) and National Socialists (Nazis) were prohibited from openly pursuing their goals via the instrumentalities of their respective political parties, individuals in either rank frequently established bonds with each other in the face of the common enemy, and especially so when they shared the same prison cell. One of these individuals was Bruno Kreisky, whose illegal activities on behalf of his party, renamed Revolutionary Socialists (RS) during its clandestine period, had earned him a prison sentence for high treason. There, in the artificial atmosphere of prison solidarity, the young Kreisky managed to earn the respect of a number of Nazis who, like him, had been convicted for illegal activities against the government. One in particular proved to be so appreciative of a service rendered him by Kreisky that he managed to obtain Kreisky's release from the Gestapo in 1938 shortly after the installation of the Nazi regime in Austria.³ Kreisky left Vienna in September 1938, before Munich, before *Reichskristallnacht*, with a valid German passport unmarked by a "J" to identify him as a Jew. His parents remained in Vienna, but he was able to help them emigrate to Sweden in 1940 and thereby escape the deportations to Poland that were moving into high gear about that time.

In Sweden, Kreisky did not consider himself a Jewish or, for that matter, an Austrian-Jewish refugee. He viewed himself as a Socialist who was temporarily prevented by his 'Jewish origins' from carrying out his political mission within the borders of his native state. Kreisky was proud of his opposition to a weak, despicable Austrian political regime that had landed him in prison. His brief encounter with the brutality of the Third Reich only reinforced his political convictions.⁴ He had left Austria defiantly, with his head held high, always surrounded by loyal, trusting friends as well as a caring, loving family. His *Weltanschauung* was intact, and he was confident that the international Socialist movement would not overlook him. Despite the setbacks administered to it by a rising fascism, the Socialist International was still a movement to be reckoned with, and Kreisky's organizational competence, idealism and proven loyalty showed that he could be depended on to work for the cause under the most adverse of circumstances.

Kreisky did indeed make a name for himself in Austrian Social Democratic emigré circles; but he never quite moved into the forefront of the SI during the war years. Possibly this failure was due to his having learned in Sweden the politics of compromise as well as the need for solid popular support for even the most beneficial social welfare policies. He began to see the future of socialism in his native country only in a solid alliance with old fashioned Austrian patriotism.⁵ Consequently, this was the direction into which most of his plans and actions turned. In Sweden, at the end of the war and afterward, he worked indefatigably to provide relief programs for Austrian children. Earlier he had organized aid for German prisoners of war who had escaped their Russian captors, if they could prove that they were Austrian rather than *Reichsdeutsch*. He made no distinction between members of the *Wehrmacht* and those of the *Waffen-SS*. His goal was to establish an emigré 'rainbow coalition' of former Socialist trade unionists, Catholic conservatives, and farmers in order to obtain recognition from the Allied powers as a government-in-exile. In this effort he was in competition with the London-based contingent of Socialist emigrés still steeped in the ideas of a more sharply defined class struggle and rather indifferent to attempts to revive the defunct first republic. Kreisky doubted that the London group, which consisted mostly of the old Jewish SDAP leadership, could command much attention from those who had chosen to remain in their homeland after it became part of Hitler's Germany and were now in the process of rebuilding the party.[6]

Presumably, he did not see the irony of working day and night for the release and favored treatment of members of the German military while those whose 'Jewish origins' he shared were roaming Europe, together with other 'displaced persons' by the tens of thousands, in search for food and shelter. He certainly was aware of the horrible consequences of Nazi persecution of the Jews and had learned of the fate of his relatives, at least twenty of whom died in extermination camps. But Kreisky's *Weltanschauung* was still much too secure and confident at that time to engage in any kind of sentimental self-analysis. If anything, it reinforced his conviction that only his socialist ideal could create a better world in which such horrors would not be repeated. Possibly, Kreisky considered the Jews' victimization a result of their failure to understand that the old fundamentals such as religion were no longer applicable in a world that was dying all around them. Even though later Kreisky would frequently refer to his perished relatives as proof that he had not been left untouched by the horrors of the Holocaust, at the time when these horrors were first revealed he appeared to have little interest in them.

His personal life in Sweden represents an interesting dichotomy in this respect. He had married the very charming and attractive daughter of a wealthy Jewish-Swedish businessman who himself had been an Austrian emigrant early in the century. Soon after his arrival in Stockholm, Kreisky was able to obtain a materially and ideologically satisfying job in a consumer cooperative. He also worked as a journalist, and he had access to a wide circle of influential people in government and business, several of whom were Jewish. Thus as an emigrant, Kreisky had succeeded in making the difficult leap toward acceptance within a different civic and political culture—yet always in the context of his cherished socialist ideas. He was adaptable in every respect except one: he refused to forget his Austrian social democratic roots since they were the conceptual framework in which he had grown to maturity. He had jettisoned Judaism long ago when as a 16-year-old he had his name removed from the rolls of the Viennese Jewish Federation (*Kultusgemeinde*). Even before that, given the total assimilation of his parents, his contact with the religious side of Judaism was hardly significant. It is clear from most of his writings that being a Jew was for him never an existential question but rather one of purely personal and cultural preference. Consequently, he always looked to his Austrian roots as the determinant factor in fashioning his personal and political goals. Later, in his memoirs and interviews he liked to boast of his genealogy on his mother's side, which could be traced all the way back to the Thirty Years War and showed his ancestors as loyal Austrian subjects, albeit of 'the Jewish persuasion.'[7]

Kreisky was fiercely defensive not only of his Austrian identity but also of all attempts to decry Austria as forever tainted by its Nazi past. After the war, during his service as a low-ranking diplomat in Austria's Stockholm embassy, Kreisky at one time considered himself importuned by a reporter who invariably portrayed Austria in an unfavorable light. His patience having reached the breaking point, he invited his caller, over the phone, to commit an obscene act.[8] This incident had no bearing on Kreisky's future career as a public servant, but it does take on significance when looked at in the light of other, later encounters by Kreisky with individuals critical of him. In the letter complaining to the Foreign Ministry about Kreisky's undiplomatic invitation, the writer admits to his critical reporting but insists that it is not always easy to write objectively about a country that, knowingly and quite enthusiastically had been part of Hitler's war machine. This consideration must have surfaced occasionally in Kreisky's consciousness as well. Thus, when Kreisky was confronted by someone who raised this issue, even only inferentially, with all its moral and ethical dimensions, he would explode beyond reason and become abusive as he did toward his caller in 1949, and again much later, in 1975, when he publicly accused Simon Wiesenthal of being a Nazi collaborator. By the time the war ended and with it his status as a refugee, Kreisky had recognized that at times even his socialism would have to yield priority to his Austrian identity and that specifically Jewish concerns would no longer play any role in his intellectual framework. He had earlier refused the request of his bride's parents to be married in the traditional Jewish manner, insisting emphatically on only a civil ceremony; neither the birth of their son Peter—who was not circumcised—nor that of their daughter, Susan—raised any questions of religious observance or identity.[9] Kreisky's secular agnosticism, and presumably that of his wife, Vera, was obviously firmly in place.

Thus, even though the man who was sworn in as the first Socialist chancellor of the Second Austrian Republic had never made any secret of his Jewish origins, it would have distorted his ideological framework to single out 'Jewishness' as part of his political identity. Yet it will always be a subject for speculation how others perceived Kreisky in the context of his religious as well as political background. The man who entered the Social Democratic Party of Austria as an activist at the age of 13 and worked his way up the ladder of the party *apparat* as a talented organizer was elected at the age of 22 to the position of director of its Youth Education Program. Ignoring risks, he followed the party into illegality, an action that resulted in his being convicted of high treason and sentenced to prison at the age of 25.[10]

For six years after war, he could not return to Austria with any expectations of again serving the party. Instead, Kreisky was sidetracked into the diplomatic service at a fairly low rank with very little hope of serving any place other than in Stockholm, where his contacts were considered most useful to the newly established Austrian republic.[11] Fortunately, Kreisky did have a small but very loyal support group of party comrades with whom he had shared the halcyon days of the movement in 'Red' Vienna before the war and who managed to keep his name alive somehow on the patronage rosters of the hierarchy. Eventually, shortly before his fortieth birthday, an opening occurred in Vienna in a minor office within the Economic Policy Division of the Federal Chancellery. The Socialist vice-chancellor, who was also chairman of the SPÖ, could finally be persuaded to 'bring Kreisky home' to Vienna. Whether it was outright anti-Semitism or just the fear of anti-Semitic reaction that kept Kreisky away for so long from the inner circle of Austrian Socialist politics would be difficult to determine—and might also be irrelevant in this context. To be sure, he had made enemies during the war years when first espousing the cause of Austrian independence; his attempts at a 'rainbow coalition' had appeared to some as a benign way of pacifying the Communists at a time when Socialist policies dictated a much more uncompromising stand against the Communist Party. But undeniably, the party leadership under Adolf Schärf as vice-chancellor and party chairman was wary of putting someone of well-known 'Jewish origins' into an exposed party post at a time when the road to an absolute majority lay only in the chiefly Protestant, German-Nationalist, indeed ex-Nazi voter pool to the right. Most probably it was a combination of all these factors plus the keen competition for top party positions in the immediate post-war years among aspirants of the old SDAP who had survived the war at home. Moreover, Kreisky's versatility, academic credentials, and proficiency in foreign languages made him an ideal choice for maintaining a small but firm foothold in that previously off-limits diplomatic service. Thus, there were a variety of reasons why he encountered such difficulties in obtaining a position that measured up to his political expectations. Anti-Semitism was a constant, if not necessarily a decisive, factor.[12]

The man chiefly responsible for keeping Kreisky 'politically alive' was Franz Olah. The two were bound by a close friendship that went back to their work as district captains for the SAJ (*Sozialistische Arbeiterjugend*, Socialist Workers Youth) during the 1930s. Olah had spent seven years in Dachau from which he returned at the end of the war to resume his political career. By the time Kreisky arrived in Vienna, Olah had already established a solid power base that cut across party and trade union lines with clear aspirations for leadership of the party and the country.[13] They both recognized that the SPÖ had to be pried loose from its Austro-Marxist moorings and guided toward the right if it intended to gain an absolute majority. The friendship between these two very complex and in many respects different personalities holds the key to Kreisky's later political success. Though there is no written record to that effect, many close to Kreisky insist that he had no illusions following his return to Vienna about overcoming anti-Semitic prejudices sufficiently to carve out a major position in the party hierarchy.[14] Yet by attaching himself closely to Olah's political aims he hoped to be able to minimize this obstacle. Olah's goal was to keep the SPÖ's options open by making sure that the small third party, the FPÖ, would be kept organizationally alive by diverting to it large sums of money from trade union funds under his control.[15] To provide further guarantees for the FPÖ's political future, he promised to bring about a change in the electoral laws, which discriminated heavily against the representation of small parties in parliament. Olah's machinations were bitterly opposed within the party, but Kreisky stood solidly with Olah in this intra-party struggle. It was a struggle that Olah could well have won had it not been that his unbounded ambition had urged him to concentrate as much power as possible in his own hands. Possessed of a brusque, frequently vulgar, and at times even brutal personality, he managed to antagonize both friends and foes in his quest for absolute power. Once installed as Minister of the Interior in the last coalition cabinet, Olah overreached himself. He used that post to assure the neo-Nazis in the FPÖ that their pre-1945 record in Hitler's political machine would no longer constitute a threat to them after Olah assumed the chancellorship.[16] That was too much even for an opportunistic SPÖ leadership; it closed ranks, succeeded in having Olah removed from his cabinet post and within a few weeks expelled from the SPÖ. It was the 'Olah Affair' that contributed heavily to the SPÖ's defeat in the 1966 election. Kreisky stood by his fallen comrade to the last and disavowed him only when, during the election campaign of 1966 Olah formed his own party, which, echoing the disruptive politics of the First Republic began to inject hatred, suspicion, brutality, and overt anti-Semitism into the political contest.[17] Surprisingly enough, Kreisky managed to survive the SPÖ's defeat with his political integrity intact (he had, after all, served successfully as Foreign Minister since 1959 with policies that had gained Austria international respect) and in control of the political power base that Olah had bequeathed to him. Thus, Kreisky emerged at the 1967 Annual Party Congress as the compromise candidate for the party stewardship who was expected to lead the party to victory in 1970.

At the meeting of the 1967 Party Congress in which Kreisky was elected to the Chairmanship of the Austrian SPÖ, few could match Kreisky's governmental experience and moderate political views. Nevertheless, Kreisky's election to the all-important post of party leader was far from being a foregone conclusion. Kreisky himself, when first approached on that subject, displayed a becoming reticence, freely admitting that the Austrian voter might still be reluctant to elect someone of his 'Jewish origins', and that, consequently, he did not want to be a liability to his party's efforts at regaining its dominant position in government.[18] Indeed, when Kreisky's name was submitted in nomination at the Annual Party Congress in February 1967, the motion gave rise to a most acrimonious debate concerning his person and credentials. Cutting references were made to his highly non-proletarian background, raising at least by innuendo his 'Jewish origins.'[19] Kreisky's personal popularity and his immaculate record in a party that had just undergone the most wrenching experience of its political existence carried Kreisky to victory as party leader. But many, including Kreisky, knew that had it not been for his ignominious expulsion, Olah would have been standing where Kreisky now stood. It was far from a unanimous decision; indeed it may have been the most lopsided vote by which a leader had ever been elected in the Austrian Socialist party.

From the foregoing it should be clear that the chancellor-designate's reaching out to the third party after the election of 1970, instead of reinstating the time-honored coalition with the People's Party, did not require any great leap of political imagination. Olah and Kreisky had anticipated such a situation much earlier, though few in Kreisky's own party and even fewer in the major opposition party really believed that Kreisky—not the least because of his 'Jewish origins'—would take such a step. However Kreisky, by-passing the time-honored coalition, instead turned to the strategy of a minority government, which required only the tacit cooperation of the third party. He entered into a written agreement with Friedrich Peter, FPÖ chairman, in which the SPÖ pledged to fulfill conditions posed by the FPÖ in return for that party's promise not to join with the ÖVP in a vote bringing down the minority government. Foremost among these conditions was the change in the electoral law that had acted as a restraint on the size of the parliamentary representation of small parties. Soon after Kreisky's minority government assumed office, the new electoral law was passed easily with the combined votes of the SPÖ and FPÖ. The reform saved the FPÖ from disappearing as a parliamentary party and many years later actually enabled the Green Party to enter parliament. If Kreisky at the time had difficulty in overcoming any moral scruples about the Nazi past of much of the FPÖ leadership, he certainly kept such doubts to himself. It is likely that he did not, because, as he let it be known repeatedly, that party represented primarily the liberal and anti-clerical wing of the middle classes. Since the new program of the SPÖ adopted in 1958 had already infused the concept of the social welfare state with a generous dose of free enterprise capitalism, Kreisky saw no reason to stay aloof from the FPÖ or, worse, to regard it as an outcast in the democratic state. In fact, he was even then certain that the FPÖ, strengthened in its economic liberalism, would emerge as the tolerant partner of the Socialists, much like the situation Kreisky had observed during his years in Sweden. Kreisky failed to see that the historical antecedents of such cooperation—including a shared religious background—were hardly the same in Austria as in Sweden. Furthermore, he dismissed the German-Nationalist element in the FPÖ as a factor in determining that party's political direction. For the immediate future however, Kreisky's strategy paid off handsomely. Left to develop and apply without interference his liberal economic and social program, which did not neglect the interests of small businesses and farmers that formed the mainstay of the FPÖ, Kreisky was able to call for another election much sooner than the opposition had anticipated. That election of 10 October 1971 was a personal triumph for Kreisky. For the first time in the history of the First and Second Republic of Austria a socialist party received more than 50 percent of the popular vote and an absolute majority of seats in parliament. In the United States, the *New York Times* hailed the Austrian vote as confirmation "that anti-Semitism had ceased to be a decisive factor in Austrian politics." [20]

But Kreisky was less worried about anti-Semitism as a factor than making clear his intention to leave the time of recrimination and discrimination behind. Such reassurance was important to the nearly one-third of the population which, at one time or another, had actively supported the Hitler regime until its ignominious defeat. Shortly after the new chancellor had announced in April 1970 the cabinet appointments to his first and minority government, the Jewish Documentation Center in Vienna, headed by Simon Wiesenthal revealed that four out of the eleven cabinet positions were held by former members of the NSDAP (*Nationalsozialistische Deutsche Arbeiter Partei*, National Socialist German Workers Party), better known as the Nazi Party.[21] Former members of that party had been accepted before into positions of responsibility after the Second Republic had achieved its full independence following the withdrawal of the Allied occupation troops. But this was the first time that Nazi party membership could be found among those of cabinet rank. One of these cabinet members, Hans Öllinger, Minister of Agriculture, had also been a member of the Waffen-SS during the war, in a unit that had engaged in documented atrocities against civilians in conquered villages and towns. Despite the outcry that immediately followed these revelations, Kreisky remained unapologetic for his action and publicly referred to Öllinger as victim in a typical Austrian tragedy that affected those Austrians who wanted to face their past unafraid.[22] However, Kreisky did order an investigation whose results showed that an earlier inquiry into Öllinger's past by the Allied Control Commission of Austria had produced no information of his having committed any war crimes. The chancellor referred to remarks in his inaugural address where he had stated that every citizen must have the right to reconsider his political views, including those held during the Nazi period, in the light of later experiences and knowledge.[23] Kreisky's firm and open handling of this incident did not harm him greatly with the Austrian public, possibly because the opposition party, the ÖVP, noted that Kreisky was not prepared to exploit the situation by dragging former Nazis in its ranks into the limelight of public controversy. If the chancellor admitted to anything, it was that he had not been sufficiently informed, originally, about Öllinger's past. Perhaps somewhat more sensitive than Kreisky in this matter, Öllinger, pleading a recurrent heart ailment, preferred to resign shortly after his chief had come so forcefully to his defense. He was succeeded by another former member of the Nazi party who, however, had never belonged to any of the other 'elite' troops of the Third Reich.

Thus, the composition of the first Kreisky cabinet remained unchanged—four ex-members of the Nazi party out of eleven. Their exact membership numbers were released by the Jewish Documentation Center, together with a list of *Aktionen* (operations) engaged in by the SS detachment to which Öllinger had belonged for a time. It was the beginning of the public confrontation between the Austrian chancellor of self-proclaimed Jewish origin and Simon Wiesenthal, who had hunted down Adolf Eichmann, in his role as scourge of all unrepentant Nazis. Wiesenthal, like Kreisky, was an Austrian citizen and registered voter, with political sympathies that were mainly on the side of the People's Party (ÖVP). Kreisky, in an interview with a Dutch newspaper called the head of the Jewish Documentation Center a 'Jewish Fascist', a term he later retracted.[24] Wiesenthal was referred to again at the annual SPÖ congress in June 1970, the 'Victory Congress' at which, incidentally, Leonard Bernstein provided the musical entertainment. With Kreisky's obvious approval, Wiesenthal was accused of using the Jewish Documentation Center for spying and of practicing 'star chamber' methods on solid Austrian citizens.[25] Kreisky and his supporters obviously did not consider that, without a thorough investigation into the background of former Nazis, the absence of criminal activities might never be established. But Kreisky's questionable cabinet choices were soon overshadowed by his determined and successful efforts to gain the absolute parliamentary majority in the election of 1971. His next and much more explosive encounter with the Nazi hunter did not take place until 1975, when it brought into focus the whole moral basis of Kreisky's *Weltanschauung* and remained as his personal problem until his death fifteen years later.

In 1975, Kreisky began to prepare for a marginal election result with the possibility of another coalition, by entering into negotiations with Friedrich Peter, the head of the FPÖ. Peter had always been sympathetic toward the SPÖ and had maintained cordial relations with Kreisky for many years. If a coalition between the two parties were to come about, Peter would naturally assume the post of vice-chancellor. A few days before the election, scheduled for 5 October 1975, Simon Wiesenthal turned over to the President of the Austrian Republic, Rudolf Kirchschläger, information purporting that Peter had been a member of an SS extermination squad.[26] Wiesenthal presumably did this to keep the President from accepting such a coalition government, an action that would have been entirely within the exercise of presidential constitutional discretion. As it turned out, the election held on 5 October 1975 brought Kreisky an absolute, if razor-thin parliamentary majority, thereby again voiding any dependence on a coalition with the right-wing FPÖ. Wiesenthal now decided to make his findings public.[27] Peter admitted that he had served with the unit in question, but categorically denied ever having participated in any of the criminal actions attributed to this group. Wiesenthal countered that he never accused Peter of actual participation in these war crimes but would leave it to others to draw their own conclusions. Now Kreisky went on the offensive, charged Wiesenthal with 'character assassination' and hinted that if Peter had deliberately concealed part of his past so had Wiesenthal.[28] Wiesenthal's actions, Kreisky claimed, were of political benefit to the People's Party and contributed to the revival of anti-Semitism. He carefully distinguished Wiesenthal from other Austrians, characterizing him as an implacable foe of the Second Republic. Kreisky went so far as to criminalize Wiesenthal's behavior, alleging that he too, cooperated with the Nazis and had been known "by some persons to be a Nazi agent."[29] At that point Wiesenthal pressed libel charges against the chancellor, who had indicated he would, if necessary, forego his parliamentary immunity to prove his accusations in court. When at a press conference an Israeli reporter inquired what exactly Kreisky meant by that and similar assertions, the chancellor erupted. In a rare outburst, he admonished the reporter that he was not to be interrogated, that "the Jews presumed too much when it comes to my person [...] and I am not here to vindicate myself as if I were a defendant standing in front of the Jewish, the Israeli public." In a private aside later to this same reporter, the chancellor, possibly in an attempt to be witty, remarked: "If the Jews are a people, they are a wretched people." (*Wenn die Juden ein Volk sind, so ist es [sic] ein mieses Volk.*) The Israeli correspondent later leaked the story to the German news magazine *Der Spiegel* which spread it over three columns under the headline: "Kreisky: The Jews—A Wretched People."[30] Though the editor of the magazine apologized to Kreisky for featuring the story in this manner, Kreisky objected and in a letter to the editor called the implication drawn from his remark a complete falsification of his views. "A people that is not 'a people'," he wrote, "cannot be a 'wretched' people either. Individuals who are, [i.e. wretched (*mies*)] exist in every people—and they do exist without distinction as to their origin, race, religion and community of fate." [31]

It was at this point, several weeks after the elections, that all the individuals involved seemed to recognize the dangerously embarrassing domestic as well as international consequences of this encounter. It was time to defuse the situation. Especially the Socialist party, just barely victorious in the last election, became aware that, unchecked, this affair could lead to defeat in the midst of victory. Kreisky, who had previously offered to shed his parliamentary immunity to achieve a judicial resolution of his and Wiesenthal's accusation, declined to take that step. An attempt at a parliamentary inquiry into Wiesenthal and his documentation center was quashed when it was realized that this would be the first time in the history of the republic that such an investigation targeted a private person rather than a member of government or a government agency.[32] Cooler heads began to intervene: the president of the Jewish Federation of Vienna approached the Jewish industrialist Karl Kahane, a personal friend of Kreisky's, and together they prevailed on the two antagonists to arrive at a compromise. Kreisky agreed to retract his libelous statement alleging Wiesenthal's collaboration with the Nazis, and the Nazi hunter agreed to drop the suit. The two parties to the controversy entered into these actions simultaneously.[33] A suit brought by Kreisky against the news magazine *profil*, also for defamation of character, went up all the way to the European Court of Human Rights. It was decided in favor of the magazine, which had claimed violation of freedom of the press.[34] In 1986 Wiesenthal revived his slander suit against the now retired chancellor when Kreisky repeated his earlier accusations against him in an interview with *profil*.[35] Three years later the court decided against Kreisky, who was fined AS 270,000, the largest fine ever levied in Austria against a defendant in a libel suit.[36] Dr. Kreisky, already ailing under the illness that was to claim him less than nine months later, never commented publicly on the verdict. However, in an interview with an Austrian journalist not long before his death, Kreisky referred once more to his relationship with Friedrich Peter. He said he believed that Peter had turned away from Nazism, and defended him because: "It appeared to me to be a terrible injustice that this decent man, Peter, should have played such a part. The assertion that he was such a dangerous man must still be proven to me. [...] It is my point of view that whatever it is, needs first to be proven. Nothing has been proven to this day." [37]

Kreisky's relations with Israel operated on an entirely different plane. Though obviously never a Zionist, Kreisky was fully in sympathy with the existence of the Jewish state and probably was as well or better informed about the internal political problems of that state as any other non-Israeli Jew who had relatives there.[38] When he became chancellor, he continued the operations of a transit camp for Soviet Jews in Austria on their way to Israel, despite reports of the danger such an operation posed for inviting Arab terrorist intervention. In the wake of an Arab terrorist attempt that, thanks to Kreisky's quick and forthright action, remained bloodless, he agreed to close this camp.[39] He did not, however, interdict the continued transit of Soviet Jews, stipulating only that from then on the operation had to be entirely under the jurisdiction of Austrian authorities. The fact that Israel during the first half of Kreisky's chancellorship was governed by the socialist Labor Party was, of course, very important in guiding Kreisky's attitude toward that state. The Israeli Labor Party, together with other socialist parties including the Austrian SPÖ, was a member of the Socialist International. It was Kreisky's firm belief that this organization owed a special loyalty to a sister party. Thus, for him the defusing of Arab-Israeli tensions was the key to solving the Middle East conflict, and he felt responsible for showing the Israeli Labor Party how that could best be achieved. A first step in that direction, he declared, was to give the Arab view an opportunity to be heard by the Socialist International which, until that time, had been exclusively oriented toward the Israeli side of the issue.[40] Soon after the October (Yom Kippur) War, Kreisky was instrumental in having the Socialist International approve the creation of a 'Fact-finding Mission for the Middle East' as a member of which he visited the countries in that conflict-ridden area, including Israel, in 1974, 1975, and again in 1976.

The results of all three missions were spelled out in a final report submitted to the Socialist International in 1977, to which the Austrian chancellor wrote the introduction and whose final recommendations also bore the imprint of Kreisky's thoughts. Kreisky favored the creation of a Palestinian state, though he was aware of the insecure economic condition of that state unless, initially, it received financial support from its oil rich Arab neighbors. He also recognized that the existence of such a Palestinian state was bound to diminish the 'messianic' character of Israel, no longer distinguishing it greatly from its Middle Eastern neighbors. Social, economic, and cultural tensions among Israel's population would surface and demand attention that could no longer be diverted to an external enemy. Normalization of relations was absolutely necessary as a first step in the direction of peace; otherwise dramatic changes could be expected in the Arab world that would present new threats to Israel's existence. "I am deeply convinced," Kreisky concluded his introductory observations, "there will be no insurmountable difficulties, and [...] if Israel, on her part, is prepared to recognize the Palestinian people and its right to live [...] the Palestinians will withdraw the declaration calling for the destruction of Israel."[41] With this report the Socialist International showed for the first time that there existed a real interest in Western Europe in the Arab point of view in their conflict with Israel. It was a harbinger of the European Community's later involvement in the Middle Eastern peace process. One thing was clear: for Kreisky the Palestinians were obviously no different in their national aspirations than were the Jews or any other ethnic group. In the early 1970s that was a view not yet generally accepted outside the

Middle East and certainly not among diaspora or Israeli Jews. For that view, Kreisky had to accept condemnation by the Israeli media and contempt in much of the American press. His popularity abroad declined even further when he granted limited diplomatic status to the PLO in its dealings with international organizations in Vienna, even though other West European countries had acted similarly earlier.[42] The aim of Kreisky's decision was to raise the respectability of the PLO, enabling it to enter into serious diplomatic negotiations. In this way he hoped to bring about the de-radicalization of that organization. Kreisky also went on record welcoming the peace process initiated by Sadat with his visit to Israel, but he remained skeptical of the efforts at Camp David since they did not address directly the rights of the Palestinian people.

Kreisky provided additional ammunition for his critics when, in 1979, he became the first Western head of state officially to receive Yassir Arafat, chief of the PLO. Kreisky's ostensible purpose was to arrange a meeting between Arafat and Willy Brandt, who was attending a session of the North-South Commission in Vienna as chairman of the Socialist International. This initiated the first formal contact between the SI and the PLO and from Kreisky's point of view was simply another mission in his role as head of a truly neutral state to facilitate contacts between representatives of important organizations whose influence reached far beyond their immediate territorial jurisdictions. For Israel and most other countries of the West, however, it was not only the substance of the talks but also the cordial manner with which the Austrian head of state received the PLO Chief that gave cause for indignant reactions. Upon his arrival at the Vienna airport, Arafat was given a most affectionate embrace by his host who, later, dismissed this demonstrative enthusiasm as simply the time-honored way of exchanging greetings in the Middle East. It was, of course, more than that. After an initially cool first meeting with Arafat during the SI Fact Finding Mission, Kreisky began to warm to the colorful Palestinian leader, possibly because he detected in him similar attitudes toward the creation of an independent Palestinian state that had once moved Kreisky toward an independent Austria during *his* period of 'exile'. Kreisky was, in effect, flaunting his 'Jewish origins' to prove to the world that another kind of Judaism could exist separately from that represented by Israel. His actions were taken to prove either apostasy or statesman-like 'moral courage' by a Jew taking on the indomitable Israelis.

Probably the loudest and most hostile reaction internationally was caused when Kreisky, as the first and only leader of a Western government, invited Colonel Quaddafi of Libya to meet with him in Vienna in 1982.

Kreisky received Quaddafi with all the honors due a foreign head of state at a time when the Colonel was under sharp attack by the United States for promoting world-wide terrorism. Although Kreisky tried to explain away his diplomatic intimacy with Quaddafi by alluding again to the broker role of a neutral state, in this case it was more likely he expected some very concrete commercial benefits for the struggling Austrian economy. In any event, his Libyan guest took full advantage of the public forum offered him to engage in some furious verbal attacks against the United States. This led to the first serious official discord between Austria and the United States. The U.S. State Department formally and vigorously objected to this new direction which Austrian neutrality appeared to be taking under its charismatic chancellor.

However by that time, Kreisky's word had lost much of its impact outside the Arab world, especially when he referred to Israel. Kreisky had, in 1978, given an interview to a British journalist in which, enraged over Prime Minister Begin's dilatory tactics in his negotiations with Sadat, Kreisky had characterized the Israeli leader as "a little lawyer from Warsaw with the soul of a narrow-minded shopkeeper."[43] Later Kreisky expanded on that remark by calling Israel a "police state that was run by men with a Fascist mentality." Eventually he regretted the frankness of these remarks but he never denied having made them. When challenged directly about them he was fond of quoting a passage from a biography of Ben Gurion in which that revered Israeli leader had compared Begin to Hitler.[44] Though no 'outsider' would ever have dared to make such a comparison, Kreisky felt comfortable enough as "insider," that is, as someone with sufficient credentials of his Jewishness, to cast these kind of aspersions on the head of the Jewish state. It was obviously one of his less than statesman-like observations. The unforgiving reaction to Kreisky by Israel in this and similar incidents may bear out the supposition that no matter how Kreisky viewed himself in this conflict, the Israelis regarded him forever as the fratricidal member of a Jewish family.[45]

Kreisky fully appreciated the existence of a secure homeland to which Jews, such as his brother, his aunt and others could emigrate in order to escape persecution and where they could live securely and with dignity.[46] But he also recognized, possibly sooner than most, that a continuous state of war between Israel and its neighbors would only work to the detriment of that country's well-being, eventually endangering its viability altogether. As head of a permanently neutral country that had known the plight of occupation by foreign powers, but also as an individual who had experienced the terror of persecution, Kreisky regarded it as his moral duty to bring about a positive dialogue between Jews and Arabs. Philosophically, Kreisky had no problem in distancing himself from that conflict since for him Judaism constituted a body of religious convictions to be accepted or discarded at will and certainly not the belief system of an ethnically or racially distinguishable group of people. The ethnic, pseudo-racist characterization of all Jews, regardless of their national origins, was by Kreisky considered a return to National Socialist doctrine of racial purity. He was convinced that the extreme nationalism that threatened to drive Israeli politics could be reigned in only by the judicious application of reason, tolerance, and moderation. His familiarity with the Austrian example had taught him that small states especially should not fall victim to the polarizations caused by extreme nationalism, since that frequently led to the intervention by the major powers.

It is difficult today to regard Kreisky's attitude toward Israel as anything but the result of the kind of clear and rational thinking whose intent it is to clarify justifiable demands on both sides. Looked at from Kreisky's vantage point, it was precisely his Jewish origins that impelled him to open up the Arab-Israeli problem to public scrutiny and to well-meaning, constructive criticism. Nothing, however, moved him to maintain, for that same reason, any solidarity with religious Judaism. Marxism, socialism, and democratic socialism were the categories that determined his thought processes, aided by the rationalist underpinning of a purely secular education. Kreisky in formal interviews and statements referring to the fate of the Jews under the Nazi regime invariably expressed his sympathy and understanding for the agonies of that time. But he seemed incapable of realizing how offensive his wooing of votes from former Nazis would prove to surviving victims of Nazi persecution, violating, in their eyes the memory of those who, like Kreisky's relatives, had lost their lives to Nazi terror. This lack of sensitivity was more likely the reason for his violent reaction to Wiesenthal, or to the accusations levelled against him by Israeli diplomats and politicians, rather than assertions of his 'self-hatred', 'Jewish anti-Semitism', and hostility toward his parents, especially his mother. There is absolutely no evidence for any of these assertions. He simply had no use for religious practices that interfered with the way of life he had charted for himself. It is possible that during the last years of his life the anomaly of having been perceived as the lone 'Jew' in an essentially 'Jewless' environment surfaced in his thinking. He suffered greatly from his physical illness and referred to it frequently as a 'punishment' visited upon him. He tended to blame others for having brought on the afflictions from which he suffered.[47] These are not the attitudes of a man at peace with himself and the world. Maybe he imagined that the reluctance with which 'his' party, the SPÖ, to which he had dedicated his life, accepted first his presence and then his leadership, and the cool treatment extended to him after retirement, were somehow connected to his "Jewish origins."

Most likely Kreisky's own attitude toward Judaism was still mired in the nineteenth century premise that if religious sanctions were no longer acceptable, one discarded that religion and, in the case of Judaism, thereby also shed the Jewish identity. Today, however, Jewish identity is no longer in question, at least no more so than that of any other ethnicity, due to the existence of a Jewish state and a vigorous, healthy debate surrounding the nature of religious Judaism. Kreisky was truly a child of his time: the time of the alienated Jew who until the appearance of Hitler could no more conceive of Auschwitz than of a state governed by Jews. The modern Jew today is no longer constrained by either/or alternatives. Today there is no longer one norm of Jewish existence that has to be followed rigorously. As a modern Israeli philosopher phrased it, "[T]here are Orthodox and secular Jews, Conservative and Reform Jews, Zionist and anti-Zionist Jews, and nuances, and subcategories within all of these [...]. Judaism today is determined by the ways Jews actually live it, and not by one compulsory model."[48] Maybe today the young Kreisky would have found a niche in this variegated spectrum and still left his mark on history. In the Israel of today, even the Jewish non-conformist lives as an accepted and respected member of that society.

NOTES

1. Kurt Steiner, *Politics in Austria* (Boston: Little, Brown & Co., 1972), ch. V. See also Adam Wandruszka, "Österreichs politische Struktur," in *Geschichte der Republik Österreich*, ed. Heinrich Benedikt (Munich: Oldenbourg, 1954), 289 ff, which calls attention to the historical continuity of the ideological division into three 'camps' or '*Lagers*.'

2. See Josef Buttinger, *In the Twilight of Socialism* (New York: F.A. Praeger, 1953), 74-76 ff; also Jack Jacobs, "Austrian Social Democracy and the Jewish Question in the First Republic," in *The Austrian Socialist Experiment*, ed. Anson Rabinbach (Boulder: Westview Press, 1985), 157-160; and Helmut Gruber, *Red Vienna* (New York: Oxford University Press, 1991), 25-27.

3. Bruno Kreisky, *Zwischen den Zeiten* (Vienna: Kremayr & Scheriau, 1986), 250-53.

4. Discussion of Kreisky's personal views are based on my interview with Egon Breiner, 17 December 1990 in Los Angeles. Breiner, like Kreisky, had been a functionary in the Socialist Workers Youth (*Sozialistische Arbeiter Jugend*, SAJ) of the SDAP in Vienna and had shared with him the early years of exile in Sweden. Kreisky's Swedish period is well documented in Oliver Rathkolb & Irene Etzersdorfer, eds., *Der Junge Kreisky, Schriften, Reden, Dokumente 1931-1945*, Schriftenreihe der Stiftung Bruno Kreisky Archiv, vol.I, (Vienna: Verlag Jugend und Volk, 1986).

5. Rathkolb/Etzersdorfer, *Der Junge Kreisky*, 251 ff; cf. also his memoirs, especially Kreisky, *Zwischen*, chs. 12-14; additional information on Kreisky's political role in Sweden was obtained in the above cited interview with Breiner.

6. Rathkolb/Etzersdorfer, *Der Junge Kreisky*, 184 ff.

7. Kreisky, *Zwischen*, 87-98.

8. Copy of a letter to the then Foreign Minister, Karl Gruber, dated 7 July 1949, signed by Gustav Deutsch, Kreisky Archiv. This letter is also referred to, obliquely, in Bruno Kreisky, *Im Strom der Politik: Der Memoiren zweiter Teil* (Vienna: Kremayr & Scheriau, 1989), 59.

9. Interview with cousin Anke Kreisky 9 August 1990; Ms. Kreisky, daughter of Rudolf, brother of Bruno's father, is, like her mother, the former Polish countess Zofja von Nikiel before she married Rudolf, a devout Roman Catholic.

10. Documents from the treason trial are reprinted in Rathkolb/Etzersdofer, *Der Junge Kreisky*, 41-69; English press accounts appeared in *The Times* (London) 17 March 1936, and *Daily Herald*, 21 March 1936, both also reprinted in ibid., 81-89. When, during an early interrogation, Bruno was asked by an infuriated prosecutor why he was willing to sacrifice himself for "those Jews" [presumably in the SDAP leadership], Kreisky only thought that was "funny," see *ibid.*, 46.

11. Kreisky, *Zwischen*, 408-10.

12. That anti-Semitism was a most likely factor in the party's dilatory behavior is maintained by Friedrich Stadler, ed., *Vertriebene Vernunft* (Vienna: Verlag Jugend & Volk, 1987), 313-23, where he documents that only a handful, maybe even less than that, of emigrated Jewish professionals returned to their native country; a negligible number were journalists, former SDAP functionaries, who because of language difficulties had found it impossible to pursue their craft in their countries of refuge.

13. On Olah's political career, see Wilhelm Svoboda, *Franz Olah, Eine Spurensicherung* (Vienna: Promedia Verlag, 1990); for Kreisky's own comments on his friend, see, *inter alia, Im Strom,* 358-61 and 382-404.

14. Interview with Heinz Fischer, Chairman of the SPÖ parliamentary caucus, 13 July 1990; also with Nicholas Scherk, former Secretary to the Kreisky cabinet, 18 July 1990.

15. Svoboda, *Olah*, 49-55

16. Ibid., 85 ff.

17. Bruno Kreisky, "Der Fall Olah," in *Arbeiter Zeitung* 26 February 1966, in which he wrote that Olah's speeches were designed "to incite the lowest instincts of narrow-minded Philistinism gone berserk." In 1989, nearly six years after his retirement, in a TV interview, the former chancellor reiterated his friendship with Olah emphasizing that his policies as chancellor had been conceptualized earlier by Olah and himself, Johannes Kunz, *Erinnerungen* (Vienna: Kremayr & Scheriau, 1989), 183-4.

18. Kreisky, *Im Strom*, 390; in an interview with the author shortly after Kreisky's death, Dr. Rudolf Kirchschläger, the former President of the republic told this story: at a meeting of SPÖ leaders, sometime during the period leading up to Kreisky's election as party chairman, Kirchschläger noticed that Kreisky was wearing heavy gold cufflinks with his initials BK. He teasingly asked Kreisky whether the letters meant that he was already anticipating becoming *Bundes Kanzler* (Federal Chancellor). Kreisky smiled back and said: "Go on, you don't really believe they're going to elect a Jew to be chancellor"! (Aber gehn's weg, Sie glauben doch net, dass die wirklich an' Juden zum Kanzler wählen!)

19. Zentralsekretäriat der SPÖ, *Protokoll des 19. Parteitags der SPÖ, 3. Oktober 1968*, (Vienna, 1967), 65 ff.

20. *New York Times*, 11 October 1971, Editorial.

21. Simon Wiesenthal, *Recht nicht Rache* (Frankfurt: Ullstein Verlag, 1988), 357.

22. Kreisky continued to defend Öllinger's appointment long after the case had disappeared from the headlines; at a rally in Klagenfurt, provincial capital of Carinthia and then as now [1992] a stronghold of right-wing, radical elements, the chancellor stated: " What is important is what a person does today and not what he did 30 years ago because of some false ideas,[...] as long as he didn't commit a crime." cited in *Kreisky Reden*, vol.II (Vienna: Verlag der Österreichischen Staatsdruckerei, 1981), 258.

23. "Regierungserklärung I," Nationalrat 27 April 1970, *Reden*, II, 1.

24. The term was reported as having been used in the Dutch newspaper, *Vrij Nederland*, 4 July 1970; Kreisky's denial was issued in *Arbeiter Zeitung*, 7 November 1970; and cf. with comments on this and similar incidents in M. v. Amerongen, *Kreisky und seine unbewältigte Gegenwart* (Vienna, 1977), 51 ff.

25. SPÖ Zentralsekretäriat, *Protokoll des 21. Parteitags der SPÖ* (Sieges [*Victory*] Parteitag) (Vienna, 1970), 83 ff.

26. The full range of notorious activities engaged in by the SS-Infantry Brigade, including forceful liquidation of the civilian population in the rear of the front line, of which Peter's regimental unit was a member, were published later by Wiesenthal in his *Informationsbulletin No.16 des Dokumentationszentrum des Bundes jüdischer Verfolgter des Naziregimes*, 31 January 1975; 1-2.

27. Wiesenthal, *Recht*, 363. In his press conference, Wiesenthal accused Peter of having deliberately omitted his service record from his official biography.

28. *Die Presse*, 10 November 1975.

29. *Die Presse* 3 December 1975; a similar statement was made by Kreisky on 18 November 1975 as reported in *Die Presse* 19 November 1975.

30. *Der Spiegel*, 17 November 1975, p. 22.

31. *Der Spiegel*, 24 November 1975, p. 12.

32. See Hans R. Laurer, *Der Parlamentarische Untersuchungsausschuss* (Vienna: Verlag Manz, 1984), 123 ff.

33. *Die Presse*, 10 December 1975.

34. "Judgment in Lingens Case (12/1984/84/31)" in vol. 103, Series A, *Publications of the European Court of Human Rights* (Cologne: Carl Heymann Verlag, 1987).

35. *profil*, 8 May 1986, pp. 25-31.

36. Wiesenthal offered to drop the case in return for a formal apology from the former chancellor. Kreisky declined, with the remark: "I am too old to apologize to anyone for anything." Interview with Simon Wiesenthal, 13 July 1990, at which time Wiesenthal also provided a copy of the verdict against Kreisky.

37. Elisabeth Horvath, *Ära oder Episode* (Vienna: Kremayr & Scheriau, 1989), 154.

38. This observation was made by Ingo Mussi, Press and Information officer in the Kreisky cabinet from 1970 to 1976, in an interview with the author on 24 July 1990.

39. The facts of this terrorist attack are chronicled fully in *The Events of September 28th and 28th 1973*, A Documentary Report, issued [in English] by the Federal Chancellery, Vienna, Austria 1973, 92 pages; the political dimensions of this attack are analyzed critically in a forthcoming biography of Bruno Kreisky by this author.

40. Kreisky, *Im Strom*, 307-9.

41. *Report of the Socialist International Fact Finding Mission to the Middle East*, Introduction by Bruno Kreisky, published by Socialist International, London, Circular No. B 14/77, 7 October 1977, 2-8.

42. Hans Thalberg, "Die Nahostpolitik," in *Die Ära Kreisky*, Erich Bielka et al., eds. (Vienna: Europa Verlag, 1983), 314 ff.

43. *Die Furche* 15 September 1978, which reports on an interview with James Dorsey of the Dutch newspaper *Trouw*; excerpts are also reprinted in B. Kreisky, *Das Nahost Problem, Reden, Commentare, Interviews* (Vienna: Europaverlag, 1985), pp. 59-62.

44. Kreisky, *Im Strom*, 346.

45. Kreisky's own feelings on that issue are well illustrated by a remark he once made to a personal friend: "*Was wollen die von mir? Das Jüdische gehört zu mir wie meine beiden Hände!* [What do they want of me? Jewishness is as much part of me as are my two hands] and he lifted his hands in the air." Interview with E. Breiner, 17 December 1990; a similar remark was also related to the author by Professor Victor Weisskopf of MIT, a former school-mate of Kreisky, in a telephone conversation, 5 May 1990.

46. See especially his comments to that effect in *Im Strom*, ch.12, 298-300; also, during his visit in Israel as a member of the Fact-Finding Commission, Kreisky again met his brother Paul whom he had last seen in 1938 but with whom he had been in touch and provided with much needed financial support. Kreisky particularly enjoyed meeting Paul's son who visited with him dressed in the IDF uniform, a fact that he related with great pride to friends upon his return to Vienna. Interview with Ingo Mussi, Press & Information Officer for the Kreisky cabinet 1970-76, 24 July 1990.

47. *profil*, No. 32, 9 August 1990, p. 18; and see Horvath, *Ära*, 104, where Kreisky names his one-time Vice-chancellor Hannes Androsch as being the cause of a stroke he suffered some years earlier. Androsch confirmed that Kreisky believed this in an interview with the author on 30 July 1990.

48. Yirmiyahu Yovel, *Spinoza and Other Heretics* (Princeton: Princeton University Press, 1989), 197; Yovel's work focuses on the dilemma of the existential Jew, typified by Spinoza, unable to escape his condition, yet incapable of finding any real suitable alternative. Bruno Kreisky's quest as individual and politician unquestioningly fits into this category.

The Foreign Policy of the Kreisky Era*

Otmar Höll

Introduction

When after the Second World War, Austria was freed from the Nazi regime by the Allied Forces in the spring of 1945, the prime goal of all political forces in government was to regain political independence and full sovereignty as soon as possible. Ideological differences between the two great political camps—differences that had led to great human misery during the interwar period and finally to the occupation of the Austrian territory in 1938 by Hitler's troops were pushed back.[1] The two great parties, the Austrian People's party (ÖVP), a Christian democratic, conservative party and the Social Democratic party (SPÖ) formed a series of "Great Coalition-Governments" between 1945/47 and 1966. Considering Austria's corporative political structure of that period, the political system did not produce an effective parliamentary opposition, and thus had, as Hans Morgenthau put it, "a disastrous effect upon the public mind" for whomever the people vote, "the government and its policies are not likely to change."[2] It was also a general constant of the Second Austrian Republic that foreign policy was practiced as a "consensual matter," that is, in full agreement by the two great parties. Undoubtedly, Austrian foreign policy of the whole postwar period, which was a success-story compared to the interwar-period, was to a great extent dominated and framed by a single person, Bruno Kreisky.

Kreisky, born 1911 in Vienna as a son of a well-to-do Jewish family, studied law and economics and was forced to go into exile to Sweden in 1938 after five months of imprisonment by Hitler's Gestapo[3] because of his political activities for the Social Democratic movement. There he worked with the Swedish Konsum-cooperative. As a correspondent for several Western newspapers, he organized on commission of the Swedish government a number of international aid initiatives and became acquainted with other exiles of the *Kleine Internationale* (Small International), above all with Willy Brandt. Later, Brandt and Kreisky were close political collaborators and became good friends. When in 1951, after five years of work as member of the Austrian Foreign Service in Stockholm for building up the Austrian mission in Sweden, he came back to Vienna with his family, he soon became the deputy director of President Körner's cabinet. In that capacity, he also functioned as a political adviser to the president. Two years later, Kreisky became state secretary, the second man in the foreign policy division of the Austrian chancellory, and during the next years he took part in the negotiations for the Austrian State Treaty. In 1959, Kreisky took over and founded the Federal Ministry of Foreign Affairs under the chancellorship of Julius Raab. He held that position until 1966, when the coalition between ÖVP and SPÖ eventually ended. After the SPÖ was defeated in the 1966 elections, Kreisky was elected the party's leader in 1967. The SPÖ won the 1970 elections by a relative majority of parliamentary seats. But only one and a half years later Kreisky succeeded in gaining absolute majority and successfully fought two subsequent campaigns in 1975 and 1979.[4]

When Kreisky started his chancellorship in 1970, he was already a well-experienced foreign affairs politician: thirteen years' experience as state secretary and as foreign minister lay behind him. Nonetheless, a period of even greater influence on Austrian foreign policy and of international influence still lay ahead of him.

What are the reasons for Bruno Kreisky's restless engagement in international politics? What are the events during his socialization period that could explain his way of thinking, his analytical precision, his intuitive assessment and above all his deep feelings of solidarity with weak or poor people and suppressed societies? Indeed, most of these formative factors can be found in his early childhood and during that period of his life when he developed to political maturity. This period of socialization spanned from the First World War through his years of exile in Sweden. It was during the First World War that he, as a child, became acquainted with the cruelty of war, which he would never forget.[5] Intellectually and emotionally he was heavily influenced by the liberal-Jewish and tolerant tradition of his bourgeois home.[6] His early political activities in the Social Democratic movement made him an unreserved admirer (with the exception of the *Anschluß-Frage*) of the Austro-Marxist politician Otto Bauer, and during the months of imprisonment in the Austrofascist and Nazi regimes he had plenty of time to become intensively acquainted with the ideas of Marxism.[7] His social feelings were developed during his early school years, when many of his companions did not even have enough to eat, and so Kreisky's parents allowed him to help them by giving small meals.[8]

The painful results of the interwar-period in Central Europe, beginning with deep economic crises, mass unemployment, social unrest,[9] and ending with fascist political power and finally war, combined with Kreisky's Swedish experiences of a democratic and social-liberal society made Kreisky an advocate of social democracy.[10] He was also struck by Sweden's not-allied and independent position in foreign affairs and its liberal, democratic and social organization which had a great impact on the political self consciousness of the young Austrian Social Democrat.[11] The period of political formation was finished in the early 1950s and Kreisky— from the viewpoint of close collaborators—would modify his political *Weltbild* only slightly during the whole of his subsequent active political life. The prime objective of Kreisky's foreign policy activities was to ensure Austria's political independence and the security of its people, which, in his view, could only be reached if welfare and social peace on the domestic front were guaranteed. But above all, these goals had to be embedded in a lasting peace in the whole of Europe and in its system of power balance between the Western and Eastern blocs.[12] All other activities such as Kreisky's globally-oriented active foreign policy, his North-South initiatives, his engagement in the Middle East conflict, were ranked second to the prime objectives of Austrian security interests and European détente.[13] Kreisky's ideological position was deeply rooted in Western, liberal democratic traditions. His motto concerning the East-West conflict was that Austria should strive for maximum confidence in the West and a minimum of distrust in the Eastern bloc.[14]

Austria's policy of good relations with her neighbors was an attempt for détente in Central Europe: early normalization of Austria's relations to Hungary after the suppression of the 1956 people's revolt, to Yugoslavia since 1960, or to countries like Poland and Rumania as well as the successful internationalization of the South Tyrol conflict under the auspices of the United Nations in 1960.[15] Kreisky's fertile contacts in the United States, culminating in an intensive series of lectures there,[16] contributed to strengthening Austria's international reputation. Kreisky took a well-balanced, progressive stance in the discussions about decolonization; this stance is documented in his lecture given in the General Assembly of the United Nations in September 1966.[17] His friendly and trusting relations with great leaders of the non-aligned movement like Pandit Nehru, Kwame Nkrumah and Leopold Senghor and others raised Austria's image in that part of the world that became so important in the 1970s especially within the United Nations framework.[18] Bruno Kreisky as state secretary and as minister of foreign affairs had already laid the foundations before 1966 for his 1970s active policy of neutrality.

Determinants of Austrian Foreign Policy between 1970 and 1983

For many observers of the Austrian political scene, the foreign policy of the phase between 1970 and 1983 was but the realization of the theoretically and practically developed strategies of the 1950s and 1960s. Austrian foreign policy, a highly consensual political matter between the two great parties ÖVP and SPÖ, must be understood in terms of continuity and consensus.

Phases of Foreign Policy

This fourth period of Austrian postwar foreign policy,[19] the so-called period of the Kreisky era, lasted until 1983. It can be structured into three phases: the first phase lasted from 1970-1975 and can be characterized as the final reconstruction phase of Austrian foreign policy directed towards political independence and stability as well as a preparatory phase of a more globally-oriented policy.[20] Foreign policy activities concentrated on European neighborhood policies on the one hand and, on the deepening of relations toward developing countries of the South and the first membership in the Security Council of the United Nations in 1973-74 on the other hand. The second phase, from 1975-1981, is marked by an opening of the foreign policy scope with a more globally-oriented direction of initiatives. Among these are Kreisky's intermediative activities in the Middle East conflict, his proposals for a massive transfer of resources from the industrialized to the developing countries in the form of a "New Marshall Plan"[21] and the Cancun summit of 1981, the only meeting of leading heads of states of the (Western) North and the South in that decade. The last years of his active political life from 1981-1983 can be understood as a phase of a regressive foreign policy record within a changing and partly deteriorating international environment and increasing domestic criticism by the great opposition party.[22]

This whole period was to a large extent dominated by Bruno Kreisky, who relied on three non-party member foreign ministers, the two diplomats Rudolf Kirchschläger and Erich Bielka and the constitutional expert Willibald Pahr. There are ironic anecdotes in which Kreisky had stated that he would not interfere in foreign policy matters, with the exception of the East-West affairs, the North-South relations and the Middle East conflict as well as development policy, meaning that almost nothing was left for the foreign ministry. However, retrospectively analyzed, it seems that Kreisky never directly intervened in the everyday policy-making of the foreign ministry. But nonetheless he was *the* representative of Austrian foreign policy of that time. In the wake of Kreisky's more or less spectacular initiatives, he could rely on his own personal national and international contacts, his own channels of communication and—above all—on an eagerly listening domestic and international media public; a great number of journalists were greedy to learn from Kreisky's analysis, proposals and critiques of foreign policy events. Undoubtedly Kreisky's initiatives ranked high in the interest of Austrian and foreign mass media. These are some of the reasons that Austrian foreign policy of that period was closely identified with the creative and innovative activities of Bruno Kreisky.

Neutrality, Policy of Neutrality and Active Foreign Policy

The opposing bloc systems that emerged out of World War II divided Europe into two zones of interest. The rising hegemonic powers, the United States and the Soviet Union, were afraid that an independent Austria "might soon be swallowed in the Soviet bloc" or "might join NATO" respectively.[23] As a first sign of decreasing tensions between the blocs after Stalin's death in 1953, Austria succeeded in establishing itself as a permanently neutral state, one that would not involve itself in the power game between East and West.[24] The important Austrian contribution to peace in Europe lay in its function as a stable and independent political actor keeping the two bloc forces apart in Central Europe, and in fact functioning as a "secret ally of the West."[25] On the other hand, Austria was interested in the stability of a balance of power between the military systems on the lowest possible level because that would minimize the chance of an outbreak of war. That also meant having an interest in slowing down the arms race and keeping the confidence between the blocs as high as possible. However, the capacity of such support in sustaining a balance of power and encouraging détente between the blocs were rather limited for a small, neutral country. What it could do was to establish channels of communications, arrange events where political talks on a high or summit level could take place or try to make proposals in the search for conflict resolutions.

From the very beginning, after it had declared its permanent neutrality, Austria intended to conduct a more active foreign policy than Switzerland.

Therefore, it joined (unlike Switzerland) the United Nations in December 1955 and the Council of Europe in April 1956. Kreisky's positive appraisal of the neutral status came out of the conviction that it was the only possible way not to endanger Austria's unity and to regain political independence.[26] He wrote in an article in *Foreign Affairs* of January 1959: "At no time have we been in doubt that Austrian neutrality is only a function of an international equilibrium, and that it would be in grave danger whenever this equilibrium was disturbed. It follows, then, that Austrian foreign policy must always aim to help maintain the balance of power by contributing in all ways possible toward lessening international tensions."[27] His understanding of neutrality was an active, dynamic one. It was situated between the more passive understanding of the Swiss and the more active and flexible one of the Swedes, which was characterized as "not-allied." The Austrian understanding of neutrality and of neutral policy developed more towards the Swedish model.

It was in 1968 that the then-international secretary of the SPÖ, Walter Hacker, wrote in a contribution about neutrality that it "should become a dynamic, active kind of neutrality." Austria should "with all its might, step in to stabilize and preserve peace everywhere in the world."[28] This was also an expression of deep changes in the value structure of the Austrian social fabric. It was particularly the young segment of society in Austria which at that time developed a more internationalistic approach of solidarity toward the Third World. Kreisky as a politician in opposition actively took up these questions.

A change toward a more active, globally-oriented Austrian foreign policy had started some years before the first SPÖ government took power in 1970. Because of the breakdown of the negotiations on an association arrangement between Austria and the EC in 1967,[29] Kurt Waldheim, the second foreign minister of the ÖVP government, developed a new pattern of a small state foreign policy, putting more weight on a globally-oriented, active policy and less weight on its military security component, based on structures Kreisky had already prepared in the early 1960s.[30] Characteristic of this new pattern were extensive visits and contacts with other countries, with more emphasis on the multilateral dimension, especially in the United Nations, and above all, intensified interests in developing countries.[31]

The SPÖ governments continued in this direction, but also developed distinctive patterns. The notion of a globally-oriented, active neutrality policy became the norm of the Kreisky era that had begun in 1970. In his second initial governmental speech on 5 November 1971, Kreisky explicitly stated that a successful foreign policy was "the best guarantor of neutrality and security in times of peace." In the first half of the 1970s, however, the international context had changed toward a diminishing of tensions between the superpowers,[32] and the Kreisky government profited from having more room to maneuver.

In the field of economic integration with Europe, Austria, together with Switzerland and Sweden, signed free-trade treaties with the EC. These treaties covered all industrial, but no agricultural products and services.

On the multilateral level, Austria improved its profile in the United Nations[33] and above all in the CSCE process.[34] The Austrian candidate Kurt Waldheim became—with the strong support of Bruno Kreisky—General Secretary of the United Nations twice, in 1971 and 1976, and Austria was for a first term elected as a non-permanent member of the U.N. Security Council (1973/74). Austria's voting behavior in the 1970s in the U.N. General Assembly showed a slight weakening in its Western orientation and some inclination toward the Third World and the "like-minded countries" group (see Appendix 1). This fact is not surprising, since the Third World represented a large majority in the United Nations, and—especially in the 1970s—many votes in the General Assembly were related to North-South questions. The high commitment to the United Nations is also reflected in the great number of Austrian soldiers who took part in peacekeeping operations of the United Nations in the Middle East and Cyprus.[35]

But Austria in that period was not only strengthening its international profile in the multilateral dimension and gaining in its foreign policy experience; it was also taking more independent bilateral initiatives. Austria was not bashful in taking limited risks, as was demonstrated on 28 May 1971 by its being one of the first countries to recognize the People's Republic of China;[36] Austria also recognized the German Democratic Republic on the day of the signing of the *Grundlagen* Treaty (21 December 1972).

It was in the second phase of the Kreisky era that the notion of an active policy of neutrality, which was often used interchangeably with Austrian foreign policy, was extended as a means to strengthen international détente. The reason for such preemptive international peace policies was the awareness of how difficult the situation of a neutral country in a geographical position like Austria's could become in times of actual conflicts.[37] It was not by chance that Bruno Kreisky's engagement in the North-South conflict was recognized as a contribution to decreasing tensions between the North and the South. It was his conviction that mass poverty in the Third World was a severe danger to world peace and would make societies in the South susceptible to communist approaches. Kreisky openly criticized the harsh position of the United States government toward the Third World, not only in the economic field but also in its stance in the Middle East conflict. On the other hand, he did not join his close friend Olof Palme who was a fierce critic of the United States' engagement in Vietnam. Kreisky's moderate position as vice chairman of the Socialist International was appreciated by U.S. President Richard Nixon.[38] That was part of the very pragmatic, and as Kreisky might have seen it, responsible attitudes toward the Great Western superpower whose "heavy responsibilities all over the world" he recognized "even though some times a little chill may creep down our spine."[39]

Austria's contribution to international peace and security was not restricted to Europe alone. By conducting an active policy of neutrality, Austria tried to contribute to the maintenance of peace and security throughout the entire world, which at that time was still dominated by the precarious balance of deterrence of the bloc systems. Not all initiatives were ultimately successful, but it was to a great extent Bruno Kreisky who enlarged Austria's profile in the international system far beyond its size.[40] Austria had a leading role in mediating in the Middle East; it tried to moderate in global crisis situations such as the Iran hostage affair, the Soviet invasion in Afghanistan and Central America. Austria hosted important political summits in Vienna as well as being a turn table for many emigrating Soviet Jews and Eastern dissidents.

Foreign Policy in East-West Relations

The East-West conflict was the most important referential conflict configuration and therefore the main determinant of Austrian foreign policy until the end of the 1980s. Not only were its relations to both superpowers constrained by that conflict; its neighborhood policy and its European policy were affected as well. A case analysis on the European system level of that time might lead to the conclusion that Austria's entire neutral foreign policy can be fully explained by the constraints of that conflict. While Austria's permanent neutrality was a function of that conflict, however, at no time was it understood in terms of an ideological equidistance.[41] Its commitment to Western pluralistic democracies was clear. Bruno Kreisky himself stated that he was a "declared adherent of a policy of containment, not of an ideological appeasement policy."[42] In his view, it was containment that paved the way towards détente.[43] Insiders of that period report that the Soviet ambassador in Vienna complained that it had been easier for him to get concessions from the former Klaus government than from Chancellor Kreisky or Foreign Minister Kirchschläger.

Bruno Kreisky was a true "Atlanticist" despite his critical remarks on United States' foreign policy in the Middle East conflict during the Carter administration and on the conservative turn that came about with Ronald Reagan's presidency.[44] He appreciated the democratic achievements of U.S. society and accepted the hegemonic position of the United States. Since the United States had taken over the leading role in the world economy in the wake of the First World War, Kreisky claimed, "it is unthinkable that a country as big as the USA and with such tremendous economic and moral resources would be free to decide if it wants to play the role or not.... However, America...carries the great political and moral responsibility for the destiny of the world. ... History has already decided."[45]

Kreisky's appreciation of the United States' policy toward Europe centered on two recurring elements. The first was the adequacy of her policy of containment: "This policy of erecting bulwarks against Soviet expansion was the most constructive contribution made by the United States to the maintenance of world peace."[46] The second was the Marshall Plan; this, in Kreisky's words, was "a bold enterprise of economic assistance ... [and] it was a brilliant political idea to save democracy in Europe."[47]

Undoubtedly, the policy of strengthening détente was at the center of Austrian foreign policy during the whole Kreisky era. In a period of détente, the superiority of democracy over communist dictatorship could best be proven.[48] The position toward the Soviet Union was characterized by mutual respect, with Austria trying to minimize distrust in its independent policy towards the Soviet Union. For the Soviet Union, Austria was, despite its different social and political system, not a real, fully-integrated part of the "Western World."[49] It was more or less the waiting room to the West.

In all the common communiques that were published after official visits in the 1960s and 1970s, it was stated that the relations and recognition of peaceful coexistence were "based on the basis of mutual appreciation and non-interference in domestic affairs."[50] This wording characterized a truly sensitive relation, but on the whole, a satisfactory one for both sides. In the 1970s, Austrian foreign policy followed the patterns set in the late 1950s and 1960s. Due to an active policy to strengthen détente in Europe, the exchange of official visits with the Warsaw-Pact countries even increased, especially between 1974 and 1980.

It was Kreisky's firm conviction that détente was not only favorable for democracies but also supportive for an improvement of the humanitarian situation in East European countries, especially in the Soviet Union. Thus Austria (followed by Finland), was the first Western government to support the Soviet Union's initiative in proposing the organization of a Conference on Security and Cooperation in Europe (CSCE) as early as in 1966; the CSCE had already been formally proposed by the Soviet Union in the early 1950s.[51] Austria for many years rendered considerable services to emigrating Soviet Jews[52] and, to a lesser degree, to political dissidents from Eastern countries. Kreisky's intrinsic anti-communist attitude, which he openly demonstrated in his speech on the occasion of the signing of the Helsinki-Final Act,[53] and Austria's open support for East European refugees and dissidents (especially members of the "Charta 77"), represented also a common understanding of mainstream Austrian foreign policy at that time.[54]

The Austrian "neighborhood policy" is a reflection of the East-West conflict.[55] Towards Austria's Western neighbors, the Federal Republic of Germany, Italy (after the settlement of the South-Tyrol conflict in 1969) and Switzerland relations were without tensions, so there was no need of an official neighborhood policy. Transboundary relations would function without restrictions. Relations toward the two countries (CSSR and Hungary) that belonged to the Warsaw Treaty Organization (WTO) and, in the south, with non-aligned Yugoslavia, can be characterized as more or less "sensitive." Austro-Hungarian diplomatic relations were improving after some years of deterioration spurred by the suppression of the 1956 people's revolt with Soviet tanks.[56] Since 1964, when an Austrian governmental delegation led by Bruno Kreisky visited Budapest, relations steadily changed into a "special case"[57] among Austria's relations to Eastern countries.

The relations with Czechoslovakia were overshadowed by a historical legacy going back to the sixteenth-century Habsburg empire. The 1968 suppression of the reformist experiment of the communist Dubcek government, known as "Prague Spring" by Soviet troops, gave rise to yet further problems, finally "freezing" Vienna's relations with Prague. Above all, inside fighting between a more liberal and a Stalinist faction within the Czechoslovakian Communist Party (CCP) made improved relations between Austria and Czechoslovakia almost impossible.

The relations with Yugoslavia, though steadily improving in the 1960s, were damaged by the failure of Kreisky's efforts to fulfill old commitments stemming from Article 7 of the State Treaty vis-à-vis the Slovene and

Croatian minorities in Carinthia. His deployment of bilingual place-name signs, proved a tragic political failure[58]: the Carinthian riots of 1972 and, as their consequence, the dismantling of the bilinual signs led to a year-long deterioration of Austro-Yugoslav relations and to a number of mutual notes of protest between the Vienna and Belgrad governments.[59] The improvement of these relations after 1978 was not strongly related to the excellent cooperation of Austria and Yugoslavia in the neutral and non-aligned group in the CSCE process.[60]

As mentioned above, it was an important aim of Austrian foreign policy of the Kreisky era to gain maximum confidence in the West and minimum distrust in the Eastern bloc. Charles DeGaulle's European vision had a great impact on Kreisky, who soon recognized the importance of a differentiated policy of détente between East and West on the basis of a rough military balance between the blocs.[61] For him this balance seemed to be an essential element for European and thus also for Austrian security policy. For a small country like Austria, situated on the demarcation line of the European divide, it was of vital importance to keep channels of communication between the antagonists open, to promote the dialogue between East and West, and above all, not to isolate the great Eastern power.[62] This Austrian position is reflected in an increasing official visitors' program in Eastern countries: the number of visitors doubled and further tripled over those in the 1960s between 1974-1982 (see Appendix 2). Together with neutral and non-aligned countries (the N+N group), Austria played a dynamic and bridge-building role in the CSCE process as long as the blocs needed a mediating broker. Austria in that period was also actively participating in and contributing to the Council of Europe[63] as well as being a prominent part of the U.N. Economic Council for Europe.

Austrian Foreign Policy in the North-South Conflict

Although in its past imperial history Austria *did* take part in the conquest, exploitation and integration of overseas territories into world markets, which today are known as the less developed countries,[64] the Austria of the Second Republic profited in its relations to these countries from its image of having had a "non-colonial past."[65] Examples can be found throughout history of Second Republic—Austria received vital support from Third World countries. In 1953, for example, India supported Austria's efforts for the signing of the State Treaty by sounding out whether Moscow would accept a neutral Austria after Prime Minister Pandit Nehru and Austrian Foreign Minister Karl Gruber—in spite of the resistance from Julius Raab and the SPÖ—discussed the matter in the famous Swiss tourist spot Bürgenstock. Furthermore, many developing countries supported Austria's and Kreisky's attempts to internationalize the South Tyrol conflict within the United Nations,[66] opted in great number for Vienna to become the third U.N. resident city, and last but not least, after the start of the Kreisky era, supported the election of Kurt Waldheim as secretary general of the United Nations and Austria's appointment in the security council in 1972.

In spite of the above-mentioned historical contacts, after the First and the Second World Wars, Austria had little of a communicative infrastructure to link it with developing countries overseas; initial attempts to develop a policy toward these countries can be found only after 1955 when Austria regained its full sovereignty and became a member of the United Nations.[67] It was not just the Austrian engagement in the U.N. decolonization process but also other initiatives (like the foundation of the Vienna Institute for Development in 1962 as an instrument of contact and public information, or the very early statement of the then-Foreign Minister Kreisky at the World Trade Conference (UNCTAD) in 1964 in Geneva) that increased Austria's reputation in these countries and helped to show that the newly-acquired political independence of Southern states required a kind of a new "Marshall Plan" for economic development.[68]

In the initial phase of the Kreisky era, the opening of Austrian foreign policy toward the countries of the Third World—which had already been further developed under Foreign Minister Kurt Waldheim—was intensified based on the first contacts of Bruno Kreisky with most important leaders of the South in the early 1960s. In the period of 1970-1983, twelve diplomatic missions in Asia, Africa and Latin-America were opened up, and the official diplomatic visiting program was extended, especially with Asian and Arab countries. In 1977 and 1982, Latin-American countries were for the first time included in the Austrian visiting program.[69] These activities were not only a friendly gesture (for example, in 1970 Austria participated for the first time in the third summit of the non-aligned movement in Lusaka); they also manifested Austria's changing interests.[70] Austria accepted the status of a guest also in all following N & N summits.

The active and mediating position in the North-South conflict found its most apparent expression in Bruno Kreisky's personal engagement in the Middle East conflict.[71] Most of Kreisky's Middle East initiatives were first developed inside the Socialist International, which was one of the most pro-Israeli political forces after World War II. For the Socialist International, Israel was an asset for the advance of social democracy in Africa and Asia until the beginning of the 1970s. From 1973 onwards (i.e. after the Yom

Kippur War) that assessment changed. In November 1973, Kreisky addressed a conference of party leaders in London with the formula of the "legitimate rights of the Palestinians."[72] In spite of Israeli President Golda Meir's bitter objection, Kreisky's proposal to send a fact-finding mission of the Socialist International under his guidance to the Middle East was accepted. The mission visited the Middle East on three occasions: in March 1974, February 1975 and March 1976; it came to the conclusion that the partnership with the Arab world should be strengthened, the PLO be recognized and that a Palestinian State in Gaza and the Westbank should be advocated.[73] The Israeli Labor party's position in the Socialist International became relatively isolated.

From the end of the 1970s onward Kreisky's Middle East initiatives were mainly launched in the framework of the Austrian government's policy. In October 1979 Kreisky announced to the General Assembly of the United Nations the forthcoming recognition of the PLO by Austria. This recognition—extended in March 1980 by the Austrian Chancellor on behalf of the federal government—gave the PLO international status as the representative of the Palestinian people. The Austrian recognition of the PLO caused a major international controversy and forced the Austrian authorities to specify the meaning of their step.[74] "Self-determination" was redefined as the right of the Palestinians to an independent state and to be represented by the PLO.

Kreisky's Middle East activities and his understanding of the precarious situation of the Palestinian people as well as some of his innovative proposals, not only led to a temporary deterioration in Austria's relations with the government and the Congress of the United States[75] in the mid-1970s but also to much criticism from the domestic parliamentary opposition. Kreisky tried to downplay the—sometimes—intransigent elements of the PLO and explain that recognition concerned merely the right to establish a state. The Austrian step had major repercussions not only in the Middle East: it was highly welcomed by Arab states and subjected to a demarche by the Israeli government. In addition, Kreisky's mediating role was highly recognized worldwide.

In spite of Kreisky's support of the Palestinian case and his later activities in promoting dialogues and encounters between Israelis and Palestinians, Austria was several times the object of Palestinian terrorist incidents.[76]

Austria's disproportionate role in the Middle East conflict was due to the personal ambitions of Bruno Kreisky. In Kreisky's view, the conflict at the southern and eastern fringes of the Mediterranean basin and its possible repercussions on European security was important enough to risk major international controversies. Kreisky was sure to have advanced the case of the Palestinian people, but remained frustrated and misunderstood concerning Israel and the Israeli Labor party.

For the entire Kreisky era it is significant that the important measures were personally initiated by Bruno Kreisky, executed through his own contacts and channels and extensively discussed by the mass media.[77]

This is especially true with the Cancun summit of October 1981. The summit concept had been proposed in the much-discussed report of the North-South Commission,[78] edited by Willy Brandt, "to organize a North-South summit for survival." Willy Brandt had asked Kreisky to organize such a conference. Together with the Mexican president Lopez Portillo Kreisky organized the global summit in Cancun. It was the intention that Kreisky's conception of a "New Marshall Plan for Third World Countries"[79] would be the center of the discussion; Kreisky hoped that the almost-broken-down North-South dialogue could be recovered at this summit. Unfortunately, Kreisky got sick and was unable to attend the conference.[80] His absence was disastrous for the summit: the meeting of heads of states and governments from eight industrial and fourteen developing countries lacked his dynamic force which could have made a great success out of the event.

Austrian foreign policy in the North-South conflict of that period was not without considerable contradictions and ambiguities. Despite recurrent affirmations to increase the weak performance of the Austrian Official Development Assistance (ODA) and to strengthen its weak administrative infrastructure, the ODA did not gain in importance.[81] It was not only Kreisky but also politicians from other parties who justified the low aid level of ODA, arguing that the developing-countries' lobby within the Austrian population was not strong enough to promote an increase of ODA aid. This argument runs counter to the respectable private aid performance carried out by ecclesiastical and other organizations as well as the highly-ranked development aid of that period, as opinion polls show.[82]

During the 1970s, Austrian voting behavior in the United Nations was similarly ambiguous.[83] On the one hand, there was a tendency to vote along with the majority of the developing countries on substantial decisions—Austria being a member of the "like-minded countries" group in the United Nations.[84] On the other hand, the Austrian delegation would vote on *financial* decisions more in accordance with the majority of industrial states, meaning that Austria in general voted in favor of substantial but against financial Third World demands.

Parallel with the economic and political decline of the Third World, the increasingly harsh and conservative position of the new U.S. government under President Ronald Reagan in North-South relations and parallel with continuous stagnant economic tendencies in the industrial states that made the 1980s a "lost decade" for development politics, the global engagement of Austrian foreign policy also declined. Bruno Kreisky's retirement from his active political life after the loss of the absolute majority of the SPÖ in 1983 accelerated this process.

Economic Elements of Austrian Foreign Policy

In general, the Austrian economic record of the post-Second World War period can be characterized as the typical success story of a small European industrialized state.[85] In spite of a steadily growing linkage of the Austrian economy with world markets and a resulting higher degree of dependency on international business cycles, Austria was able to enlarge its political room to maneuver. Supportive factors of the positive record in the Austrian social-political fabric were, among others, a relatively large public sector with long-term economic perspectives (concerning profitability and job security) controlled by the government, a highly flexible small-to-medium-sized private sector, and corporative political structures based on the consensus of top representatives of organizations of employers and employees (called "social partnership").

During the 1970s and 1980s economic relations of national economies were increasingly internationalized on the global scale; from 1974-75 until the beginning of the 1980s a thorough slow-down of economic development in the industrial states occurred.[86] The Austrian overall record during that period of crisis was quite remarkable until the end of the 1970s. For some years, in spite of the global economic crisis, Austrian economic policy was recognized as a positive international example of a successful Keynesian, anti-cyclical policy.[87] It was based on the shared societal values of social peace in connection with a high rate of employment and an active policy of domestic adjustment to international changes on the one hand and on close integration into the EC-markets after the free-trade-treaty of 1972 on the other hand. One might say that throughout the 1970s Austria, in following path of political intervention, was successfully able to uncouple from the worst effects of the global economic crisis. At the beginning of the 1980s, the limits of such an economic policy became obvious and Austrian economic development, measured in terms of significant economic indicators and of Austria's status of positive internationalization[88] (see Appendix 3), fell behind comparable European states like Finland, Sweden and Switzerland. In the mid-1980s the critics made the economic policy of the Kreisky government liable for these setbacks.

The dynamics and structures of foreign economic relations in the Kreisky era can be characterized as follows (see Appendix 4):[89] Austria as a small industrialized country is heavily dependent on foreign trade. The export percentage of Western countries (that is, OECD countries) declined slightly until the mid-1970s and increased in the following period. Still of prime importance were the EC and especially the Federal Republic of Germany's markets. The percentage of exports to Third World countries had increased since 1972-73 but declined after 1985 to the level of the 1960s. The increase of the exports in Third World countries at that time was the result of high income revenues, especially of the OPEC countries because of an increased price level of crude oil. Since 1974 the relations to the OPEC countries were continuously intensified, not the least because of Kreisky's fabulous image in that part of the world; in 1980, the percentage to OPEC countries of the total Austrian exports to developing countries was almost 50 percent.[90] In the midst of the 1980s that the foreign trade with newly industrializing countries gained in importance.

Austrian exports to Eastern Europe (which in the inter-war period reached a level of one third of the overall export volume) fell—as a consequence of great economic problems of the socialist countries in that period and due to Austria's deliberate policy of "Westernization." The export level was approximately 13 percent in the 1950s and between 12 and 17 percent in 1965-1975; in 1988 the percentage was down to only 9 percent and is still shrinking. The Austrian export structure with regard to the developing countries (and to certain extent also to Eastern Europe) was that of a typically Western industrialized country: low-processed goods (commodities, fuels and agricultural products) were imported, processed goods and technology intensive products were exported. The foreign trade structure toward the higher industrialized Western countries was just the opposite. Above all, the Eastern European states are, to a great extent, debtors of the Austrian finance system. The typical foreign financial status vis-à-vis the foreign countries traditionally shows Austria as a debtor of short term credits to Western countries and as a long term creditor to Eastern European countries.[91] Andreas Unterberger recently charged that a great percentage of these Eastern debts had been latent subsidies for Austrian nationalized industry.[92] Another annoying fact was that the percentage of the energy imports from countries of the Eastern bloc was rather high (in the second half of the 1980s almost 100 percent of the gas imports had been imported from the then-Soviet Union, and coal imports have been varying annually between 30 and 80 percent).

The foundation of the EC in 1957 was a challenge for Austrian integration policy. The great coalition government first opted for the creation of a great European free trade area. When this attempt proved a failure,[93] Austria, together with other six European states, founded the EFTA in 1960. Attempts at a multilateral bridgebuilding between EC and EFTA in the 1960s were not successful, and the political fight of the Austrian parties between the "right" supporters of a further approach towards the EC and the "leftist" group of those who opted for a continuation of EFTA would determine the integration debate for years.[94]

During the SPÖ single-party government, in July 1972, bilateral free-trade treaties were concluded between the EFTA countries and the EC in the field of industrial products. The Austrian treaty was less comprehensive than the association treaty that was intended during the 1960s. Although the non-tariff barriers were not touched, the damage for Austrian industry proved to be by far smaller than was expected in the 1960s if full membership could not be reached. The Austrian export economy, however, profited from the easy access to EC-markets.[95]

At the beginning of the 1980s, the phase of stagnating "eurosclerotic" development in the EC was overcome, and first steps towards a common West European market were taken. In the opinion of the Austrian government, this could mean that the profits for Austria, which could be realized through the free trade treaty of 1972, might be lost. It was Willibald Pahr's successor in the post of foreign minister, Erwin Lanc, who since May 1983 set the course for an intensified approach towards Western Europe.[96]

There were two more events at the beginning of the 1980s which increased the pace of Austria's foreign policy approach toward Western Europe. First after 1982, it was the U.S. government, that put pressure on certain European states, including Austria, because of high-tech exports to the Eastern bloc, originating from American technological development, which were listed under the tightened control of the COCOM provisions.[97] Second, another aspect overshadowed the economic relations towards the United States: with reference to the provisions of GATT, the United States government prohibited the levying of an oil-seed customs duty, under the protection of which an Austrian oil-seed production could have been erected. It seems more than probable that behind both interventions were both political and considerable economic interests of the United States.

Critics of the Kreisky Era

The notorious "consensus in foreign policy" that guided with only some exceptions the Second Austrian Republic still existed on basic objectives during the entire period of the foreign policy of the Kreisky era; yet, as Karl Gruber has stated, it was almost destroyed "over irrelevant matters."[98] The increasing criticism of Austrian foreign policy starting in the middle of the 1970s was at first mainly directed toward the chancellor's Middle East policy. Kreisky's Middle East engagement since that time led to disagreement between the governments of Austria and the United States. The ÖVP, worrying about a possible deterioration of relations with the Western superpower, took up this criticism. But in spite of such ÖVP critiques, the foreign policy of the Kreisky government [99] could rely on relatively broad support in the Austrian public as opinion polls showed.[100]

At the same time, the Austrian international lawyer Konrad Ginther[101] criticized the absence of a strong military component in Austria's foreign policy. Instead of putting stress on the military defense component, Ginther detected a strong emphasis on a positive peace or active neutrality policy to reach global peace and détente. Thus, in his view, the Austrian understanding of neutrality had approached the idea of peaceful coexistence, an ideologically empty formula, promulgated by Soviet foreign policy. Alfred Verdross, on the other hand, argued that a neutral country, being above all a member of the United Nations, could not abstain from all international conflicts and therefore must through an active neutrality policy "be instrumental in the strengthening of an overall peace and international security." The interpretation of a positive definition of peace be oriented according to the principles of Western democracies.[102]

But the main political controversies were carried out between the two great parties. In October 1978, the ÖVP started its criticism by formulating her foreign political foundations as a motion for resolution in parliament; this was seen as her "foreign political doctrine."[103] In December of the same year, the SPÖ followed with a comparable declaration of principles.[104] Applications were presented to a parliamentary subcommittee for consideration. Since there were no agreements to be reached between the two parties, the initiative petered out. The other initiative, the "council for foreign affairs" which was founded in 1976, also failed to elaborate a common foreign policy line of the government together with the opposition party.[105] Parallel with the deterioration of the economic and political international framework, the domestic criticism of Kreisky's foreign policy became increasingly severe. Representatives of the ÖVP not only complained about an increasing "anti-American tendency," "neutralism," and a dangerous reinterpretation of neutrality as "equidistance"[106] between the blocs, but also about the North-South and development policies as an "international hypocrisy and individual image neurosis" of Bruno Kreisky.[107] Andreas Kohl[108] criticized the SPÖ for cultivating a "détente euphoria" and "a total equation between foreign and neutrality policy." In addition, Khol argued that dissent about the definition of détente characterized the whole of the period of the 1970s;[109] the election of Ronald Reagan, as president of the United States, however, had initiated a completely new phase of détente.[110]

The opposition's critique was in most cases directed toward Chancellor Bruno Kreisky himself. Until 1978, the debate had been relatively moderate and differentiated. However, it became evident for the ÖVP that the international profile of Kreisky's foreign policy created a voting bonus for the SPÖ. The internationally high reputation of the chancellor was appreciated by the Austrian public. Still, in January 1977 the then-chairman of the ÖVP Josef Taus, mentioned in a speech before the Austrian Foreign Policy Association, that the principle of a common foreign policy was still kept during the first phase of the single government of the SPÖ, that is until 1975.[111] Only very carefully did he intimate that this consensus might be questioned for the second half of the 1970s. In the middle of 1978, demands were raised in the ÖVP that the party had to finally start to develop a foreign policy line of her own.[112] From now on critics became more and more alert, with the ÖVP developing a strong international infrastructure inside her party organization.

After the beginnings of the 1980s, global tensions steadily increased with the Teheran hostage affair, the invasion by the Soviet Union of Afghanistan and the declaration of martial law in Poland. Austrian foreign policy and especially Bruno Kreisky actively tried to mediate between the conflicting parties. At the same time the Austrian foreign ministry and Kreisky cooperated closely with countries of the non-aligned movement and *inter alia* a meeting was arranged between Kreisky and the Libyan President Mohammed Gadaffi. In 1979, the Austrian foreign ministry also officially recognized the PLO as the representative of the Palestinian people. All these activities were heavily criticized by the ÖVP.[113]

The controversy heated up during the next years. In 1981, set off by a contribution of Andreas Unterberger, a journalist of the conservative daily news *Die Presse*, the controversy was continued in the form of written pamphlets.[114] Unterberger criticized the three-fold "mythologization" of Austrian foreign policy: neutrality, détente and Bruno Kreisky. Referring to Unterberger's critical remarks, Ludwig Steiner, the then-foreign political spokesperson of the ÖVP in parliament, took a critical stance towards the foreign policy of the SPÖ government. He criticized the *Kreisky'sche Effekthascherei*[115] (Kreisky's fishing for effects); but contrary to Unterberger's statement he declared that "twenty-five years after" the conclusion of the State-Treaty it was still true that "our neutrality ... was not a catch-phrase, not a means and no myth." Andreas Khol conceded in the same number of the *Europäische Rundschau* that the social democratic policy in the interpretation of détente had acted "bona fide, in good faith." The SPÖ had followed the "universal mainstream" of that time. Above all, he stated, the Kreisky government had been able to establish a respected place for Austria in Europe.[116] The controversies continued until 1983; but in the electoral campaign of the 1983 spring elections, the ÖVP, despite its criticism, refrained from raising foreign policy issues.[117]

Concluding Remarks on Foreign Policy after 1983 and Kreisky's Late Activities

After Kreisky's retirement, a small coalition government followed from 1983 until 1986. The governmental responsibility of the SPÖ and her small partner the FPÖ, under the chancellorship of Fred Sinowatz was still following more or less in the footsteps of the 1970s and sometimes seeking Kreisky's advice. Austrian foreign policy in the short ministerial era of Erwin Lanc was confronted with a moving international environment. It started to rearrange some of its variables and afterwards changed important determinants. The times of a risk-taking, globally-oriented and "interventionist" foreign policy of the Kreisky era were gone. The European environment changed as well; the "new European dynamic" of the EC, as a consequence of losing economic ground in relation to North America and the Pacific region (above all Japan), became a challenge for the small industrialized EFTA states.[118] The main objectives of that new era were more heavily stressed, a policy directed toward Austria's neighboring states, and Europe; the military component of its security policy was strengthened again. This period of Austrian politics was not only characterized by a number of publicized scandals also noticed abroad; it was shaped by a phase of squaring off by the opposition against the Kreisky era.[119]

Kreisky's influence on concrete foreign policy issues began to diminish. His state of health had deteriorated in 1981. That was one of the reasons that he left the government after the loss of an absolute parliamentary majority in the wake of the 1983 elections. In the following years the record of his international contacts on high political levels, a great number of invitations to important conferences, interviews and lectures, his activities as vice-president of the Socialist International, as president of scientific and political institutions, the Austrian Institute for International Affairs, the Vienna Institute of Development and the educational institute of the SPÖ (the Renner Institute), show how intensively he tried to take an active part on the international and Austrian political scene and to remain effective.[120] It was especially the North-South dialogue, humanitarian activities and his interest in international social issues that were in the center of his activities during this last phase.

Kreisky remained interested in the Middle East, although the assassination of Arafat's close companion Issam Sartawi, who had become a close friend of Kreisky's, and the resettlement of the PLO headquarters from Beirut to Tunis caused some frustration vis-a-vis Arafat and the PLO.[121] But Kreisky was still instrumental in Israeli-Palestinian negotiations for an exchange of war prisoners that took place in 1983 (six Israeli against 4700 Palestinians) and 1985 (three Israeli war prisoners against 1150 Palestinian war prisoners and others). He still believed that there was a chance to reach the stage where political negotiations and mutual recognition could be possible. Many of his proposals pointed in the right direction or were taken up later on.

In 1986 Kreisky also agreed to chair the international scientific "Commission on Employment in Europe". The Commission published first results in 1989,[122] proposing measures against mass unemployment in Western and Eastern Europe. The report was, among others, also given to the president of the EC commission Jacques Delor, in connection with establishing the "social dimension" of the Common Market.

During the discussions about the ÖVP presidential candidate of 1986, Kurt Waldheim, Kreisky at the beginning of the campaign accused the World Jewish Congress of "exaggerated interference" and even accused "some Austrians of Jewish origin"[123] of having had a Nazi-fascist past. In later stages of the campaign he began to keep a greater distance from Kurt Waldheim whom he had staunchly supported in his candidacy for U.N. secretary general in the early 1970s, not knowing about Waldheim's position and activities in the Balkans during the Second World War. This might partly mirror Kreisky's ambivalence in connection with his own Jewish descent and his complicated relations with Israeli politicians and politics and with Austrian Jews over almost his entire lifetime.[124] After all, the election of Kurt Waldheim as federal president of Austria and the international reactions in the mass media, together with a number of scandals mentioned above, tarnished Austria's image abroad, bringing it to an all-time low in the second half of the 1980s.

One could finally ask whether anything remains in Austria's foreign policy from the Kreisky era since Kreisky's views had been highly appreciated by most governmental officials of the Austrian foreign service. For many reasons it no longer seems to be the case. Considering the external dimension, the international environment has changed profoundly. Moreover there were two decisive internal events that deeply divided the officials of the foreign ministry and, as a consequence, destroyed traditional values and loyalties as well as the corporate social internal structures of the 1970s—the election of Kurt Waldheim as Austrian president and the discussions about full membership in the EC. At the end of the 1980s only little could be traced back to the Kreisky era. But one could ask further: would the present Austrian foreign policy look different with Bruno Kreisky as its main representative? Taking into account Kreisky's high amount of pragmatism, his intuitive sensitivity, and his ability to move domestic constraints and gain more room to maneuver, one could realistically argue that his foreign policy of today would differ strongly compared to that of the 1970s and early 1980s. But it would also be quite different from its present shape.

Because of his weak state of health and because of differences of opinion with the politics of the SPÖ and its leaders—he never agreed that the ÖVP should take over the foreign ministry after 1986—Kreisky retired from all official positions (as president of honor of the SPÖ, as president of the Renner Institut, the Austrian Institute for International Affairs and the Vienna Institute for Development). He still remained active on the international scene as a private elder statesman, as a lecturer and as a well-informed and wise interpreter of international and domestic political affairs. When he died in late July 1990 he had been the conscience of Austrian public life for a generation.

The Kreisky era undoubtedly was the most significant and active period of Austrian foreign affairs since 1955. Despite some failures, it succeeded within an international, quickly-changing framework in realizing creative policies; positive aspects obviously were predominant. It is still not contested that this kind of foreign policy contributed a lot to establishing a profile of Austrian society, an image within the international system, which was both unknown before and after Kreisky and disproportional to the size of the country. It was to a great extent because of the abilities and the international reputation of Bruno Kreisky, his perseverance in communicating in spite of controversial dialogues in the domestic as well as in the international arenas. For the first time in Austrian history after World War II, someone had awakened the interest of the Austrian people in foreign affairs.[125] Kreisky managed to establish little Austria within the international environment as a respected partner. It will be difficult for Kreisky's epigones to live up to such high standards.

* The article is based on the extant literature about Austrian foreign policy between 1950-1983, on archival materials, and on speeches by Bruno Kreisky. In researching this era, I was fortunate to having had the chance to speak to several persons who were close collaborators of Bruno Kreisky. I should like to thank Erwin Bielka, Peter Jankowitsch, Rudolf Kirchschläger, Peter Kreisky, Erwin Lanc, Georg Lennkh, Gabriele Matzner, Ingo Mussi, Thomas Nowotny, Willibald Pahr, Oliver Rathkolb, Alois Reitbauer, Margit Schmidt and Hans Thalberg.

NOTES

1. Cf. the "Lager"-theory of Adam Wandruszka, "Österreichs politische Struktur," in *Geschichte der Republik Österreich*, ed. Heinrich Benedikt (Vienna: Verlag für Geschichte und Politik, 1977), 289-485, and Rudolf Steininger's interpretation of the Austrian Society of the Second Republic with the concept of "Versäulung," due to external threats, the experience of World War II and the lasting Allied occupation. Besides its well-known aspects of distinct lines of cleavage between subcultures - the clerical and the socialist "camps" ("Lager")—the notion "Versäulung" ("pillarization") means restriction of authority for the leading political parties and forced involvement into the political decision-making process by other power groups of society. "Polarisierung und Integration. Eine vergleichende Untersuchung der strukturellen Versäulung der Gesellschaft in den Niederlanden und in Österreich," in *Politik und Wähler*, eds. René König, Erwin K. Scheuch and Rudolf Wildenmann, vol.14 (Maisenheim am Glan: A. Hain, 1975), 254 ff.

2. Hans J. Morgenthau, *United States Policies in Austria. A Report Prepared at the Request of The Department of State*, Washington, D.C., October 1, 1951. mimeo.

3. In January 1935 Kreisky had been imprisoned also by the Schuschnigg-Regime; he was condemmed for high treason in the "Sozialistenprozeß" of March 1936 and released not before June 1936, a fact deeply and traumatically rooted in Kreisky's memory.

4. Austrian foreign policy of the period of the Second Republic is discussed in several articles. Among others see Renate Kicker, Andreas Khol and Hanspeter Neuhold, eds., *Außenpolitik und Demokratie in Österreich. Strukturen—Strategien—Stellungnahmen* (Salzburg: Neugebauer, 1983); Helmut Kramer, "Aspekte der österreichischen Außenpolitik (1970-1985)," in *Der österreichische Weg 1970-1985. 15 Jahre, die Österreich verändert haben*, eds. Erich Fröschl and Helge Zoitl (Vienna: Europaverlag, 1986), 187-199; "Wende in der österreichischen Außenpolitik? Zur Außenpolitik der SPÖ—ÖVP—Koalition," in *ÖZP* 17 (1986): 117-131; "Strukturentwicklung der Außenpolitik (1945-1990)" in *Handbuch des politischen Systems Österreichs*, eds. Herbert Dachs, et al., (Vienna: Manz, 1991),

637-657. Specific contributions on the Kreisky era can be found in Erich Bielka, Peter Jankowitsch and Hans Thalberg, eds., *Die Ära Kreisky. Schwerpunkte der österreichischen Außenpolitik* (Vienna: Europaverlag, 1983); Herbert Denk and Helmut Kramer, "Außenpolitik und internationale Solidarität. Die Außenpolitik der SPÖ von 1945-1986," in *Auf dem Weg zur Staatspartei. Zur Geschichte und Politik der SPÖ seit 1945*, eds. Peter Pelinka and Gerhard Steger (Vienna: Gesellschaftskritik, 1988), 267-292; Oliver Rathkolb, "Sozialistische Außenpolitik(er) in Österreich 1945-1959," in *Die Bewegung. 100 Jahre Sozialdemokratie in Österreich*, eds. Erich Fröschl, Maria Mesner and Helga Zoitl (Vienna: Passagenverlag, 1990), 499-514. For critical appraisals from the side of the then-oppositional conservative party, see among others Andreas Unterberger, "Die Außenpolitische Entwicklung," in *Politik in Österreich. Die Zweite Republik: Bestand und Wandel*, ed. Wolfgang Mantel (Vienna: Böhlau, 1992), 204-239.

5. See Paul Lendvai and Karl Heinz Ritschel, *Kreisky. Portait eines Staatsmannes* (Vienna: Zsolnay, 1974), 27.

6. For Kreisky's political biography see the first volume of his autobiography, *Zwischen den Zeiten* (Vienna and Berlin: Siedler-Kremayr, 1986).

7. Ibid., 351.

8. Lendvai and Ritschel, 28.

9. As a proof of Kreisky's post-Keynesian thinking in his last years, see his introductory remarks in the report of the Kreisky Commission, *Zwanzig Millionen suchen Arbeit. Ein Programm für Vollbeschäftigung in den 90er Jahren* (Vienna: Passagenverlag, 1989), 14.

10. See the "Stockholmer Erklärung of the Austrian Social Democratic group in Stockholm," in Bruno Kreisky, *Zwischen den Zeiten,* 1986, 391. Kreisky's understanding of "social democracy" is well-documented in the introduction of the published dissertation of Christoph Butterwegges, *Austromarxismus und Staat* (Marburg, 1991), 9 ff.

11. Kreisky's Swedish exile is documented in his biographical remarks *Zwischen den Zeiten*, 1986, 365-386.

12. See Kreisky's article in *Foreign Affairs* (January 1959): 269-281.

13. See Bruno Kreisky, *Reden*, vol. I (Vienna: Österreichische Staatsdruckerei, 1981), 621-629.

14. See Bruno Kreisky, *Im Strom der Politik. Der Memoiren zweiter Teil* (Vienna and Berlin: Siedler-Kremayr, 1988), 186.

15. For the important role of Bruno Kreisky in the resolution of the South-Tyrol conflict with Italy see Felix Ermacora, *Südtirol und das Vaterland Österreich* (Vienna-Munich: Amalthea, 1984), 82-91.

16. Rathkolb, "Sozialistische Außenpolitik(er)" (1990), 499.

17. Kreisky, *Reden*, vol. I, 180 ff.

18. Bruno Kreisky's understanding of North-South relations is extensively discussed by Jankowitsch, in Bielka, Jankowitsch, Thalberg, (1983), 259-261.

19. The previous periods are, first, 1945-1955 with the main task of the reconstruction of Austria's economy as well as her political independence and sovereignty; 1955-1966, the time of great coalition governments and the establishment of confidence within Central Europe and with the signatory powers; then 1966-1970, the period of the majority government of the ÖVP with a further opening up of the scope of Austrian foreign policy.

20. This phase structure follows *grosso modo* the more comprehensive contribution of Denk and Kramer, 267-292; especially see 276-281.

21. See Heinz Fischer, "Muss Österreichs Außenpolitik revidiert werden?," in *Europäische Rundschau* 9 (1982): 3-12 and Helmut Ornauer, "Ein Marshall-Plan für die Dritte Welt?," in *Österreichisches Jahrbuch für Politik (ÖJP) 1982*, eds. Andreas Khol and Alfred Stirnemann (Munich: Oldenburg, 1983), 207-273.

22. For the increasingly critical Austrian discussion see the series of contributions in Andreas Unterberger, "Mytholigisierung der österreichischen Außenpolitik," in *Europäische Rundschau* 9 (1991): 89-96 and the following answers by Andreas Khol, Heinz Fischer, Ludwig Steiner, Thomas Nowotny und Gregor Woschnagg.

23. See Karl Zemanek, "Austria's Policy of Neutrality: Constants and Variables," in *The European Neutrals*, eds. Hanspeter Neuhold and Hans Thalberg, 1984, 17-23.

24. It was as early as 1953 that the newly-elected chancellor, Julius Raab, tried to find a solution for Austria's independence in concluding a direct agreement with the Soviet Union by offering the neutralization of Austria. This call for ideological neutralization was heavily criticized by politicians from the German CDU/CSU as well as from the FDP but cheered from the German Social Democrats (SPD). However, the Austrian Socialist Party objected to Raab's view. See Oliver Rathkolb, "Austria's 'Ostpolitik': Early Détente Efforts, 1955-1965. Honest Broker or Double Agent?" (Paper prepared for the sixteenth Annual Conference of the German Studies Association, Minnesota, 1-4 October 1992), 4 and 8.

25. See Gerald Stourzh, "The Origins of Austrian Neutrality," in *Neutrality: Changing Concepts and Practices*, eds. Alan T. Leonhard and Nicholas Mercuro (Lanham: University Press of America, 1988), 38-40.

26. Kreisky, *Reden*, vol.I, 145.

27. Bruno Kreisky, "Austria Draws the Balance," in *Foreign Affairs* (January 1959), 277; he made similar arguments in a 1973 lecture in Warsaw. See Kreisky, *Reden*, vol. II, 313.

28. See Walter Hacker, "Neutralität im Atomzeitalter," in *Probleme der österreichischen Politik*, vol.2 (1968), 85 ff.

29. See Paul Luif, *Neutrale in der EG? Die wirtschaftliche Integration in Westeuropa und die neutralen Staaten* (Vienna: Braumüller, 1988), 40.

30. Kramer, "Strukturenentwicklung," 646.

31. Paul Luif, "Die internationale Politik der österreichischen Volkspartei," in *Schwarzbunter Vogel. Studien zum Programm, Politik und Struktur der ÖVP* (Vienna: Junius, 1985), 211. "Indicators" of an active foreign policy are given in Olav Elgstrom, "Active Foreign Policy as a Preventive Strategy Against Dependence," in *Small States in Europe and Dependence*, ed. Otmar Höll, 1983, 262-280.

32. Undoubtedly the position of a small neutral country in times of high tension between power blocs is especially precarious. In the 1970s there existed a broad political consensus on basic values guiding Austrian foreign policy such as human rights, the rule of law, strengthening of détente and social market economy.

33. See Silvia Michal-Misak, "Österreich in den Vereinten Nationen," in *Österreichische Zeitschrift für Politikwissenschaft* (ÖZP) 19 (1990): 379-395.

34. See Hanspeter Neuhold, ed., *CSCE: N+N Perspectives* (Vienna: Braumüller, 1987).

35. Austrian peacekeeping operations are restricted to cases in which all conflicting parties would agree, to the mediating exercise.

36. Austria did not follow the example of Italy and Canada which had accepted the inclusion of the phraseology "Taiwan is an integral part of the territory of China" within the recognition communiqué. Since 1959 Kreisky's position towards the "two Chinas" had been quite different than that of the United States. He had opted for the integration of continental China into international world politics.

37. Kreisky, *Reden*, vol.II, 436 f.

38. See Karl Gruber, "Freunde im Westen," in *Die Ära Kreisky*, eds. Erich Bielka, Peter Jankowitsch and Hans Thalberg, 1983, 117-142 and Kramer, "Aspekte der österreichischen Außenpolitik" (1986). Foreign Minister Rudolf Kirchschläger officially protested against the Christmas Eve bombardment of Hanoi. Kreisky disagreed with Kirchschläger postition and criticized him for the protest.

39. Kreisky, "Austria Draws the Balance," 281.

40. Henry Kissinger, *Memoiren 1968-1973*, vol.I (Munich: Bertelsmann, 1979), 1204.

41. See even Julius Raab in his speech of 26 October 1955 on the federal constitutional neutrality law: "Neutrality commits the state, but not the individual .... Neither does the law imply a commitment to ideological neutrality." (cited by Kreisky, "Austria Draws the Balance," 276). The year before, Raab's position was more in the opposite direction as he would have accepted ideological neutralization as a price for independence. See Rathkolb, "Austria's 'Ostpolitik'," 9.

42. Kreisky, *Reden*, vol.II, 863. Under the pseudonym "X" in the U.S. journal *Foreign Affairs* (1947), the "creator" of the notion and the policy of "containment", George F. Kennan, demanded a strong U.S. stance against communism. Through military and economic aid for allies of the United States in the neighborhood of the "Iron Curtain," communism should be "contained."

43. Ingo Mussi, "Bruno Kreisky und der schöpferische Dialog mit den Vereinigten Staaten," in *Die Ära Kreisky*, eds. Erich Bielka, Peter Jankowitsch and Hans Thalberg (1983), 128 f.

44. Ibid., 136 f. The beginning presidency of Ronald Reagan was a turn also in the domestic Austrian discussion insofar as some ÖVP-representatives euphorically interpreted that fact as a "new phase in global détente policy." See Andreas Khol, "Zur Kritik und Bestandsaufnahme der österreichischen Außenpolitik," in *Europäische Rundschau* 9 (1981): 111. On Kreisky and Reagan see also the Rathkolb essay in this volume.

45. See Kreisky, *Reden*, vol.I, 466.

46. Ibid., 462.

47. Ibid., 461.

48. See Kreisky, *Reden*, vol.II, 875.

49. After a decade of intensive negotiations, the Soviet Union had agreed to a fully sovereign Austria and to the conclusion of the State Treaty on 15 May 1955 only when it was made clear that Austria would not join Germany (see Art. 4 of the State Treaty—*Anschlußverbot*) and would become a permanent neutral country (*nach dem Vorbild der Schweiz*). On 26 October 1955 Austria, out of its own free will, declared its permanent neutrality, following its non-binding committment in the Moscow Memorandum in April of the same year. See Gerald Stourzh, *Kleine Geschichte des Staatsvertrages* (Graz: Styria, 1975), 170-172.

50. See Heinrich Siegler, ed., *Österreich. Chronik 1945-1972* (Vienna: Siegler, 1973), 126.

51. See Otmar Höll, "Kleinstaatliche Außenpolitik am Beispiel der N+N Gruppe," in *ÖZP* 15 (1986): 294. Austria withdrew its proposal to host the main conference in Vienna after the invasion of WTO troops in Czechoslovakia in August 1968. In July 1970, Foreign Minister Rudolf Kirchschläger sent a memorandum to all participating states proposing Vienna only as the negotiation place for the preparatory talks.

52. See John Bunzl, *Gewalt ohne Grenzen. Nahost-Terror und Österreich* (Vienna: Braumüller, 1991).

53. Cf. ÖZA 4/1975, pp. 232-234. A "clean" version is given in Kreisky *Reden*, vol. II, 490-493.

54. Heinrich Haymerle, "Die Beziehungen zur Grossmacht im Osten," in *Die Ära Kreisky*, eds. Erich Bielke, Peter Jankowitsch, and Hans Thalberg, 1983, 193.

55. Austria's neighborhood policy is analyzed in Andreas Khol, "Österreichs Beziehung zu den Nachbarstaaten," in *Außenpolitik und Demokratie in Österreich*, eds. Renate Kicker, Andreas Khol, and Hanspeter Neuhold, 1983, 371-409 and Hans-Georg Heinrich, "Österreichische Nachbarschaftspolitik--ein Mythos?," in *ÖZP* 17 (1988): 155-168.

56. The Soviet Union at an early stage showed great interest in improved relations between Austria and Hungary as Bruno Kreisky states ("Austria Draws the Balance," 279). Moscow gave early evidence through diplomatic channels that improved relations with the West for Budapest "leads through Vienna."

57. See Hans-Georg Heinrich, "Die Entwicklung der österreichisch-ungarischen Beziehungen," in *die Beziehungen zwischen Österreich und Ungarn: Sonderfall oder Modell?*, ed. Zdenek Mlynar (Vienna: Braumüller, 1985), 21-29.

58. This event is well documented in Helmut Fazekas, Die (Kärntner) Minderheitenfrage und Österreichs Beziehungen zu Jugoslawien. Vienna, mimeo, 1983; Hanns Haas and Karl Stuhlpfarrer, *Österreich und seine Slowenen* (Vienna: Löcker und Wögenstein, 1977); Theodor Veiter, *Die Kärntner Ortstafelkommission. Arbeit und Ergebnisse der Studienkommission für Probleme der slowenischen Volksgruppe in Kärnten von 1972-1975* (Vienna: Braumüller, 1980); Otmar Höll, ed., *Österreich--Jugoslawien. Determinanten und Perspektiven ihrer Beziehungen* (Vienna: Braumüller, 1988).

59. See Otmar Höll, *Österreich-Jugoslawien. Determinanten und Perspektiven ihrer Beziehungen* (Vienna: Braumüller, 1988), 230-235.

60. See Otmar Höll, *Österreich—Jugoslawien* (1988), 234.

61. The European concept of Charles de Gaulle (cooperation from the Atlantic to the Urals) provided for a special role of Austria as a mediator between Western and Eastern Europe. See Oliver Rathkolb, "Austria and European Integration after World War II, *CAS,* Vol. I (1993), 54f.

62. Above all, Kreisky carried out an intensive humanitarian "silent diplomacy," intervening directly with Eastern politicians over individual human rights cases. This discreet form of intervention was quite successful and lasted until his death in 1990.

63. See Waldemar Hummer and Gerhard Wagner, eds., *Österreich im Europarat 1956-1986. Bilanz einer dreißigjährigen Mitgliedschaft* (Vienna: Verlag der österreichischen Akademie der Wissenschaften, 1988).

64. After the death of Emperor Maximilian I in 1519 his successor Charles V was able to unite his Spanish- as well as the Austro-Habsburg dominions; in 1863 the brother of Emperor Francis Joseph I Archduke Maximilian was appointed as Emperor of Mexico; also cf. Alexander Randa's book on the—unsuccessful—attempts of the Austro-Hungarian monarchy to conquer overseas colonies, *Österreich in Übersee* (Vienna 1966).

65. See Wolfgang Benedek, "Österreichische Außenpolitik in den Nord-Süd-Beziehungen," in *Außenpolitik und Demokratie in Österreich*, eds. Renate Kicker, Andreas Khol and Hanspeter Neuhold (Salzburg: Neugebauer, 1983), 321-370; Otmar Höll, "Entwicklungspolitik," in *Handbuch des politischen Systems Österreichs*, eds. Herbert Dachs, et al., 1991, 690-704; Anselm Skuhra, "Austrian Aid: Policy and Performance," in *European Development Assistance*, vol.I, *Policies and Performance*, ed. Olav Stokke (Tilburg: Tilburg Press, 1984), 65-87.

66. For the important part, Bruno Kreisky played in the resolution of the South-Tyrol-conflict see Felix Ermacora, 1984.

67. See Peter Jankowisch, "Österreich und die Dritte Welt," in *Die Ära Kreisky*, eds. Erich Bielka, Peter Jankowitsch and Hans Thalberg, 1983, 257-292.

68. A general survey on the Austrian development policy is given by Höll "Entwicklungspolitik," 690-704.

69. See Paul Luif, "Außenwirtschaftpolitik," in *Handbuch des politischen Systems Österreichs*, eds. Herbert Dachs, Peter Gerlich et al., 1991, 767 f.

70. The decision to participate in the Lusaka summit was taken partly from an expected spin-off that developing countries would support Austria's intended election into the security council of the United Nations. The decision to be a candidate for the security council was made alone by the foreign minister at the time, Rudolf Kirchschläger, without previously informing Kreisky.

71. See Hans Thalberg, "Die Nahost-Politik," in *Die Ära Kreisky*, eds. Erich Bielka, Peter Jankowitsch and Hans Thalberg, 1983, 293-322.

72. Ibid., 293, 303.

73. John Bunzl, 1991, 47.

74. See *Österreichische Zeitschrift für Außenpolitik* (ÖZA) 1 (1980): 53 f; 2 (1980): 125 f; John Bunzl, 1991, 61.

75. Kreisky's role in the Middle East was not only criticized but also highly accepted in the United States; some of his early proposals (such as direct negotiations between Palestinians and Israeli) became reality many years later. Considering the diplomatic recognition of the PLO by the Austrian foreign ministry, critics in the U.S. Congress stated that this was "an attempt of a small country to extend its profile." See Kramer, "Strukturentwicklung," 648.

76. John Bunzl, 1991, 50 ff.

77. Lendvai and Ritschel, 1974, 323-346.

78. North-South Commission, ed. Willy Brandt, *A Program of Survival: Common Interests of the Industrial and Developing Countries* (German ed.: Cologne: 1980), 36 ff.

79. Kreisky's first reference to build up a Marshall Plan for developing countries can be found as early as in his speech in 1958 at the occasion of an international diplomatic seminar in the Kleßheim Castle near Salzburg. See Kreisky, *Reden*, vol.I, 61-68; see also Dorit Fischer, "Ein Marshall-Plan für die Dritte Welt. Der österreichische Vorschlag zu einem verstärkten Ressourcentransfer," in *ÖZP* 10 (1981): 139-152; Helmut Ornauer, 1983, 207-273.

80. Among the most famous participants were U.S. president Ronald Reagon, the French president Francois Mitterand, the British prime minister Margaret Thatcher, the Japanese prime minister Zenko Suzuki, the Chinese prime minister Zaho Ziyang, the Indian prime minister Indira Gandhi, the Tanzanian president Julius Nyerere and the Canadian prime minister Pierre Elliott Trudeau, who in the absence of Bruno Kreisky, chaired the Conference.

81. Otmar Höll, *Österreichische Entwicklungshilfe 1970-1983. Kritische Analyse und internationaler Vergleich* (Vienna: Braumüller, 1986).

82. Otmar Höll, "Problembereiche von globaler Bedeutung," in *Das außenpolitische Bewußtsein der Österreicher*, eds. Hanspeter Neuhold and Paul Luif (Vienna: Braumüller, 1992), 131 f.

83. Manfred Moschner and Franz Quendler, Das österreichische Abstimmungsverhalten in den Vereinten Nationen 1976-1980 (Vienna: mimeo, 1983.)

84. See Anthony J. Dolman, "The Like-Minded Coutries and the North-South Conflict," in *ÖZP* 10 (1981): 153-163.

85. For a general overview on European small states' research see Otmar Höll, *Small States in Europe and Dependence* (Vienna: Braumüller, 1983).

86. See Helmut Kramer, ed., *Österreich im Internationalen System*, 161-190.

87. There was a vivid discussion about the "Austrian model" going on in the late 1970s and early 1980s. As example, see among others Peter Katzenstein, "Dependence and Autonomy: Austria in an Interdependent World," in *ÖZA* 19 (1979): 241-255; Walter Lang, "Krisenmanagement durch Neokorporatismus," in *Politische Vierteljahresschrift* 21 (1981): 6-25; see also the Rothschild essay in this volume.

88. See Waltraut Urban, "Österreichische Direktinvestitionen in der Dritten Welt und Lateinamerika," in *Zeitschrift für Lateinamerika* 35 (1988): 67-83; Claudia Pichl, "Internationale Investitionen. Verflechtung der österreichischen Wirtschaft," in *Wifo-Monatsberichte* (March 1989): 161-176.

89. See Helmut Kramer and Otmar Höll, "Österreich in der internationalen Entwicklung," in *Handbuch des politischen Systems Österreichs*, eds. Herbert Dachs, et al., 1991, 50-69; Paul Luif, "Außenpolitik," 1991, 677.

90. See Höll, "Entwicklungspolitik," 1991, 696 and Mehdi Fallah-Nodeh, Austria's Relations with the OPEC Countries 1960-1990 (Vienna: mimeo, 1992). At the occasion of official visits it became quite usual that Bruno Kreisky was accompanied by a number of top level businessmen of the Austrian national and private enterprises. Arrangements with financial groups of the AOPEC-countries were helpful to build the Vienna International Center of the United Nations and the Austrian International Conference complex. Kreisky actively used his political influence and Austria's good reputation in that area (at that time) to strengthen the Austrian economic record.

91. Hans Kernbauer, "Internationale Konjunktur—und Währungsverflechtung," in *Österreich im internationalen System*, ed. Helmut Kramer, 1983, 115; on Austria's trade with Eastern Europe, See also Felix Butschek, "EC Membership and the Velvet Revolution," in *CAS* 1(1993): 62-80.

92. Unterberger, "Die außenpolitische Entwicklung," 1992, 231.

93. For the Austrian integration efforts in the 1960s see Luif, *"Neutrale in die EG?"* (Vienna: Braumüller, 1988), 94-116 and Rathkolb in *CAS* 1(1993): 42-67.

94. See Peter Katzenstein, "Trends and Oscillations in Austrian Integration Policy since 1955: Alternative Explanations," in *Journal of Common Market Studies* 14 (1975): 171-197.

95. See Unterberger, "Die außenpolitische Entwicklung," 1992, 233.

96. See *ÖZA*, 3-4, 1983, 179.

97. See Paul Luif, "Die internationale Politik," 1985.

98. Karl Gruber, 1983, 104.

99. Palestinian terrorist incidents were partly seen as a "by-product" of Kreisky's Middle East policy, but other European countries with less outspoken positions were even more often the objects of such attacks. If one considers Austria's role as a turn-table for emigrating Soviet Jews, one can easily imagine that Kreisky's Middle East engagement and contacts were an asset.

100. See Helmut Kramer, "Zur Rolle der öffentlichen Meinung in der Außenpolitik," in ÖZP 13 (1984): 141-164; see also Kramer, 1988, 279.

101. Konrad Ginther, *Neutralität und Neutralitätspolitik. Die österreichische Neutralität zwischen Schweizer Muster und sowjetischer Koexistenzdoktrin* (Vienna: Springer, 1975), 141.

102. Alfred Verdross, *Die immerwährende Neutralität Österreichs* (Vienna: Geschichte und Politik, 1977), 73.

103. See the application of the ÖVP No. 120/A from 19 October 1978 (II-4314 of the enclosure to the protocol).

104. See the application of the SPÖ No. 11/32/A from 5 December 1978 (II-4417 of the enclosure to the protocol).

105. Heinz Wittmann, "Die Rolle des Parlaments und der Parteien in der Außenpolitik," in Kicker, Khol and Neuhold, eds., *Außenpolitik*, 1983, 135 ff.

106. Foreign minister Willibald Pahr used that notion of "equidistance" on 12 May 1980 in a speech among a group of Austrians living abroad. He stated, "in the future Austria will follow a foreign policy with all true respect of its affiliation and membership to the Western world, equidistantly geared towards the great powers and both bloc systems". Gregor Woschnagg, "Außenpolitik ist keine Geheimwissenschaft," in *Europäische Rundschau* 9 (1981): 117.

107. Ludwig Steiner, "Neutralität darf keine leere Hülse sein," in *Europäische Rundschau* 9 (1981): 109.

108. Andreas Khol, "Zur Kritik und Bestandsaufnahme der österreichischen Außenpolitik," in *Europäische Rundschau* 9 (1981): 111-118.

109. ibid., 116.

110. ibid., 117.

111. Josef Taus, *Außenpolitische Vorstellungen der österreichischen Volkspartei*, Vortrag vor der österreichischen Gesellschaft für Außenpolitik und Internationale Beziehungen (Vienna: Mimeo, 1977).

112. *Die Presse*, 12 July 1978, cited by Paul Luif, "Die internationale Politik der österreichischen Volkspartei," in *Schwarz-bunter Vogel. Studien zum Programm, Politik und Struktur der ÖVP* (Vienna: Junius, 1985), 212.

113. See Luif, "Die internationale Politik der österreichischen Volkspartei," 1985, 214; Kramer, "Zur Rolle der öffentlichen Meinung in der Außenpolitik," in *ÖZP* 13 (1984): 141-164; see also Kramer, 1988.

114. See *Europäische Rundschau* 1 (1981) and 2 (1981).

115. Ludwig Steiner, "Neutralität darf keine Hülse sein," in *Europäische Rundschau* 9 (1981):107.

116. Andreas Khol, "Zur Kritik und Bestandsaufnahme der österreichischen Außenpolitik," in *Europäische Rundschau* 9 (1981): 111-118.

117. See Kramer, Zur Rolle der öffentlichen Meinung in der Außenpolitik," in *ÖZP* 13 (1984): 156.

118. It may have been the Austrian initiative by minister Erwin Lanc that led to the "Luxemburg declaration" of 1984 intending a future overall European Economic Space.

119. See Helmut Kramer, 1988, 122.

120. An accurate time-table of Kreisky's activities is given in a brochure of the "Bruno Kreisky Forum for International Dialogue" (Wiener Neustadt: Gutenberg-Druck, without date).

121. See *profil* 46 (1983): 43 and *Basta* 10 (1984): 40. Kreisky accused Arafat of having withdrawn his protection from Sartawi. He also was of the opinion that the PLO headquarters should not be transferred from Beirut, but should remain in the conflicting region.

122. See Kreisky, ed., *20 Millionen suchen Arbeit. Bericht der Kreisky-Kommission. Ein Programm zur Vollbeschäftigung in den neunziger Jahren* (Vienna: Passagenverlag, 1989).

123. See *profil*, 21 April, 1986.

124. John Bunzl, Kreisky and the Middle East (Vienna: Mimeo, 1992), 10; see also the Secher essay in this volume.

125. Helmut Kramer, "Zur Rolle der öffentlichen Meinung in der Außenpolitik," in *ÖZP* 13 (1984): 141-164.

FURTHER LITERATURE

Wolfgang Benedek, "Österreichische Außenpolitik in den Nord-Süd-Beziehungen," in *Außenpolitik und Demokratie in Österreich*, eds. Renate Kicker, Andreas Khol and Hanspeter Neuhold. Salzburg: Neugebauer, 1983.

Erich Bielka, Peter Jankowitsch and Hans Thalberg (eds.), *Die Ära Kreisky. Schwerpunkte der österreichischen Außenpolitik*. Vienna: Europaverlag, 1983.

Erich Bielka, "Österreich und seine volksdemokratischen Nachbarn," in *Die Ära Kreisky*, eds. Erich Bielka, Peter Jankowitsch and Hans Thalberg. 1983, 195-231.

Willy Brandt (ed.), *Bericht der Nord-Süd-Kommission. Das Überleben sichern: Gemeinsame Interessen der Industrie- und Entwicklungsländer*. Cologne: Kiepenheuer & Witsch, 1980.

John Bunzl, *Israel und die Palästinenser. Die Entwicklung eines Gegensatzes*. Vienna: Braumüller, 1983.

John Bunzl, *Gewalt ohne Grenzen. Nahost-Terror und Österreich*. Vienna: Braumüller, 1991.

John Bunzl, Kreisky and the Middle East, Vienna: mimeo, 1992.

Christoph Butterwegges, *Austromarxismus und Staat: Politik, Theorie und Praxis der österreichischen Sozialdemokratie zwischen den beiden Weltkriegen*. Marburg: Arbeit und Gesellschaft, 1991.

Herbert Dachs, Peter Gerlich et al. (eds.), *Handbuch des politischen Systems Österreichs*. Vienna: Manz, 1991.

Herbert Denk and Helmut Kramer, "Außenpolitik und internationale Solidarität. Die Außenpolitik der SPÖ von 1945-1986," in *Auf dem Weg zur Staatspartei. Zur Geschichte und Politik der SPÖ seit 1945*, eds. Peter Pelinka and Gerhard Steger. Vienna: Gesellschaftskritik, 1988, 267-292.

Anthony J. Dolman, "The Like-Minded Countries and the North-South-Conflict," in *Österreichische Zeitschrift für Politikwissenschaft (ÖZP)* 10 (1981): 153-163.

Ole Elgström, "Active Foreign Policy as a Preventive Strategy Against Dependence," in *Small States in Europe and Dependence*, ed. Otmar Höll. 1983, 262-280.

Felix Ermacora, *Südtirol und das Vaterland Österreich*. Vienna: Amalthea, 1984.

Josef Esser and Wolfgang Fach, "Korporatistische Krisenregulierung im 'Modell Deutschland'," in *Neokorporatismus*, ed. Ulrich Alemann. Frankfurt: Campus, 1981, 158-179.

Mehdi Fallah-Nodeh, *Austria's Relations with the OPEC-Countries 1960-1990*. Vienna: mimeo, 1992.

Helmut Fazekas, *Die (Kärntner) Minderheitenfrage und Österreichs Beziehungen zu Jugoslawien*. Vienna: mimeo, 1983.

Willi Filla, Ludwig Flaschberger et al., "Soziologie der nationalen Minderheiten in Österreich - Kroaten, Ungarn, Slowenen," in *Journal für Sozialforschung* 22 (1982): 462-469.

Dorit Fischer, "Ein Marshall-Plan für die Dritte Welt. Der österreichische Vorschlag zu einem verstärkten Ressourcentransfer," in *ÖZP* 10 (1981): 139-152.

Heinz Fischer, "Muß Österreichs Außenpolitik revidiert werden?," in *Europäische Rundschau* 9 (1982): 3-12.

Konrad Ginther, *Neutralität und Neutralitätspolitik. Die österreichische Neutralität zwischen Schweizer Muster und sowjetischer Koexistenzdoktrin*. Vienna: Springer, 1975.

Karl Gruber, "Freunde im Westen," in *Die Ära Kreisky*, eds. Erich Bielka, Peter Jankowitsch and Hans Thalberg. 1983, 117-142.

Hanns Haas and Karl Stuhlpfarrer, *Österreich und seine Slowenen*. Vienna: Löcker und Wögenstein, 1977.

Walter Hacker, "Neutralität im Atomzeitalter," in *Probleme der österreichischen Politik*, vol. 2, (1968): 50-91.

Heinrich Haymerle, "Die Beziehungen zur Großmacht im Osten," in *Die Ära Kreisky*, eds. Erich Bielka, Peter Jankowitsch and Hans Thalberg. 1983, 143-193.

Hans-Georg Heinrich, "Die Entwicklung der österreichisch-ungarischen Beziehungen," in *Die Beziehungen zwischen Österreich und Ungarn: Sonderfall oder Modell?*. Vienna: Braumüller, 1985, 11-44.

Hans-Georg Heinrich, "Österreichische Nachbarschaftspolitik - ein Mythos?," in *ÖZP* 17 (1988): 155-168.

Otmar Höll (ed.), *Small States in Europe and Dependence*. Vienna: Braumüller, 1983.

Otmar Höll, "Abhängigkeit oder Autonomie: Österreich im Internationalisierungsprozeß," in *Österreichisches Jahrbuch für Internationale Politik (ÖJIP) 1984*. Vienna: Böhlau, 1985, 26-63.

Otmar Höll, *Österreichische Entwicklungshilfe 1970-1983. Kritische Analyse und internationaler Vergleich*. Vienna: Braumüller, 1986.

Otmar Höll, "Kleinstaatliche Außenpolitik am Beispiel der N+N-Gruppe," in *ÖZP* 15 (1986): 293-310.

Otmar Höll (ed.), *Österreich - Jugoslawien. Determinanten und Perspektiven ihrer Beziehungen*. Vienna: Braumüller, 1988.

Otmar Höll, "Entwicklungspolitik," in *Handbuch des politischen Systems Österreichs*, eds. Herbert Dachs, Peter Gerlich et al.. 1991, 690-704.

Otmar Höll, "Problembereiche von globaler Bedeutung", in *Das außenpolitische Bewußtsein der Österreicher*, eds. Hanspeter Neuhold and Paul Luif. Vienna: Braumüller, 1992, 131-147.

Waldemar Hummer and Gerhard Wagner, eds., *Österreich im Europarat 1956-1986. Bilanz einer dreißigjährigen Mitgliedschaft*. Vienna: Verlag der österreichischen Akademie der Wissenschaften, 1988.

Peter Jankowitsch, "Österreich und die Dritte Welt," in *Die Ära Kreisky*, eds. Erich Bielka, Peter Jankowitsch and Hans Thalberg. 1983, 257-292.

Peter Katzenstein, "Trends and Oscillations in Austrian Integration Policy since 1955: Alternative Explanations," in *Journal of Common Market Studies* 14 (1975): 171-197.

Peter Katzenstein, "Dependence and Autonomy: Austria in an Interdependent World," in *Österreichische Zeitschrift für Außenpolitik (ÖZA)* 19 (1979): 241-255.

Hans Kernbauer, "Internationale Konjunktur- und Währungsverflechtung," in *Österreich im internationalen System*, ed. Helmut Kramer. 1983, 108-117.

Andreas Khol, "Zur Kritik und Bestandsaufnahme der österreichischen Außenpolitik," in *Europäische Rundschau* 9 (1981): 111-118.

Andreas Khol, "Österreichs Beziehungen zu den Nachbarstaaten", in *Außenpolitik und Demokratie in Österreich*, eds. Renate Kicker, Andreas Khol and Hanspeter Neuhold. 1983, 371-409.

Renate Kicker, Andreas Khol and Hanspeter Neuhold (eds.), *Außenpolitik und Demokratie in Österreich. Strukturen - Strategien - Stellungnahmen*. Salzburg: Neugebauer, 1983.

Rudolf Kirchschläger, "Integration und Neutralität," in *Die Ära Kreisky*, eds. Erich Bielka, Peter Jankowitsch and Hans Thalberg. 1983, 61-95.

Henry Kissinger, *Memoiren 1968-1973*, vol. I. Munich: Bertelsmann, 1979.

Helmut Kramer (ed.), *Österreich im internationalen System. Zusammenfassung der Ergebnisse und Ausblick*. Vienna: Braumüller, 1983.

Helmut Kramer, "Zur Rolle der öffentlichen Meinung in der Außenpolitik," in *ÖZP* 13 (1984): 141-164.

Helmut Kramer, "Aspekte der österreichischen Außenpolitik (1970-1985)," in *Der österreichische Weg 1970-1985. 15 Jahre, die Österreich verändert haben*, eds. Erich Fröschl and Helge Zoitl. Vienna: Europaverlag, 1986, 187-199.

Helmut Kramer, "Wende in der österreichischen Außenpolitik? Zur Außenpolitik der SPÖ-ÖVP-Koalition," in *ÖZP* 17 (1986): 117-131.

Helmut Kramer, "Strukturentwicklung der Außenpolitik (1945-1990)", in *Handbuch des politischen Systems Österreichs*, eds. Herbert Dachs, Peter Gerlich et al.. 1991, 637-657.

Helmut Kramer and Otmar Höll, "Österreich in der internationalen Entwicklung," in *Handbuch des politischen Systems Österreichs*, eds. Herbert Dachs, Peter Gerlich et al.. 1991, 50-69.

Bruno Kreisky, "Austria Draws the Balance," in *Foreign Affairs*. (January 1959): 269-281.

Bruno Kreisky, "Die Renaissance der kleinen Staaten", in *Europäische Rundschau* 1 (1973): 5-12.

Bruno Kreisky, *Reden*, 2 vols., Vienna: Österreichische Staatsdruckerei, 1981.

Bruno Kreisky, *Zwischen den Zeiten. Erinnerungen aus fünf Jahrzehnten.* Vienna: Siedler-Kremayr & Scheriau, 1986.

Bruno Kreisky, *Im Strom der Politik. Der Memoiren zweiter Teil.* Vienna: Siedler-Kremayr & Scheriau, 1988.

Bruno Kreisky (ed.), *20 Millionen suchen Arbeit. Bericht der Kreisky-Kommission. Ein Programm zur Vollbeschäftigung in den neunziger Jahren.* Vienna: Passagenverlag, 1989.

Werner Lang, "Krisenmanagement durch Neokorporatismus," in *Politische Vierteljahresschrift* 21 (1981): 6-25.

Paul Lendvai and Karl Heinz Ritschel, *Kreisky. Portrait eines Staatsmannes.* Vienna: Zsolnay, 1974.

Paul Lendvai, "Der 'Kreisky-Effekt' und die internationalen Medien," in *Die Ära Kreisky*, eds. Erich Bielka, Peter Jankowitsch and Hans Thalberg. 1983, 323-346.

Paul Luif, "Österreich zwischen den Blöcken. Bemerkungen zur Außenpolitik des neutralen Österreichs," in *ÖZP* 11 (1982): 209-220.

Paul Luif, "Die internationale Politik der Österreichischen Volkspartei," in *Schwarzbunter Vogel. Studien zum Programm, Politik und Struktur der ÖVP*. Vienna: Junius, 1985. 202-218.

Paul Luif, "USA - Österreich: Der Konflikt um den Technologietransfer", in *Zukunft* (December 1985): 17-20.

Paul Luif, *Neutrale in die EG? Die wirtschaftliche Integration in Westeuropa und die neutralen Staaten*. Vienna: Braumüller, 1988.

Paul Luif, "Außenwirtschaftspolitik," in *Handbuch des politischen Systems Österreichs*, eds. Herbert Dachs, Peter Gerlich et al.. 1991, 674-689.

Reinhard Meier-Walser, *Die Außenpolitik der monocoloren Regierung Klaus in Österreich 1966-1970*. Munich: Tuduv, 1988.

Silvia Michal-Misak, "Österreich in den Vereinten Nationen," in *ÖZP* 19 (1990): 379-395.

Zdenek Mlynar (ed.), *Die Beziehungen zwischen Österreich und Ungarn*. Vienna: Braumüller, 1985.

Hans J. Morgenthau, *United States Policies in Austria* (A Report prepared at the Request of the Department of State, Oct. 1.). Washington, 1951 (mimeo).

Manfred Moschner/Franz Quendler, *Das österreichische Abstimmungsverhalten in den Vereinten Nationen 1976-1980*. Vienna: mimeo, 1983.

Ingo Mussi, "Bruno Kreisky und der schöpferische Dialog mit den Vereinigten Staaten," in *Die Ära Kreisky*, eds. Erich Bielka, Peter Jankowitsch and Hans Thalberg. 1983, 117-142.

Hanspeter Neuhold (ed.), *CSCE: N+N Perspectives*. Vienna: Braumüller, 1987.

Hanspeter Neuhold and Hans Thalberg (eds.), *The European Neutrals in International Affairs*. Vienna: Braumüller, 1984.

Thomas Nowotny, "Österreichs Außenpolitik in den Augen eines Konservativen," in *Europäische Rundschau* 9 (1981): 123-129.

Helmut Ornauer, "Ein Marshall-Plan für die Dritte Welt?," in *Österreichisches Jahrbuch für Politik (ÖJP) 1982*, eds. Andreas Khol and Alfred Stirnemann. Munich: Oldenbourg, 1983, 207-273.

Claudia Pichl, "Internationale Investitionen. Verflechtung der österreichischen Wirtschaft," in *Wifo-Monatsberichte* (March 1989): 161-176.

Alexander Randa, *Österreich in Übersee*. Vienna: Harold, 1966.

Oliver Rathkolb, "Sozialistische Außenpolitik(er) in Österreich 1945-1959," in *Die Bewegung. 100 Jahre Sozialdemokratie in Österreich*, eds. Erich Fröschl, Maria Mesner and Helge Zoitl. Vienna: Passagenverlag, 1990, 499-514.

Oliver Rathkolb, Austria's "Ostpolitik": "Early Detente Efforts, 1955-1965", "Honest Broker or Double Agent?" (Paper prepared for the 16th Annual Conference of the German Studies Association, Minnesota, Oct. 1-4, 1992, mimeo).

Oliver Rathkolb "Austria and European Integration after World War II", in *Austria in the New Europe, Contemporary Austrian Studies*, vol. 1, eds. Günter Bischof and Anton Pelinka. New Brunswick: Transaction Publishers, 1993, 42-61.

Manfred Schmidt, "Politische Steuerung der Ökonomie in Kleinstaaten," in *ÖZP* 10 (1981): 77-89.

Marshall D. Shulman, "Sowjetische Vorschläge für eine europäische Sicherheitskonferenz (1966-1969)," in *Europa-Archiv* 24 (1969): 671-684.

Heinrich Siegler, ed., *Österreich. Chronik 1945-1972*. Vienna: Siegler, 1973.

Anselm Skuhra, "Austrian Aid: Policy and Performance," in *European Development Assistance*, vol.I, Policies and Performance, ed. Olav Stokke. Tilburg: Tilburg Press, 1984, 65-87.

Ludwig Steiner, "Neutralität darf keine leere Hülse sein," in *Europäische Rundschau* 9 (1981): 105-110.

Rudolf Steininger, "Polarisierung und Integration. Eine vergleichende Untersuchung der strukturellen Versäulung der Gesellschaft in den Niederlanden und in Österreich," in *Politik und Wähler*, eds. René König, Erwin K. Scheuch and Rudolf Wildenmann, vol. 14. Maisenheim am Glan: A. Hain, 1975.

Gerald Stourzh, *Kleine Geschichte des Staatsvertrages*. Graz: Styria, 1975.

Gerald Stourzh, "The Origins of Austrian Neutrality", in *Neutrality: Changing Concepts and Practices*, ed. Alan T. Leonhard. Lanham: University Press of America, 1988, 38-40.

Josef Taus, Außenpolitische Vorstellungen der Österreichischen Volkspartei, Vortrag vor der Österreichischen Gesellschaft für Außenpolitik und Internationale Beziehungen. Vienna: mimeo, 1977.

Hans Thalberg, "Die Nahost-Politik," in *Die Ära Kreisky*, eds. Erich Bielka, Peter Jankowitsch and Hans Thalberg. 1983, 293-321.

Andreas Unterberger, "Mythologisierung der österreichischen Außenpolitik," in *Europäische Rundschau* 9 (1981): 89-96.

Andreas Unterberger, "Die außenpolitische Entwicklung," in *Politik in Österreich. Die Zweite Republik: Bestand und Wandel*, ed. Wolfgang Mantel. Vienna: Böhlau, 1992, 204-239.

Waltraut Urban, "Österreichische Direktinvestitionen in der Dritten Welt und Lateinamerika," in *Zeitschrift für Lateinamerika* 35 (1988): 67-83.

Theodor Veiter, *Die Kärntner Ortstafelkommission. Arbeit und Ergebnisse der Studienkommission für Probleme der slowenischen Volksgruppe in Kärnten von 1972-1975*. Vienna: Braumüller, 1980.

Alfred Verdross, *Die immerwährende Neutralität Österreichs*. Vienna: Geschichte und Politik, 1977.

Adam Wandruszka, "Österreichs politische Struktur," in *Geschichte der Republik Österreich*. Vienna: Geschichte und Politik, 1977, 289-485.

Heinz Wittmann, "Die Rolle des Parlaments und der Parteien in der Außenpolitik," in *Außenpolitik und Demokratie in Österreich*, eds. Renate Kicker, Andreas Khol and Hanspeter Neuhold. 1983, 111-142.

Gregor Woschnagg, "Außenpolitik ist keine Geheimwissenschaft," in *Europäische Rundschau* 9 (1981): 115-129.

Karl Zemanek, "Austria's Policy of Neutrality: Constants and Variables," in *The European Neutrals*, eds. Hanspeter Neuhold and Hans Thalberg. 1984, 17-23.

APPENDIX 1: The Voting Behavior of Neural and Non-aligned Countries in the UN General Assembly (Index for Between East and West Controversial Votes)

	11th Sess. 1956	13th Sess. 1958	16th Sess. 1961	18th Sess. 1963	21st Sess. 1966	23rd Sess. 1968	26th Sess. 1971
USSR*	0	0	0	0	0	0	0
German Dem. Republic	-	-	-	-	-	-	-
Cuba	91	97	0	0	4	32	18
Yugoslavia	27	27	9	23	13	35	33
Egypt	32	30	11	23	13	35	38
India	36	37	21	32	29	50	35
Pakistan	95	100	48	68	27	44	50
Philippines	93	93	74	68	73	74	60
Finland	66	47	76	82	56	79	63
Sweden	80	63	83	82	85	91	70
Austria	95	80	79	82	83	91	75
Ireland	100	63	97	91	88	94	70
Norway	80	67	91	86	92	94	75
Netherlands	100	100	100	100	94	100	83
Fed. Rep. of Germany	-	-	-	-	-	-	-
France	100	100	100	100	69	79	100
United Kingdom	100	100	100	100	100	100	100
USA*	100	100	100	100	100	100	100
Number of votes analyzed	22	15	33	11	24	17	20
% of all recorded (roll-call) votes	48.9	45.5	45.5	36.7	44.4	32.1	16.8

Note * = By definition these countries score 0 or 100 (see below).
Sess. = Session of the UN General Assembly.
All record (roll call) votes of the Plenary Meetings of the General Assembly were taken, including procedural motions and paragraph votes but excluding issues approved without vote or by consensus. From this basis those votes were selected in which the Soviet Union (= 'East') voted for, the USA, the UK and France (= 'West') voted against a resolution etc. or vice versa. Votes in which one or more of these countries abstained were absent or did not participate were not included. For the 21st and 23rd Session, Canada replaced France because of de Gaulle's anti-NATO policy.
The index was calculated in the following way:
voting with the 'West' = 1
voting with the 'East' = 0
abstaining, absent, not participating = 0.5
The values were added and then the index was calculated by assigning perfect 'Western' voting 100, perfect 'Eastern' voting 0.

Source: Paul Luif, 1986, 32f.

APPENDIX 1: The Voting Behavior of Neural and Non-aligned Countries in the UN General Assembly (Index for Between East and West Contrcoversial Votes)

	28th Sess. 1973	31st Sess. 1976	33rd Sess. 1978	36th Sess. 1981	38th Sess. 1983	39th Sess. 1984
USSR*	0	0	0	0	0	0
German Dem. Republic	0	0	0	0	0	0
Cuba	0	7	24	11	7	0
Yugoslavia	13	23	35	29	27	12
Egypt	20	23	40	37	39	25
India	20	27	47	27	25	11
Pakistan	20	30	38	31	32	20
Philippines	37	33	41	37	48	42
Finland	67	60	72	65	61	66
Sweden	77	67	74	75	68	71
Austria	77	63	78	76	64	69
Ireland	77	80	82	82	68	75
Norway	77	63	81	89	88	90
Netherlands	80	90	88	93	93	95
Fed. Rep. of Germany	83	97	99	98	97	98
France	100	100	100	100	100	100
United Kingdom	100	100	100	100	100	100
USA*	100	100	100	100	100	100
Number of votes analyzed	15	15	34	42	55	63
% of all recorded (roll-call) votes	15.6	15.6	21.9	26.1	30.9	32.6

Note * = By definition these countries score 0 or 100 (see below).
Sess. = Session of the UN General Assembly.
All record (roll call) votes of the Plenary Meetings of the General Assembly were taken, including procedural motions and paragraph votes but excluding issues approved without vote or by consensus. From this basis those votes were selected in which the Soviet Union (= 'East') voted for, the USA, the UK and France (= 'West') voted against a resolution etc. or vice versa. Votes in which one or more of these countries abstained were absent or did not participate were not included. For the 21st and 23rd Session, Canada replaced France because of de Gaulle's anti-NATO policy.
The index was calculated in the following way:
voting with the 'West' = 1
voting with the 'East' = 0
abstaining, absent, not participating = 0.5
The values were added and then the index was calculated by assigning perfect 'Western' voting 100, perfect 'Eastern' voting 0.

Source: Paul Luif, 1986, 32f.

APPENDIX 2: Official Visits in Austria and Abroad

Yearly averages per period, absolute numbers and percentages

Visits in resp. from	1956-58	1959-62	1963-65	1966-69	1970-73	1974-76	1977-80	1981-82	1983-84
NATO countries (incl. Spain), Australia, New Zealand, South Africa	2.7 (40.0)	4.0 (48.5)	2.7 (30.8)	5.3 (43.8)	5.0 (31.2)	5.7 (25.8)	4.8 (22.6)	5.5 (16.4)	8.5 (30.9)
Warsaw Pact countries (incl. Albania)	0.7 (10.0)	1.3 (15.2)	2.7 (30.8)	3.0 (25.0)	4.3 (26.6)	7.7 (34.8)	6.5 (31.0)	7.5 (22.4)	5.0 (18.2)
European neutrals and non-aligned (incl. Ireland, Liechtenstein, San Marion, Vatican)	0.7 (10.0)	2.0 (24.2)	1.0 (11.5)	2.5 (20.8)	4.0 (25.0)	3.0 (13.6)	3.3 (15.5)	5.5 (16.4)	4.0 (14.6)
Asia	2.7 (40.0)	0.8 (9.1)	1.0 (11.5)	1.3 (10.4)	1.3 (7.8)	3.7 (16.7)	2.8 (13.1)	10.0 (29.9)	6.5 (23.6)
Africa	0	0.3 (3.0)	1.3 (15.4)	0	1.5 (9.4)	1.3 (6.1)	1.0 (4.8)	4.0 (11.9)	3.0 (10.9)
Latin America	0	0	0	0	0	0.7 (3.0)	2.8 (13.1)	1.0 (3.0)	0.5 (1.8)
Sum	6.8 (100.0)	8.4 (100.0)	8.7 (100.0)	12.1 (100.0)	16.1 (100.0)	22.1 (100.0)	21.2 (100.0)	33.5 (100.0)	27.5 (100.0)

Note: All bilateral official and semi-official visits by foreign heads of states or governments and foreign ministers in Austria as well as the visits of Austrian presidents, chancellors and foreign ministers abroad have been included. Since there always exist problematic cases (especially in the 1950s), only yearly averages for each period have been reproduced.

Source: Paul Luif, 1986, 28.

APPENDIX 3: Significant Economic Indicators in International Comparison (1965-1991)

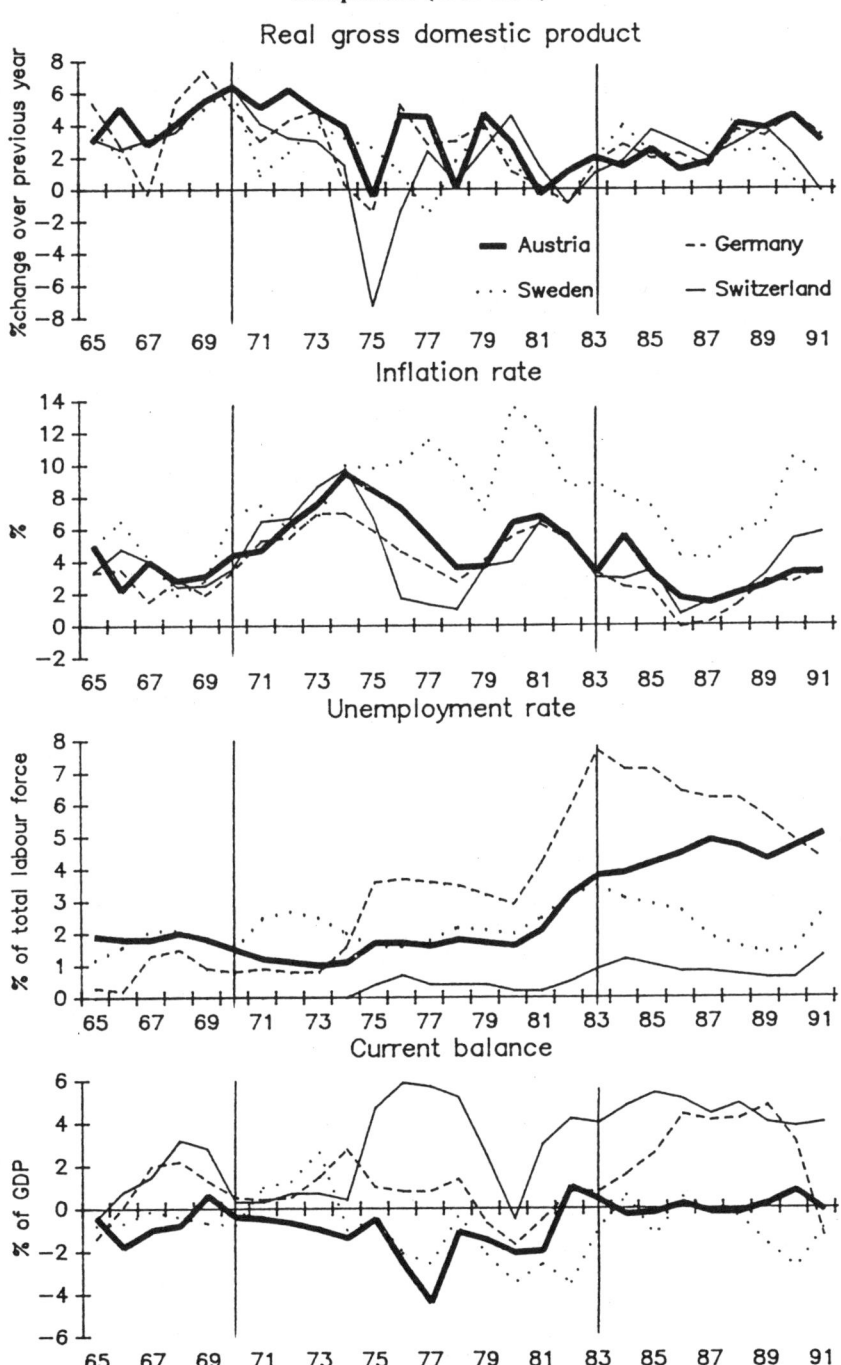

Source: Austrian Institute for Economic Research 1992

APPENDIX 4: Austrian Exports and Imports (percentages)

	1937		1958		1970	
	Imp.	Exp.	Imp.	Exp.	Imp.	Exp.
EC 1958	28.3	36.5	54.4	49.6	56.0	39.4
EC 1973 and 1981	-	-	-	-	-	-
(FRG)[1]	(16.2)	(14.8)	(39.1)	(25.1)	(41.2)	(23.4)
(FRG)[1]	-	-	-	-	-	-
EFTA 1960[2]	9.7	13.7	11.4	10.9	19.6	26.6
EFTA 1973[2]	-	-	-	-	-	-
Eastern Europe (excl. Yugoslavia)	32.0	27.8	10.8	12.4	9.3	12.9
Rest of Europe	10.0	8.1	3.4	6.5	2.7	7.0
USA, Canada, Austr., New Zealand, S. Africa, Japan	8.6	6.2	12.3	7.5	5.8	7.3
Asia	4.6	4.1	2.5	7.0	2.2	3.5
Afica	2.5	1.4	2.5	2.6	1.7	1.8
Latin America	4.3	2.2	2.7	3.5	2.7	1.5
(OPEC)	-	-	-	-	(0.9)	(1.8)
(NICs)[3]	-	-	-	-	(2.3)	(1.5)
Sum (percentage)	100.0	100.0	100.0	100.0	100.0	100.0
Sum AS 1000 million	1.5	1.2	27.9	23.7	92.3	74.3

1) The 1937 data of the Federal Republic of Germany refer to the German Reich, the 1991 data refer to the unified "Germany"
2) EFTA always includes Finland
3) NICs are Brasilia, Hongkong, Mexico, Singapore, South Korea and Taiwan

Sources: Statistisches Handbuch der Republik Österreich (Vienna: 1960 and 1973); *Statistische Nachrichten*, various volumes; Paul Luif, 1986, 29 and own calculations.

APPENDIX 4: Austrian Exports and Imports (percentages)

	1980		1984		1991	
	Imp.	Exp.	Imp.	Exp.	Imp.	Exp.
EC 1958	(58.6)	(49.4)	(57.0)	(47.2)	(61.9)	(57.8)
E C 1973 and 1981	62.2	54.4	60.4	5344	67.8	65.8
(FRG)[1]	(40.8)	(30.8)	(39.9)	(29.6)	(43.0)	(39.0)
(FRG)[1]	62.2	54.4	60.4	53.4	67.8	65.8
EFTA 1960[2]	(11.3)	(17.2)	(10.8)	(16.3)	(11.3)	(14.4)
EFTA 1973[2]	7.9	12.4	7.9	10.8	6.9	9.2
Eastern Europe (excl. Yugoslavia)	9.7	12.1	11.6	12.2	6.1	9.0
Rest of Europe	1.7	5.4	2.1	4.8	1.4	2.7
USA, Canada, Austr., New Zealand, S. Africa, Japan	6.9	4.2	7.7	6.9	9.7	5.8
Asia	6.7	6.0	4.1	7.4	5.3	5.4
Afica	3.0	4.1	4.0	3.4	2.1	1.6
Latin America	1.9	1.4	2.2	1.1	1.0	0.8
(OPEC)	(7.1)	(5.6)	(4.7)	(6.4)	(2.1)	(2.9)
(NICs)[3]	(1.9)	(0.9)	(2.6)	(0.9)	(3.0)	(1.6)
Sum (percentage)	100.0	100.0	100.0	100.0	100.0	100.0
Sum AS 1000 million	315.8	226.2	392.1	314.5	591.9	479.0

1) The 1937 data of the Federal Republic of Germany refer to the German Reich, the 1991 data refer to the unified "Germany"
2) EFTA always includes Finland
3) NICs are Brasilia, Hongkong, Mexico, Singapore, South Korea and Taiwan

Sources: Statistisches Handbuch der Republik Österreich (Vienna: 1960 and 1973); *Statistische Nachrichten*, various volumes; Paul Luif, 1986, 29 and own calculations.

Political Culture and Party System in the Kreisky Era

Peter Ulram

Introduction

The article outlines the main features of the Austrian political culture[1] in the 1970s and the early 1980s and discusses the relationship between political culture and the party system at that time. It does not suggest that there was a special "political culture of the Kreisky era" but that the Kreisky era can be better understood by looking at the then-dominant political cultural orientations. The basic argument is that these orientations constituted—among other, for example economic and socio-structural, factors—a kind of framework for the process of party competition providing more favorable conditions for the SPÖ under the leadership of Kreisky than for other political actors. Later changes in political culture (as well as in other areas of societal development) contributed to the decline of the SPÖ's electoral strength and its former hegemonic position in the party system.

This interpretation of the relationship between political culture and party system should be seen against a wider background of Austria's post-Second World War political development. Until now one can identify three distinct phases of political culture and three corresponding phases of the political, especially the party, system.[2] It should be noted, however, that there is no simple causal model suggested (a given state of political culture determining a certain balance of political force). As the argument will show, the political actors reacted and adapted in different modes to the political cultural framework—some evidently in a more, and others in a less, appropriate way.

The Political Culture of the "Social-Liberal Consensus"

The 1960s and 1970s were a period of profound social change. Because important characteristics of the traditional Austrian political culture were closely connected with the politicization of socioeconomic and cultural cleavages, these changes had an important impact on political culture. This holds especially true for the role of political subcultures ("camps") with their corresponding sociopsychological orientations (*Lagermentalität*).[3]

Between 1961 and 1981 the share of self-employed persons among the work force decreased from 29 to 14 percent while that of white-collar workers increased from 27 to 42 percent. The number of high school graduates more than doubled and that of university students grew at an even faster rate. Austria was becoming a developed industrial society with a large service sector. Of similar importance was the process of religious secularization measured by a drop of regular church attendance (from some 50 percent in the late 1950s to about one third in the early 1980s) and a doubling of the divorce rate between 1960 and 1980[4]—in a country where divorce is rejected by the dominant Catholic Church.

Even though the process of modernization was primarily undermining the social and cultural base of the Christian-conservative camp, the breaking up of social milieus, the withering away of closed ideological systems, the emergence of new values and life styles and their distribution by the mass media have had their impact on the socialist subculture too. Traditional bindings began to lose their strength; party identification decreased and so did the once life-time loyalty to one's party (see appendix 1).

A notable change also took place in the fields of political socialization and communication. Traditional socialization agencies like family and youth-organizations (of the church or the parties) were losing importance, and party-controlled networks of political information were substituted by neutrals or independent sources of political information, especially the mass media.[5]

Political participation was no longer restricted to voting or to activities within the parties and interest organizations. Grass-root movements, peaceful demonstrations, and plebiscites found a growing acceptance, mostly among younger people and the urban middle classes—even though the level of unconventional participation was lower than in other democracies and political violence remained nearly unknown.[6] Furthermore, the increase of new forms of participation did not visibly weaken the older and conventional forms. Rather than a substitution, one finds a combination or cumulation of old and new: the acceptance and practice of unconventional activities by a part of those who were also active in conventional forms of political action.[7] Electoral turnout thus remained high and party membership was probably the highest in the western world (see appendices 2 and 3).

The political agenda of the early 1970s has been described as "social-democratic" or "social-liberal."[8] Materially, it was founded upon economic growth, full employment and the expansion of the welfare state; its less material aspects included a desire for liberal reforms, easier access to higher education, the recognition of women's new role in society (see the Fischer-Kowalski essay in this volume) and the opening or "democratization" of institutions. The political system was held responsible for guaranteeing and expanding full employment, income and social security. The political parties were mainly judged according to their efforts in reaching there goals. Correspondingly, there existed widespread support for state interventionism and public spending.[9]

By international comparison as well as in absolute figures the substantive output of the government and the political parties was judged very positively. This was especially true for the core issues of "social guarantism,"[10] but even new topics like the environmental issue were not viewed as completely neglected—although the level of trust and perceived competence was here much lower (see appendix 4).

A rather different picture evolves if one changes from the positive evaluation of the political output to the fields of stylistic performance and moral qualities of the political personnel: both were judged in a negative way. Also, the working of the public administration was perceived as somehow unfair and not oriented toward the clients' needs. Subjective political competence and the perception of political efficacy was low and did not substantially change over time (see appendix 5).[11]

Dissatisfaction with certain aspects of the political behavior and the moral qualities of politicians as well as widespread feelings of powerlessness, however, did not challenge the legitimacy of the political system. Summarizing the results of the Austrian Political-Action study, Marsh makes the following observation:

> The Austrian case is particularly interesting because they recorded the lowest system responsiveness score above but now record the highest levels of political trust. It is a strange stance to take. They feel that officials and politicians ignore them but can be trusted to do what is right and care for a common collective good. It is a uniquely Austrian idea and it rehabilitates earlier ideas about political passivity in Austria being a function of public contentment.[12]

Political parties, the system of organized interest representation (*Sozialpartnerschaft*)[13] and parliament were partly criticized but their substantive performance as well as their basic necessity and functionality were appreciated.[14] The fundamental democratic institutions and principles enjoyed a high degree of legitimacy. Furthermore, the existence of a genuine Austrian nation was accepted by the vast majority of the Austrian people and was accompanied by strong feelings of national pride. The "national question," that is, the cleavage between German national and Austrian national orientations, had thus become largely obsolete. Interestingly, it was the political system itself which—in this period—was an object for feelings of national pride (see appendix 6).[15]

The once-restricted democratic consciousness became more comprehensive and citizens' activities remained no longer restricted to traditional modes of participation. Genuine anti-democratic sentiments were largely absent and political violence was virtually non-existent. There still existed, however, a strong tendency to escape political conflicts in general as well as some traits of authoritarian consciousness in minor groups. The political culture of the 1970s might thus be characterized as "a limited participatory and competitive democracy."

The Period of Social-Democratic Hegemony

Changes in the social composition of the electorate, the decline of the *Lager* and the respective increase of mobile voters, new modes of political communication—especially the overwhelming impact of the mass media—and a political agenda dominated by social welfare issues and the call for institutional reforms constituted a new framework for the process of party competition.

The ÖVP was not able to cope with this challenge. Concentrating only on technocratic reforms and economic politics, the party lacked a feel for welfare politics. Furthermore, the changes in the sociocultural field were met only in a rather reluctant way, if not viewed with open distrust. Traditional core groups of the party (the old middle classes and parts of the public employees) felt threatened by the new developments; so did the Catholic Church, which exerted a strong pressure on the *Volkspartei*.

The SPÖ, on the other hand, was not only favored by the new situation, but was also capable of adapting to it. Being the traditional representative of working class interests and the advocate of social equality and an extension of the welfare state, the SPÖ now presented itself as the representative of the so-called new middle classes.[16] The process of sociocultural secularization and liberalization was compatible by an explicit renunciation of marxist ideas in the fields of economic politics (see appendices 7 and 8).

The SPÖ's political program fostered economic growth and the expansion of welfare politics as well as the opening of the educational system to the socially ascending groups. It also adapted legal norms to changed values, promised to democratize institutions and promoted some reforms in the field of women's emancipation. The party thus responded to the main tenets of the social-liberal consensus of the 1970s and was able to form a new political coalition of interests, values and voters between the traditional socialist core groups and the new middle classes. Symbolic politics were an essential part of the SPÖ's new profile. The party presented itself as an "open one" calling for an alliance with "progressive" liberals, Catholics, intellectuals and artisans. It successfully projected itself as the party of political, social and cultural modernization. Bruno Kreisky, the party leader, can be seen as a personification of this trend symbolizing both the new values of liberal reform and the fidelity to social-democratic traditions. From a more practical point of view, the SPÖ was the party that adapted better to the new rules of media politics. Kreisky (nicknamed "the media chancellor") was the first Austrian politician who really understood the working and the importance of television in the process of political communication and image building and was certainly the only one in this period to use the new world of media communication for his political aims.

As a matter of fact, the SPÖ was not only able to dominate Austrian politics by gaining a relative majority in 1970 and absolute ones in the elections of 1971, 1975 and 1979 but even more to build up a position of political hegemony which endured for more than a decade. The hegemonical political system of the 1970s was based on several factors:

* an increase and strengthening of the SPÖ's power and influence in public administration and the public economy and in those social and economic sectors depending on the prior ones;
* a broad electoral consensus, especially by those social groups that showed considerable or increasing numerical strength in this period;
* a policy which tried—and succeeded for quite a long time—to respond to the main material and non-material demands of those groups;
* a dominant position in both the interpretation of social developments and problems and the political solutions for them. This symbolic hegemony surpassed by far the party's actual electoral strength and its positions of direct power and influence.

One should note, however, that the SPÖ's hegemony depended on economic developments and political cultural orientations that were largely outside the party's or government's capacity of steering and control. Changes in economic conditions and the orientations of the population thus were likely to affect the stability of the social-democratic coalition of interest, values and voters. Furthermore, the political-bureaucratic penetration of large sectors of civil society resulting from the political strategy of extensive state interventionism had repercussions in the political institutions. The parties, and here especially the long-time incumbent SPÖ, were infiltrated by individual and group interests. Informal old-boy networks, vested interests and veto positions were gaining importance, thus reducing the possibilities for innovative political actions. Since the electoral strength of the SPÖ depended on an uncertain coalition of voters a high degree of sensibility for developments within this coalition as well as a high responsiveness to changing demands and moods were vital. But the above-mentioned increase of structural rigidities endangered the necessary flexibility to react to new challenges and to attract the increasing number of floating voters.

The Erosion of the Social-Liberal Consensus

In the late 1970s and in the 1980s the consequences of social change were affecting the very base of the socialist electorate. Party identification decreased notably among blue-collar workers and among the SPÖ electorate in general; in addition, the party's formal and informal networks of communication and organization began to dissolve (see appendix 9).

With the dealignment process reaching the core groups, the SPÖ could no longer count on a body of loyal party adherents big enough to shield it from electoral desertion on the part of its fringe voters. At the same time, the conditions for maintaining the social-democratic voter coalition were worsening. On the one hand, economic growth slowed down significantly in the early 1980s, and on the other, the financial costs of social-welfare politics were felt by large groups of the population. Public debt limited the possibilities for state intervention, and a high level of taxation was burdening private households.

Austria faced rising unemployment—still low by international standards but high by domestic ones—and only modestly rising, if not diminishing incomes. This situation was aggravated by the crisis of the "sunset-industries," most of them in public ownership. These industries were not only strongholds of socialist voters but were also considered flagships for the so-called "Austrokeynesianism."[17]

Economic and employment problems provided the background for increasing distributional conflicts within and between the groups forming the social-liberal consensus. These conflicts gained a specific political dimension since the distribution of incomes, life-chances, and the like often depended on state action and because economic problems were felt within the area of governmental influence. Governmental politics had come to be seen as the object of entitlement demands and the distributor of advantages and (increasingly) disadvantages. In this sense, it was also the former success of social-democratic politics that began to undermine the base of the social-liberal consensus. A loss of confidence was taking place— ranging from fears about the stability of welfare programs and job security to anger about the extent, costs and bureaucratic aspects of state interventions in general.

On a more general level, the former dominant entitlement orientations lost in importance[18]; the issue agenda became more complex and contradictory. Preventing the waste of tax resources (linked with the growing desire for lower and more just taxation) and protecting the environment gained in importance. Environmental problems in particular were a cause of open conflicts. Government performance on these issues was judged much worse than that of traditional economic and social politics—and even those were no longer considered really adequate (appendices 10 and 11). Thus, both the material and the non-material foundations of the social-liberal consensus of the 1970s were eroding; its component groups were drifting apart, if not finding themselves in open conflict with one another. The SPÖ, as the dominant political interpreter and profiteer of this consensus, was gravely affected. Faced with economic problems and conflicting interests within its voter coalition the party saw a deterioration of its position as a representative of various social interests and of its image as a competent political actor (see appendices 12 and 13). The loss of substantive and symbolic domination was aggravated by evident political mistakes and by a series of intraparty-conflicts and political scandals.[19] Rising criticism from the media and public opinion in general was not met by a change in style or substance. As a consequence the SPÖ lost votes in the general elections of 1983 and 1986. Even though the party remained the largest in the country, the era of social-democratic hegemony in Austria had come to an end.

A Challenging Political Culture

New issue priorities along with significant changes in sociopolitical orientations—like the diminishing appeal of state interventionism and the formation of new political cleavages on the dimensions "public vs. private" and "job and standard of living vs. nature and environment"—are signs of a changing political culture.[20] The formerly extensive consensus on aims and methods has withered away. Of similar—probably even greater—importance, however, has been the withering of trust, a development not restricted to the output of governmental and party politics. Growing political dissatisfaction primarily has stemmed from the policy-making process and from the relationship between the citizenry and the political class. An expansive understanding of politics and a petrification of structures and outdated ways of behavior have activated the feelings of powerlessness. Negative views about the moral qualities of the political personnel—reinforced by affairs of corruption and political scandals—have created growing anger about the political parties and their representatives. The formerly latent discomfort in the Austrian party state has developed into open, emotionalized protest on the one hand and retreat from politics on the other (see appendix 14). The new political culture has shown growing moods of party weariness and dissatisfaction with established politics. Given a mobile electorate, this has meant a decrease in voting discipline and an increase in negative voting, which, in turn, has created a larger space for green-alternative and neopopulist movements (the FPÖ under Jörg Haider).[21]

The Second Austrian Republic has been characterized by a high degree of congruence of and mutual influence between political culture and political structure. The political structures of the 1950s were based to a large extent on the dominant features of the "pillarized consociational democracy." At the same time, important political innovations—the firm establishment of a sovereign and neutral nation state, social bargaining, power sharing and the spoils system (*Proporz*) during the grand coalition between ÖVP and SPÖ—helped to drive back potentially disruptive elements of the political culture during the immediate postwar years (the "national question," political hostility between the camps, not yet firmly anchored democratic norms). In the period of the social-liberal consensus the development of political structure and political culture proceeded in a congruent and mutually reinforcing way. It is also important to note that in both these phases the dominant political cultural patterns contributed not only to the overall stability of the political system but also to the establishment of specific structures of party-political hegemony: two decades of the "historical compromise" of the two camps, were followed by one-and-a-half decade of stable socialist domination (the Kreisky-era).

Compared with these periods, the 1980s and 1990s seem to be characterized by deficits in the congruence between political culture and political structure. This holds especially true for the established party system and organized interest representation whose sclerotic structures clashed with accelerating changes in orientations on political issues and the political process. As a consequence one finds clear signs of erosion on the structural side. This does not mean that the basic orientations (national identity, acceptance of democratic norms and the rules of the game) are threatened, but it does mean that the "end of the Austrian exceptionality" constitutes new challenges to the Second Republic.

As we all know, periods of political change are especially interesting times for journalists and political scientists. One should, however, keep in mind that in Ancient China the form of salutation "may you live in interesting times" was not meant as a compliment but as a curse.

NOTES

1. "Political culture" means value orientations and attitudes of individuals, groups and the society as a whole that are important for political behavior. It encompasses ideas about political norms, the view of the political process, the perception of institutions etc. There is a rich literature on the subject staring with the seminal work of Gabriel A. Almond /Sidney Verba, *The Civic Culture: Political Culture and Political Development in Five Nations* (Princeton: Princeton University Press, 1963) to later adaptions, clarifications and critical comments, e.g., Gabriel A. Almond /Sidney Verba, eds. *The Civic Culture Revisited* (Boston, 1980); Glenda M. Patrick, "Political Culture," in *Social Science Concepts: A Systematic Analysis*, ed. Giovanni Sartori (London: Sage, 1984), 265-314. For a recent comparative study of the political culture in the new Eastern European democracies see Peter Gerlich, Fritz Plasser, and Peter A. Ulram, eds., *Regimewechsel: Demokratisierung und politische Kultur in Ost-Mitteleuropa* (Vienna: Böhlau, 1992).

2. The political culture of the "pillarized consociational democracy" (consisting of closed camp-cultures founded on traditional social and political cleavages on the one hand and orientations of compromise, cooperation and mutual trust on the level of the political elites), the political culture of the "social-liberal consensus" and the present "political culture of malaise." The author has developed this argument comprehensively and empirically in Peter A.Ulram, *Hegemonie und Erosion: Politische Kultur und politischer Wandel in Österreich* (Vienna: Böhlau, 1991).

3. See Adam Wandruszka, "Österreichs politische Struktur: Die Entwicklung der Parteien und politischen Bewegungen," in *Geschichte der Republik Österreich*, ed. Heinrich Benedikt (Vienna: Verlag für Geschichte und Politik, 1954), 289-485; for a case study see G. B. Powell, *Social Fragmentation and Political Hostility: An Austrian Case Study* (Stanford: Stanford University Press, 1970). A recent comprehensive work on Austrian politics is Kurt Richard Lother and Wolfgang C. Müller, "Consociationalism and the Austrian Political System," *West European Politics* 15 (January 1992) 1-15; see also Fritz Plasser, Peter A. Ulram, and Alfred

Grausgruber, "The Decline of Lager Mentality and the New Model of Electoral Competition in Austria," *West European Politics* 15 (January 1992), 16-44.

4. See Peter A. Ulram, *Hegemonie* and Peter M. Zulehner, *Religion im Leben der Österreicher* (Vienna, 1981).

5. In the early 1960s only 45 percent of the adult population read independent newspapers; in the 1980s the figure rose to 85 percent. In the same period the importance of TV as the primary source of political information rose from 11 percent (1960s) to 67 percent (1980s). For details see Ulram, *Hegemonie* and Plasser, Ulram and Grausgruber, *Decline*.

6. See Samuel H. Barnes et al., *Political Action: Mass Participation in Five Western Democracies* (Beverly Hills: Sage, 1979); for special aspects see Sidney Verba, Norman H. Nie and Jae-On Kim, *Participation and Political Equality: A Seven Nation Comparison* (Cambridge: Cambridge University Press, 1978).

7. See Roland Deiser and Robert Winkler, *Das Politische Handeln der Österreicher* (Vienna, 1982).

8. See Ralph Dahrendorf, *Lebenschancen: Anläufe zur sozialen und politischen Theorie* (Frankfurt/Main: Suhrkamp, 1979).

9. For an extensive discussion see Fritz Plasser and Peter A. Ulram, *Unbehagen im Parteienstaat: Jugend und Politik in Österreich* (Vienna: Böhlau, 1982).

10. "Social guarantism" is a larger concept than "welfare politics." It asks for a generalized responsibility of the state for social and (sometimes) individual welfare encompassing also ideas of social equality and a continuing updating of living standards by state interventionism. See Peter A. Ulram, "Changing Issues in the Austrian Party system," in *The Austrian Party System*, ed. Anton Pelinka and Fritz Plasser (Boulder: Westview Press, 1989), 197-222.

11. See recently Fritz Plasser and Peter A. Ulram, *Staatsbürger oder Untertanen? Politische Kultur in der Bundesrepublik Deutschland, Österreich und der Schweiz* (Frankfurt: Lang, 1991).

12. Alan Marsh, *Political Action in Europe and the USA*, (abridged version of *Political Action* London: Houndmills, 1990), 167.

13. The big interest organization (trade union, chambers of labor, commerce and agriculture) have an important say in economic and social politics in Austria. The prevalent style is one of cooperation and compromise rather than of open conflict.

14. See Ulram *Hegemonie*; Peter Gerlich and Karl Ucakar, *Staatsbürger und Volksvertretung: das Alltagsverständnis von Parlament und Demokratie in Österreich* (Salzburg: Neugebauer, 1981); Peter Gerlich, "Consociationalism to Competition: The Austrian Party System since 1945," in *Party Systems in Denmark, Austria, Switzerland, The Netherlands and Belgium*, ed. Hans Daalder (London: Pinter, 1987), 61-106.

15. See Gerald Stourzh, *Vom Reich zur Republik. Studien zum Österreichbewußtsein im 20. Jahrhundert* (Vienna: Atelier, 1990).

16. The term refers to better educated white-collar workers (as opposed to the self-employed old middle classes, e.g., artisans, small businessmen).

17. The term refers to an economic policy based on commitment to a strong currency, promotion of investment and savings, income policy and the stabilization of demand by deficit spending. See Volkmar Laube, "Changing Priorities in Austrian Economic Policy," in *West European Politics* 15 (January 1992), 147-172.

18. See Ulram, "Changing Issues."

19. See Ulram, *Hegemonie*.

20. See Kurt Traar and Franz Birk, "Der durchleuchtete Wähler - in den achtziger Jahren" (Sonderheft des Journals für Sozialforschung 1987/1) and Ulram, "Changing Issues."

21. See Christian Haerpfer, "Austria," in *Electoral Change in Western Democracies*, ed. Ivor Crewe and David Denver (London: Croom Helm, 1985) 264-186; Fritz Plasser, *Parteien unter Streß. Zur Dynamik der Parteiensysteme in Österreich, der Bundesrepublik Deutschland und den Vereinigten Staaten* (Vienna: Böhlau, 1987) and Fritz Plasser and Peter A. Ulram, "Überdehnung, Erosion und rechtspolitische Reaktion," in *Österreichische Zeitschrift für Politikwissenschaft* (1992), 147-164.

APPENDIX 1: Indicators of Political Secularization

IN PERCENT OF A) THE TOTAL ELECTORATE B) ÖVP-SUPPORTERS	50s/60s	70s	80s
a) Show party identification	73	63	51
a) Are subjectively bound traditional voters	65	56	34
a) Read party newspapers	35	15	7
b) Go to church every Sunday	67	55	47
b) Live in a party-political consonant social network	+	78	60

Source: Fessel+GfK, Political Indicators and Media Surveys

APPENDIX 2: Types of Political Activity by International Comparison (1974)

IN PERCENT OF CLASSIFIED CASES	A	D	I	USA
Inactive	35	27	24	12
Only conventional participation	19	13	7	17
Conventional and unconventional p.	27	33	34	50
Only Unconventional participation	19	27	35	20

Source: Samuel H. Barnes, "Il cittadino italiano: un caso particolare?," in *Il Mulino* 35 (November/December 1985), based on Political Action data from 1974.

APPENDIX 3: Electoral Turnout and Party Membership by International Comparison

IN PERCENT OF ELIGIBLE VOTERS	ELECTORAL TURNOUT (MEAN OF DECADE)				PARTY-MEMBERSHIP (SINGLE YEARS)		
	50s	60s	70s	80s	60s	70s	80s
Austria (A)	95	94	92	92	24	22	23
Italy (I)	94	93	92	91	11	+	9
Germany (D)	87	87	89	87	3	4	4
USA-president	60	62	55	53	3	3	3

Source: Ulram, *Hegemonie*

APPENDIX 4: Issue Agenda and Evaluation of Governmental Performance by International Comparison

IN %	IMPORTANT TASK					PERFORMANCE (VERY GOOD)				
	A	UK	NL	D	I	A	UK	NL	D	I
Job security	93	83	87	93	82	90	55	50	72	18
Medical care	92	93	91	94	93	77	83	78	76	37
Crime control	92	84	87	96	93	57	62	39	37	13
Education	88	90	96	92	90	87	74	75	64	49
Environmental protection	86	81	91	82	84	41	50	40	30	25
Old age care	85	85	81	91	90	67	65	72	56	32
Housing	77	85	92	84	89	54	46	59	56	19
Sex equality	59	46	62	75	59	63	54	54	57	56

Source: Maria Weber, "Italia: Paese europeo? Una analisi della cultura politica degli itagliani in prospettiva comparata," (Milano: Angeli, 1986) based on Political Action datas from 1974.

APPENDIX 5: Political Efficacy and System Responsiveness

IN PERCENT	1974	1989
* People like me have no say in what government does	81	75
* Parties are only interested in people's votes but not in their opinions	73	73
* Those we elect to parliament lose touch with the people pretty quickly	72	78
* Politicians and public officials don't care much about what people like me think	67	68

Source: Leopold Rosenmayr, ed, "Politische Beteiligung und Wertwandel in Österreich," (Munich: Oldenbourg, 1981); Fritz Plasser/Peter A. Ulram, "Politisch-kultureller Wandel in Österreich," in Plasser/Ulram, *Staatsbürger*.

APPENDIX 6: National Consciousness and National Pride

IN PERCENT	1956	64	70/73	80/82	87	88/89
Austria is a nation	49	47	66	67	75	79
Austria is becoming a nation	+	23	16	19	16	15
Austria is not a nation	47	15	8	11	5	4
No response	4	14	10	3	3	3
Absolutely proud to be an Austrian	+	+	56	69	57	53
Mostly/rather proud	+	+	34	24	32	35
Not really proud	+	+	2	1	5	7
Not at all proud	+	+	1	1	1	2
Austrian politics are a source of national pride	+	+	+	72	27	+

Source: Plasser/Ulram, "Wandel," IMAS, Representative Surveys (1973, 1982, 1987).

APPENDIX 7: The Representation of Social Groups (1976)

BEST REPRESENTED	PERCENT SPÖ MINUS ÖVP
Blue-collar workers	+ 83
Pensioners	+ 65
Employed women	+ 61
Young people	+ 52
Families with children	+ 52
Housewives	+ 36
People like me	+ 32
White-collar workers	+ 17
The middle class	+ 10
Public employees	- 7
Farmers	- 60
Industrialists	- 63

Source: Ulram, *Hegemonie*

APPENDIX 8: Thematic Competence of SPÖ and ÖVP (1976 - 1981)

DIFFERENCE SPÖ MORE COMPETENT MINUS ÖVP MORE COMPETENT	IN PERCENT			
	1976	1977	1980	1981
Job security	+ 45	+ 43	+ 48	+ 43
Creating new jobs	+ 32	+ 34	+ 35	+ 33
Stability of prices	- 1	+ 7	+ 20	+ 18
Improving medical care	+ 17	+ 14	+ 24	+ 20
Improving financial conditions of elderly people	+ 34	+ 23	+ 25	+ 28
Law and order	+ 7	+ 8	+ 5	+ 11
Protection of environment	+ 36	+ 17	+ 15	+ 16
Prevent waste of taxes	- 22	- 20	- 14	- 14
Tax reform/ tax reduction	- 3	- 12	- 4	+ 2

Source: Ulram, *Hegemonie*

APPENDIX 9: Dealignment in the SPÖ-Electorate

IN PERCENT	MIDDLE 70s	1990	CHANGE
Blue-collar workers with party identification	65	47	- 18
SPÖ adherents with subjective party ties	74	43	- 31
SPÖ adherents living in party-political consonant network	86	57	- 29

Source: Fessel+Gfk, Political Indicators

APPENDIX 10: The Withering of Trust

IN PERCENT OF TOTAL ELECTORATE	79/80	81/82	84/85	CHANGE
Pensions will be secured for the next 10 - 15 years	69	38	26	- 43
One can be confident that the state will always pay	55	36	30	- 20
Security of full employment is not at all/not sufficiently considered by political parties	+	36	88	+ 52
Security of standard of living is not at all/not sufficiently considered by political parties	+	30	43	+ 13
The burden of taxation upon the economy is the main reason for danger to employment	30	37	46	+ 16

Source: Fessel+GfK, Political Surveys

APPENDIX 11: The Career of Political Issues (1980 - 1987)

VERY IMPORTANT ISSUE IN PERCENT	1980	1985	1987
Protection of the environment	55	76	79
Prevent waste of tax resources	51	74	76

Source: Ulram, *Hegemonie*

APPENDIX 12: Representation of Social Groups (1976 - 1985)

BEST REPRESENTED BY THE SPÖ IN PERCENT	76	80	85	CHANGE
Blue-collar workers	88	86	82	- 6
Pensioners	77	70	65	- 12
Employed women	73	69	62	- 11
Young people	68	63	58	- 10
Families with children	69	60	56	- 13
Housewives	59	51	54	- 14
People like me	57	50	42	- 15
White-collar workers	53	52	46	- 7
Public employers	40	43	35	- 5
The middle class	48	37	32	- 16

Source: Ulram, *Hegemonie*

APPENDIX 13: Thematic Competence of the SPÖ (1976 - 1985)

IN PERCENT OF THE TOTAL ELECTORATE SPÖ IS THE MOST COMPETENT PARTY FOR CHANGE	1976	1981	1985	
Job security	63	57	45	- 18
Creation of new jobs	55	49	38	- 17
Protection of environment	48	40	37	- 11
Tax reform/tax reduction	31	32	22	- 9
Prevent waste of tax resources	26	29	19	- 7

Source: Fessel+GfK, Political Surveys

APPENDIX 14: Political Dissatisfaction

IN PERCENT	MIDDLE 70s	EARLY 80s	LATE 80s	CHANGE
Have the impression that politics is always or often failing to resolve important questions	+	33	43	+ 10
Have been angry about political parties recently	+	43	68	+ 25
Think that politicians are corrupt and open to bribery	+	38	69	+ 31
Disagree with the statement: politicians are doing a good job	+	30	55	+ 25
Would like to see new parties in the political arena	10	17	47	+ 30

Source: Plasser/Ulram, "Wandel;" Ulram, *Hegemonie*

Social Change in the Kreisky Era

Marina Fischer-Kowalski

Introduction

During Kreisky's chancellorship in the 1970s Austria experienced a period of accelerated social change. Although structural social changes typically do not occur as a result of policies but as a result of underlying social and economic processes[1], the person and the politics of Kreisky are connected to these changes in at least two ways.

(1) Kreisky's political decisions were guided by a concept of modernization of Austrian society. This concept may have been inspired by his previous Scandinavian experiences. His vision was one of an egalitarian, middle-class society quite different from the Austrian socialist concept of defending the interests of the—manual—working class that had dominated, if not the policies, at least the political rhetoric of the pre-Kreisky period. Social democratic ideas were to be shared by a majority of liberal, "enlightened" citizens rather than by a class campus and their functionaries. This vision implied trust in education and urbanization and in the forcing open of frozen social hierarchies (other than the labor-capital relation) in the expectation that the intelligentsia would promote such changes. This vision fitted well into what was actually happening internationally; it permitted others to view the Austrian society of the mid-1960s as somehow "backward," and it guided political strategies that would modernize Austria into the community of the most developed welfare states.

(2) Kreisky had a much less "economistic" view of society than his predecessors and his followers.[2] He thereby deviated both from the right wing and from the left wing social democratic positions. Whereas the rightist positions sought to functionalize social processes for economic growth that in their minds depended upon sufficient fringes of profit for

stimulating capital investment (and sufficient wages to stimulate private consumption), the left wing interpreted all policies in the light of the class conflict between labor and capital and focused upon narrowing the disposition of capital over its political and distributional share. Kreisky perceived a wide range of possibilities to shape society without interfering with the basics of the capital-labor relationship. He extensively used social science research to explore these ranges, to legitimize interventions and to evaluate their effect. His slogan "democratization of all life spheres" quite intentionally circumvented the labor-capital conflict but extended to many other realms of social life. So Kreisky was a politician who intended to induce social change, and economic growth was a means rather than an end in this process.

Kreisky may just have been the right man in the right place at the right moment. But certainly he was not the politician merely to yield to objective forces and to adapt existing structures to neccessities. With regard to social structures and processes, he acted purposively, often cunningly, trying to mold them according to his vision—well aware of the rules of the game but certainly not in complete submission to them.

In 1969 Kreisky initiated a political program with the help of "1000 experts" headed by the slogan *Für ein modernes Österreich* (For a modern Austria). This program indeed preceded a phase of accelerated modernization of Austrian society. The contents of this modernization were quite in line with what nineteenth century theorists had considered the secular features of social progress. In Kreisky's administration, some of these secular modernizations reached their final stage. In the period afterwards they lost their momentum or were replaced by developments of a much more multifaceted character, lacking the directedness of an evolutionary progress.[3]

In the following sections I shall explore the impact of these developments on two basic fields of social organization: the organization of private reproduction, that is, of family and gender roles, and the organization of the labor market. With regard to the latter I shall concentrate on the transition process from traditional to modern forms of labor and on the social and political management of vertical inequalities.

Bringing Familialism to a Close— and Supporting Women's Liberation
Familial Reproduction and Demographic Transition

Modernization of family structures is generally understood to mean nuclear family with a small number of children, just enough to reproduce the population. The modern family no longer includes a lot of dependent persons unable to marry and raise children of their own or large numbers of children used as family-helps.

In the social democratic tradition, marriage and family had always been looked upon with mixed feelings. They were recognized and valued as a central concern of the populace, but at the same time made responsible for the subjugation of women and the oppression of sexual liberties. The Kreisky solution to this dilemma was to support marriage and child bearing, but mitigate the consequences. He introduced financial supports attractive enough for the founding of a family to raise marriage to a statistical peak[4] and bring the preceding decrease of birth rates to a halt. At the same time, he established a female Secretary of State for Women's Affairs and supported her quite aggressive strategies against the discrimination of women. And he backed his long-term minister of justice in executing a program decriminalizing sexual deviance, facilitating of divorce, liberalizing abortion and birth control and raising the legal status of illegitimate children.

These policies were adopted at the end of a secular process that had lasted about two hundred years: the demographic transition from an abundant form of demographic reproduction (many births and many and early deaths per stock unit) to a relatively thrifty form (fewer births, late deaths). Both patterns of reproduction render a more or less static population, if migration processes are disregarded. During the transition process a number of highly dynamic changes occur, though. Typically the death rates slow down before the birth rates do. This disparity creates a rapid population growth, as was the case in Austria around the turn of the century. At a later stage of this transition process there is a phase of "overaged" population: old people (who had still been born in the phase of high birth rates but already declining death rates) outnumber young people, thereby threatening the financial basis of pension schemes. This stage, although somewhat distorted due to the losses of the world wars, had been reached in the pre-Kreisky period. In the 1970s the (seemingly) final balance of this transition process was achieved. Life expectancy, after another, rather unexpected rise during the 1070s[5], had arrived at about seventy years for males and seven years more for females, and the ideal pattern of two births per female life was firmly established.[6] To get married and raise children had become the universal way of life for almost everyone. Had the number of people never getting married been close to one third before the First World War, the estimates for the early 1970s amount to 95 percent of people marrying at least once in their lives. These proportions had never been reached before and would not occur thereafter. Until the mid-1970s, the age of the first marriage was continuously decreasing, and so was the percentage of children born illegitimately. Marriage was even predominant in the sense that people getting divorced were almost invariably remarrying. Divorces had been rising continuously, though, since the early 1960s.[7] The nuclear family household reached its peak with about 80 percent of the total population sharing their daily lives with a partner (and maybe children).

This golden age of marriage and nuclear familiy living was, of course, not a uniquely Austrian phenomenon, but a phase common to all of the more highly developed OECD countries (see appendix 1). And it did not last very long: from the mid-1970s onward one can observe many indications of a counter trend; but this trend rather implies a fragmentation of the previous patterns than the establishment of a new one (see appendix 1).

What comes after nuclear family living is unclear. Obviously, there is an increase in the proportion of singles in the younger age groups; in Austria, the increase has been even more marked than for the OECD average. There is also a further and continuous decrease in the number of children born per female (amounting to an average of 1.5 by the beginning of the 1990s, well below net-reproduction of the population). The age of marriage has gone up, and the rates of marriage have declined massively so that demographers today estimate one third of the population to remain unmarried all their lives. The proportion of illegitimate children again amounts to one quarter, and divorces keep rising while re-marriage is becoming scarce. There exists no positively filled ideological image of modernization of the patterns of household living any more; the ongoing process of diversification and individualization[8] is being accepted but does not constitute a political goal.[9]

Levelling out Sexual Inequalities

The Kreisky era coincided with a relative peak of the women's liberation movement. Strong forces "from below," organized outside of the political parties and within the parties (particularly the Social Democratic party) demanded and supported policies against the discrimination of women. Two governmental reports (one in 1975, the other 1985—*Frauenberichte der Bundesregierung*) analyzed the living conditions of women in Austria. According to these reports the most important developments seem to be as follows:

(a) A gradual loosening of the association between familial phases of the life cycle and female employment. Female employment before had followed Myrdal's so called three-phase model (education/employment—child rearing—employment), rendering women poor chances to reenter the labor market after disruption. Now, however, these cyclical differences started to level out; married women and mothers experienced the highest increase in employment rates, and interruptions of the working life due to children became shorter despite social policies to support mothers of small children economically.[10] Austria being a country of traditionally high female employment, however the overall rise in female employment during this period was—internationally compared—rather low.[11]

(b) The general expansion of the educational system worked very much in favor of women. Many of the political measures during the Kreisky era intended to equalize educational chances between the social classes and regions (such as free access to schools and universities, granted schoolbooks and transportation) mainly increased the equality between the sexes. In the period concerned, the educational disadvantage of girls was levelled out: they gained almost equal access to further education after secondary school. They even reached high school graduation (*Matura*) over-proportionally and had the same chances to enter university education as males though with a lesser chance of graduating. A very strong horizontal differentiation between the sexes persisted nevertheless: although co-education was strongly promoted politically, the invasion of females into traditionally male educational realms (and the invasion of males into female realms) happened only at a very slow pace.[12] Given the qualification-specific rates of female employment (with university graduates having the highest rates) educationally the female labor force was almost equally qualified as the male; but this was honored little in employment status and not at all in income (see below).

(c) The 1970s saw a marked change in the structure of female employment, even more marked than for men. The number of female white collar employees increased sharply at the expense of an equally sharp reduction of family-helps (see appendix 2). This occupational status had been the most typical for females in the past. It had implied the highest dependency of women upon their husbands and involved working hours more often than not exceeding 60 hours per week.[13] Here again we find a secular modernization process coming to an end (see appendix 2).

Within the other occupational groups contradictory changes took place. Among blue-collar workers (whose overall number and proportion within the female labor force showed a slow decrease) a process of devaluation of female labor can be registered: more often than before females serve as unskilled laborers. Their number and proportion among skilled labor decreases. Among the sharply rising numbers of female white-collar employees, however, the proportions in the upper levels show the highest increases.[14] These changes are even more marked among the younger employees, partly due to improved education.[15] By the end of this period there nevertheless still exists a remarkable discrimination against women within white collar work: even equal education does not provide both sexes with the same occupational chances (see appendix 3).

Thus, in terms of the occupational hierarchy the female labor force has become more polarized during the 1970s than ever before. This, on the other hand, is not the case for income: male wages exceed female wages (standardized by working time) by 30 percent, and this disparity has remainded constant for the last three decades.[16] In income level relative to their male counterparts, female laborers have improved and female white-collar employees have declined. The female income pyramid contracted.[17]

(d) One core problem of the female role associated with family, namely the highly unequal distribution of labor in the household and with children, in nineteenth century theories of modernization could not even have been imagined to be subject to social change. And indeed for a long time it proved resistant. As the governmental report on women in Austria critically comments, in 1983 still almost 90 percent of all adult women organize a household (compared to 7 percent of the men), half of which are households with children.[18] Only 29 percent of the women who have a partner receive a daily help from him, whereas 57 percent are hardly ever helped by their partners in household work. This distribution has changed only marginally between the years 1977 and 1983. What has changed though is the frequency with which fathers look after their (preferably elder) children: regular care increased from 30 percent to 54 percent in this 6-year period.[19] As may be gathered from appendix 4, between 1969 and 1983 quite a remarkable restructuring of the working time of both sexes has taken place.

In 1969 employed females had had an extra thirty-six-hour-week of work in household and child care, amounting to as much as an eighty-working-hour week including their jobs. Employed males only contributed seven hours a week to household and children, thus having an excess of twenty-six hours per week of disposable time over females. This equals twenty-five weeks of extra holiday per year! This discrepancy was reduced during the following decade: male household participation increased to nine hours a week, while the female share went down, absolutely and relatively. In 1983 the male working week (job plus household) amounts to an average of three hours less, the female working week to fourteen hours less than in 1969.[20] The resulting difference between the sexes still corresponds to fifteen weeks of extra holidays per year for men—but a redistribution of labor within little more than a decade, and of tasks that had been considered "female" for all of human history, may still be called an important social change.

(e) The access of females to political and economic power has not improved during this period. As the analyses of the governmental report show, the political representation of women on all levels remained basically constant in the period 1970-1983.[21] Among the members of parliament there is a steady 17 percent-minority of females throughout this period, the same as in the second chamber (*Bundesrat*). In the (nine) regional parliaments the female proportion rose from a meager 7 percent (in the pre-Kreisky period) to 10 percent in the early 1980s. Among the members of the national and the federal governments, the female proportion shows no increase and varies around 6 percent. Probably the same holds true for the proportion of females in the top ranks of business, the media, and the administration.

A New Middle Class Society on the Basis of Employed Labor for Everyone?

The transformation of all forms of labor into wage labor is considered a core process of modernization.[22] Fourastié's three-sector-model reshaped social democratic views upon this process: contrary to Marx, they did not expect from this change a general impoverishment (*Verelendung*[23]), but a promising dynamics of tertiarization providing most employees with nice, middle-class jobs and living conditions. Both the international and the Austrian developments since the end of the Second World War had strongly confirmed this conviction. But the Kreisky era may be considered the last phase in which such developments happened at a significant pace (or even speeded up temporarily). With regard to the structure of the labor force one may not call this period a turning point to the same extent as with familialism, though; the developments thereafter kept the same direction. But I would claim that by strongly losing momentum they changed their quality.[24]

The Absorption of the Traditional Sector of the Labor Force

The substitution of traditional forms of labor, that is, of labor in the form of self-employment, family-help, seasonal farm labor and the work of dependent housewives in modern forms of employed labor had always been welcome to social democracy. It meant a quasi-automatic increase of their clientele: small property owners and peasants and, to some extent, also dependent housewives had always tended to vote conservative. And it suited the social democratic understanding of modernization. Accordingly the most fundamental strategies of social democracy were directed toward making employed labor a secure mode of subsistence, as well as providing for age, sickness, childbearing and unemployment. These strategies had been successful to the degree of making employed labor gradually a more attractive and reliable form of living than the dependency upon (small) property or upon a partner in marriage.

During the Kreisky era important benefits were added: the general fourty-hour week (that had been decided upon already by the conservative government in 1969) was introduced along with a guaranteed minimum of four weeks of holiday per year (1976); unemployment payments and pension schemes were improved.[25] With good reason the 1970s are considered a phase of expansion of the welfare system in Austria.[26]

In combination with prosperity, wage growth and the structural dynamics of displacement of small property by medium and large capital,[27] this period also saw an accelerated absorption of traditional forms of labor by employed labor (see appendix 5).

The data presented in appendix 5 are organized in a somewhat unconventional form. The "traditional sector" includes housewives who are normally not considered part of the labor force.[28] From a theoretical point of view it is legitimate to include them, though: housework is certainly a necessary part of social labor, provides those who do it with a full time job, and constitutes the basis of subsistence for women without an income of their own. The traditional sector also includes blue-collar farm laborers but not the white-collar farm employees rising in numbers in connection to modern, industrialized forms of agriculture. Appendix 5 demonstrates the massive decline of the traditional sector, comprising 60 percent of the labor force in 1951 and shrinking to one third in 1981.[29] During the 1980s this decline is less marked. The number of self-employed outside of agriculture even rises, which in this century has never happened before. On the other side, the increase of employees is remarkable and accelerates between 1971-1981. But then their number stagnates.[30]

It is a matter of discussion whether this situation represents only a temporary slowdown of structural modernization due to declining rates of economic growth and increasing unemployment, or whether it is one of the symptoms of a quite fundamental crisis of capitalist development, as for example Lutz argues. He analyzes the cycles of economic prosperity and stagnation during the last 100 years in terms of the exchange modes between the modern sector of the economy and the traditional sector. He concludes that the postwar phase of prosperity was largely a result of neutralizing the "reserve army mechanism" Keynesian and welfare politics and utilizing the traditional sector for the supply of appropriately socialized labor and cheap goods of daily consumption—thereby using it up, absorbing it. With the end of this "internal imperialism," another phase of prosperity may only be achieved by qualitatively new mechanisms not in sight yet. If Lutz's analysis is correct, the Kreisky era coincided with a turning point in development.[31]

One obvious symptom is the rise in unemployment. Whereas it was possible to keep unemployment very low during the 1970s (lower than 2 percent, which was about half of the OECD average[32]), it started to rise in the early 1980s and more than doubled up to 1985 to remain around 5 percent since then (see appendix 6). In the last years of the Kreisky government, strong efforts were made at stimulating investment and active labor market policy (training programs, creation of "experimental" jobs) as well as relieving the labor market by premature pensions. These efforts ultimately led to an enormous increase in public debt; by 1984, cuts in public expenditures were considered inevitable, announcing the "crisis of the welfare state."

The Irrestible Rise from Blue Collar to White Collar Labor

The vertical differentiation among employed persons, and particularly between blue- and white-collar labor, was remarkable during the Kreisky era and persisted thereafter. The main social democratic answer was not a levelling out of these differences, but a promise of chances of mobility and equalization of chances for such mobility. This procedure was supported by the expectation of a constant increase of the white-collar share, until perhaps traditional blue-collar work would be eradicated altogether. Unfortunately this change did not occur; on the contrary, structures started freezing by the end of the Kreisky era as they did in other OECD-countries,[33] and so the golden times of upward mobility came to an end. Upward mobility by some then had to be paid for by downward mobility of others, thereby intensifying competition. This, thirdly, was accompanied by an ideological and political decline in the representation of blue-collar workers, and led to an increase in alienation and resentment towards the political system in general and the Social Democratic party itself. In the 1970s the party had had to worry about how to win over the ambitious parts of the middle class; now they had to worry about how to keep the resignative and resentful parts of the blue-collar working class.

Concerning vertical differentiation according to occupational status, the Kreisky government has financed a whole series of studies that paint a picture of inequality in which the unequal distribution of income is only a minor factor.[34] Median white-collar wages supersede blue-collar wages by about 20 percent; the difference increases though when looked upon separately for males and females.[35] Large differences exist regarding the quality of work: environmental influences detrimental to health, occupational strains or the range of disposition over one's work performance.[36] Of course there are also large differences with respect to job security. In all cases blue-collar workers are worse off, and in many cases even skilled workers are worse off than the lowest ranges of white-collar employees. This mirrors itself in subjective work satisfaction as presented in appendix 7.

These vertical differences persisted, despite some political efforts at equalizing the legal status of blue-collar and white-collar employees during the 1970s and up to now.[37] So if the occupational status and the working conditions of the majority of blue-collar workers were not satisfying to them and did not promise to improve (apart from some reduction in working time and increases in income), what else could the dissatisfied strive for, but individual mobility? The traditional dream of skilled laborers, namely to found a small enterprise of their own, had hardly ever materialized in the period after the Second World War.[38] But the modern dream, to rise into the ranks of technical or administrative employees, could be realized by relevant fractions (about 20 percent of all blue-collar workers within a decade[39]). As Haller[40] demonstrates, upward mobility generally increases for the cohorts entering the labor force in the second half of the 1960s, and at the same time downward mobility declines.[41]

The chances of realizing mobility hopes invested into one's children were even better. Although the strong hierarchical segregation of the Austrian school system persisted (despite attempts of the Kreisky government at a reform integrating secondary schools), the explosion of school enrollment during the 1970s, supported by liberal measures such as free fare, free schoolbooks and transportation, conveyed a feeling of upward social mobility to the lower classes. If the parents suffered from the strain, the children at least would be better off. And although differences in educational chances according to social origin did not decrease substantively, there was a strong "elevator effect."[42] By the end of the 1970s almost half of the children of blue-collar workers had obtained white-collar jobs (and more than 80 percent of the children of white-collar workers had remained in this status[43]).

That the promise of mobility chances could be kept without endangering those that had arrived at a middle-class position already was due to structural changes. As may be gathered from appendix 8, there was a remarkable increase in white-collar work during the 1970s: almost half a million additional white-collar jobs were created. Contrary to a widespread prejudice, the number of blue-collar jobs did not decrease, though.[44] Among males, blue-collar work still clearly dominates (see appendix 8).

Since the beginning of the 1980s the growth of white-collar work slows down markedly, and the pleasant constellation comes to an end. The rise from blue-collar to white-collar employment from now on is no more the result of a structural drag, but a matter of individualized competition. On top of that, blue-collar workers bear the main load of rising unemployment (see appendix 6). Thus, their present existence has not become any better compared to a decade ago, and their future has lost its promise. Their political representation had continuously declined: in 1956, one third of all members of parliament had come from blue-collar occupations; in 1968 it was 18 percent and by 1976 it had declined to 14 percent (among the socialist members the quota was 61 percent, 34 percent and 26 percent respectively[45]). What else can be expected but resignation and resentment?

Conclusion

The Kreisky era appears to have been something like the "golden age" of modernization in Austria. Secular processes connected to a notion of social progress culminated and produced conditions both for prosperity and social peace. Most of these processes took the same course in all highly industrialized countries, but in Austria they were more condensed into one specific period, and well-supported by politics. The trouble, though, was that these processes were considered steady and ongoing. This was obviously not the case, but the political fantasies did not reach beyond them. So towards the end of this phase several crashes hit as quite a surprise: unemployment, a financial crisis of the welfare state, mass resistance against technological progress causing environmental destruction and a susceptibility of manual workers to rightist politics. The old power of the capitalist economy over social processes seems to be restored, and social "progress" has lost its direction. So in some ways Kreisky was the last emperor of good old modern society in Austria.

NOTES

1. In talking about structural social changes I must cope with a severe methodological disadvantage: For the Kreisky period I may empirically rely upon the Austrian census data (1971, 1981). Unfortunately, the results of the 1991 census have not been published yet. Thus, I am often not on safe grounds when speaking about the comparative changes during the 1980s.

2. There was even a widespread rumor among the Austrian intelligentsia that he was not really interested in economics at all.

3. Rudolf Burger, "Nach der Utopie oder man lache nicht über Fukuyama," in *Abstriche* (Vienna: Sonderzahl, 1991), 9-20.

4. Besides the apparent statistical peak in 1972, it can be shown that the birth cohort of 1935-1945 has the highest marriage rates of all times. Susanne Feigl, *Frauen in Österreich: 1975-85* (Vienna: Staatssekretariat für allgemeine Frauenfragen, 1986).

5. Peter Findl, "Ehe, Familie, Haushalt," in *Sozialstatistische Daten 1990* (Vienna: ÖSTAT, 1990), 43-76.

6. Richard Gisser et al., "Familiale Wirklichkeit aus demografischer und soziologischer Sicht," in *Familienbericht der Bundesregierung* (Vienna: BMUJF, 1990).

7. Peter Findl, "Ehe, Familie, Haushalt," in *Sozialstatistische Daten 1990* (Vienna: ÖSTAT, 1990), 43-76.

8. Elisabeth Beck-Gernsheim, *Die Kinderfrage* (Frankfurt: Suhrkamp, 1989).

9. The family report of the Austrian government in 1990 (see Gisser et al. 1990, p.82) rather vaguely talks about a "new plurality of life styles." Strangely enough, the conservative People's Party at the same time demanded the "protection of the family" to be included in the Austrian constitution. This was hard to put in practice, though: there could not yet be reached a definition of what a "family" was supposed to be.

10. Gudrun Biffl, "Entwicklung auf dem Arbeitsmarkt bis zum Jahr 2000," *WIFO-Monatsberichte no 2*, 1988.

11. Gudrun Biffl, "Entwicklung auf dem Arbeitsmarkt bis zum Jahr 2000," *WIFO-Monatsberichte no 2*, 1988.

12. Marina Fischer-Kowalski et al., "Bildung," *Frauenbericht 1985, Bericht über die Situation der Frau in Österreich* (Vienna: Bundeskanzleramt, 1985), 57.

13. According to the data of the Mikrozensus 1983 (yearly averages of factual working hours per week) 51 percent of all female familiy helps worked an average of 60 or more hours. Altogether 83 percent of them worked more than 40 hours per week.

14. Susanne Feigl, *Frauen in Österreich 1975-85*, (Based upon the data of the *Frauenbericht* 1985) (Vienna: Staatssekretariat für allgemeine Frauenfragen, 1986), 40.

15. Marina Fischer-Kowalski, *Arbeits- und Lebensverhältnisse der Frauen in Österreich - Aspekte der Veränderungen in den Siebzigerjahren* (Vienna: Research Report no. 127 of the Institute of Advanced Studies, 1980), 17.

16. Susanne Feigl, *Frauen in Österreich 1975-85*, 43.

17. Irene Wolf and Walter Wolf, *Wieviel weniger...? Einkommensunterschiede zwischen Frauen und Männern in Österreich* (Vienna: Bundesministerium für Arbeit und Soziales, 1991).

18. "Zusammenfassung," *Frauenbericht 1985, Bericht über die Situation der Frau in Österreich* (Vienna: Bundeskanzleramt, 1985), 10.

19. Susanne Feigl, *Frauen in Österreich 1975-85*, 18.

20. The only really reliable data for this subject were collected by the Microcensus in 1981. In this survey the 15,000 respondents had to register all use of time during one September day (time budget). The working hours on the job (main job plus extra jobs) differ from the yearly averages presented in 3. They amount to an average of 6.8 hours for employed males, and 5.3 hours for employed females per day. Taking these working hours on the job (instead of the numbers in 3), the yearly difference between the sexes shrinks to 432 hours/year or 7.7 male working weeks. Data comparable to this do not exist for 1969.

21. Gerda Neyer and R. Köpl, "Politik / Gesetz," *Frauenbericht 1985, Bericht über die Situation der Frau in Österreich* (Vienna: Bundeskanzleramt, 1985).

22. Marx was insightful and courageous enough to formulate this prognosis at a time when wage labor amounted to less than 10 percent of the working force in England and even less in Germany.

23. Wolf Wagner, *Verelendungstheorie - die hilflose Kapitalismuskritik* (Frankfurt: Fischer, 1976).

24. See a similar figure of reasoning with: Ulrich Beck, *Risikogesellschaft. Auf dem Weg in eine andere Moderne* (Frankfurt: Suhrkamp, 1986); Burkart Lutz, *Der kurze Traum immerwährender Prosperität* (2nd ed., Frankfurt: Campus, 1989).

25. In this period some elements of social security that had been connected to employed labor were extended to other parts of the population, such as to students, mothers/housewives and self-employed persons. But up to now the Austrian system of social security is basically an insurance system focused on employed labor.

26. Emmerich Talos, "Sozialpolitik in Österreich seit 1970," in *Der österreichische Weg 1970-1985*, ed. Erich Fröschl and Helge Zoitl (Vienna: Europa Verlag, 1986).

27. Felix Spreitzhofer, "Wer dominiert die österreichische Wirtschaft?," in *Lebensverhältnisse in Österreich. Klassen und Schichten im Sozialstaat*, ed. Marina Fischer-Kowalski and Josef Bucek (Frankfurt-New York: Campus, 1980), 321-351.

28. Of all age groups but only if they personally do not have any other source of income (e.g., wage, pension).

29. All its components have shrunk: agricultural work (self-employed, family-helps and farm laborers) by 75 percent, other self-employed by 32 percent and housewives by 11 percent.

30. Here the lack of census data really is a pity. The comparability of census data with the microcensus is somewhat limited. But I tend to trust these results since they represent a common feature of many OECD countries in the same period (Fischer-Kowalski 1985, p.27).

31. Burkart Lutz, *Der kurze Traum immerwährender Prosperität*. (2nd ed.. Frankfurt: Campus, 1989). Even if this is correct one may argue, however, that the traditional sector in terms of housewives is still fairly large, and the agricultural sector in Austria still contains traditional parts "superfluous" in view of the European integration, so that the process of absorption would not yet have to stop for lack of supply.

32. Kurt W. Rothschild, "Felix Austria? Zur Evaluierung der Ökonomie und Politik in der Wirtschaftskrise," *Österreichische Zeitschrift für Politikwissenschaft* 3 (1985): 261-274.

33. Marina Fischer-Kowalski, *The Social Structure of OECD-Countries 1960-1980 and its Implications for Selected Aspects of Wellbeing* (Vienna: Research Report no. 223 of the Institute of Advanced Studies, 1985).

34. Max Haller et al., *Strukturen der sozialen Ungleichheit in Österreich* (Vienna: Research report of the Institute of Advanced Studies, 3 vols., 1978); Marina Fischer-Kowalski and Josef Bucek, eds., *Ungleichheit in Österreich: Ein Sozialbericht* (Vienna: Jugend & Volk, 1979); Sozialstatistische Daten 1980. Beiträge zur österreichischen Statistik No. 613 (Vienna: 1981); Bundesministerium für soziale Verwaltung, ed., *Soziale Struktur Österreichs* (Vienna: Verlag für Gesellschaftskritik, 1982).

35. Sozialstatistische Daten 1980. Beiträge zur österreichischen Statistik No. 613 (Vienna: 1981), 177; Sozialstatistische Daten 1990. Beiträge zur österreichischen Statistik No. 967 (Vienna: 1990), 206.

36. See: Eva Cyba et al., "Arbeitsbedingungen und Rationalisierung," in *Lebensverhältnisse in Österreich*, reed. by Marina Fischer-Kowalski and Josef Bucek (Frankfurt: Campus, 1986), 401-28; Bundesministerium für Soziale Verwaltung ed., *Soziale Struktur Österreichs. Soziale Schichten, Arbeitswelt, Soziale Sicherung* (Vienna: Verlag f. Gesellschaftkritik, 1982); Ewald Bartunek, "Umwelteinflüsse und andere Belastungen am Arbeitsplatz," *Statistische Nachrichten* 42/1 (1987): 27-37; Ewald Bartunek, "Berufliche Tätigkeit mit schädlichen Arbeitsstoffen," *Statistische Nachrichten* 42/2 (1987): 88-93; Ewald Bartunek, "Berufsbedingte Beschwerden und Krankheiten," *Statistische Nachrichten* 42/3 (1987): 184-190.

37. For some comparisons see ibid. Max Haller, "Die Sozialstruktur Österreichs—Entwicklungstendenzen und Charakteristika im internationalen Vergleich," in *Handbuch des politischen Systems Österreichs*, ed. Herbert Dachs et al., (Vienna: Manz, 1991): 37-77.

38. Berndt Schmeikal, "Topologie und Dynamik von Mobilitätsstrukturen," *Österreichische Zeitschrift für Soziologie* 3-4 (1978): 19-38.

39. Max Haller et al., *Strukturen der sozialen Ungleichheit in Österreich* (Vienna: Research Report of the Institute of Advanced Studies, vol. 3, 1978), 709.

40. Max Haller, *Klassenstrukturen und Mobilität in fortgeschrittenen Gesellschaften* (Frankfurt - New York: Campus, 1989), 336.

41. This is a much luckier constellation than in the decades before, and much more favorable than in France and the United States at the same time, as Haller's (1991) comparisons show.

42. Marina Fischer-Kowalski and Peter Seidl, *Von den Tugenden der Weiblichkeit* (Vienna: Verlag für Gesellschaftkritik, 1986).

43. Bundesministerium für Soziale Verwaltung, ed., *Soziale Strukturen Österreichs*, 65.

44. This again is not an Austrian speciality, but common to most OECD-countries. In most countries, with the only exception of the United States, the proportion of blue-collar workers stagnated somewhere between 40-45 percent of the labor force.

45. Heinz Fischer, "Die parlamentarischen Fraktionen," in *Das politische System Österreichs*, ed. Heinz Fischer (3rd ed., Vienna: Europa Verlag, 1982), 129.

APPENDIX 1: Contracting of Families to the Nucleus - and Then?

% of the population in nuclear families (pairs with/without children)	1960	1970	1980
OECD-Median	78%	76%	68%
Austria	75%	77%	74%

% of the population in one-person-households			
OECD-Median	4%	6%	7%
Austria	6.5%	8.5%	10%
BRD	7%	9%	12%

% of the population in single-parent families (parent and children)			
OECD-Median	6%	6%	6%
Austria	9%	7.5%	6%

Source: M. Fischer-Kowalski, *The Social Structure of OECD-Countries;* International report to OECD 1983.

APPENDIX 2: Changes in the Employment Status of Women 1951-1988

	Employees		Self-Employed	Family Helps	(N in Thousands)
	Blue-Collar	White-Collar			

In percent of female labor force

1951	37.5	18.0	11.5	32.9	(1299)
1961	36.7	27.0	11.1	25.2	(1360)
1971	35.8	37.5	10.0	16.7	(1237)
1981	33.1	49.2	10.7	7.0	(1427)
1988	28.8	55.0	8.1	8.0	(1391)

Rates of change of absolute numbers by periods

1961/51	+ 2%	+57%	-30%	-20%
1971/61	-11%	+26%	-19%	-40%
1981/71	+ 7%	+52%	+23%	-52%
1988/81	-15%	+ 9%	-26%	+11%

Source: Census-date, own calculations

APPENDIX 3: Differences in Career Patterns of Female and Male White Collar Employees

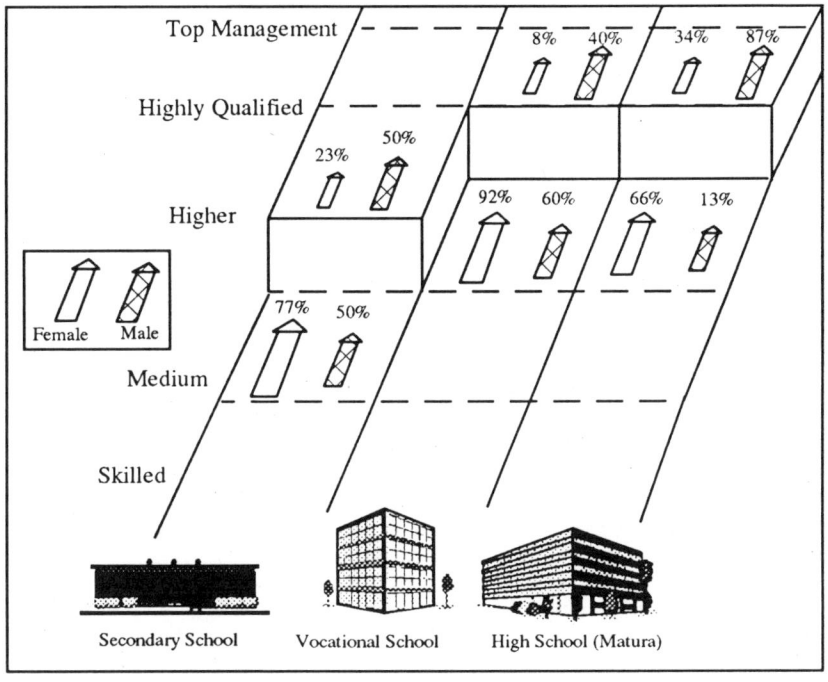

Source: ÖSTAT, Microcensus 1989, from Wolf & Wolf (1991), 45.

APPENDIX 4: Changes in Weekly Working Hours of Employed Males and Females 1969-1981

	1969 m	1969 f	1981 m	1981 f
Working time in employment[1]	47.2	44.3	42.5	38.4
Working time household & children[2]	7.2	36.0	8.0	27.5
Sum of working hours per week	54.4	80.3	51.3	65.9
Working hours per year	2829	4176	2668	3427
Difference between the sexes in hours per year		1347		759
Difference between the sexes in male working weeks		24.8		14.8

1) Microcensus: yearly averages of actual working hours/week
2) Source for 1969: Fischer-Kowalski, 1980, 56; for 1983: ÖSTAT: *Tagesablauf* (1981).

APPENDIX 5: The Absorption of the "Traditional Sector" by Employed Labor

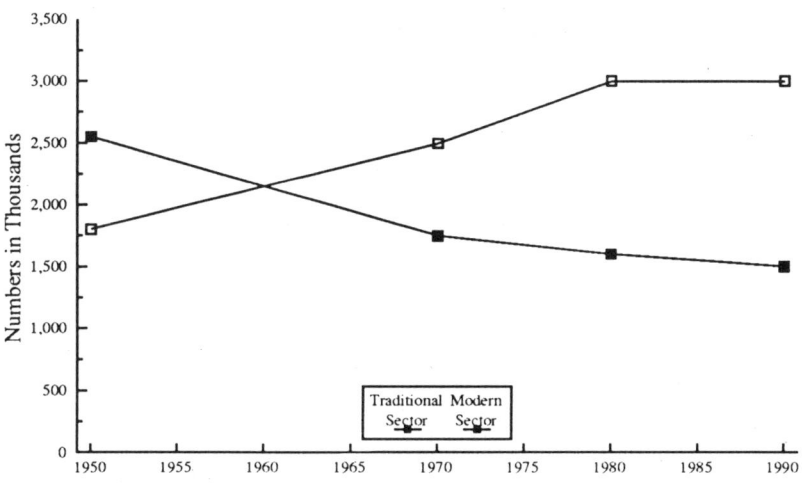

"traditional sector": self employed, family-helps, farm laborers, housewives without an own income
"modern sector": white collar and blue collar employees (employed and unemployed) with the exclusion of farm laborers

Sources: Census data 1951, 1971, 1981, Microcensus 1988 (in the version of ÖSTAT, Sozialstatistische Daten 1990, 160, corrected for comparability).

APPENDIX 6: Persons Registered As Unemployed 1970-1989

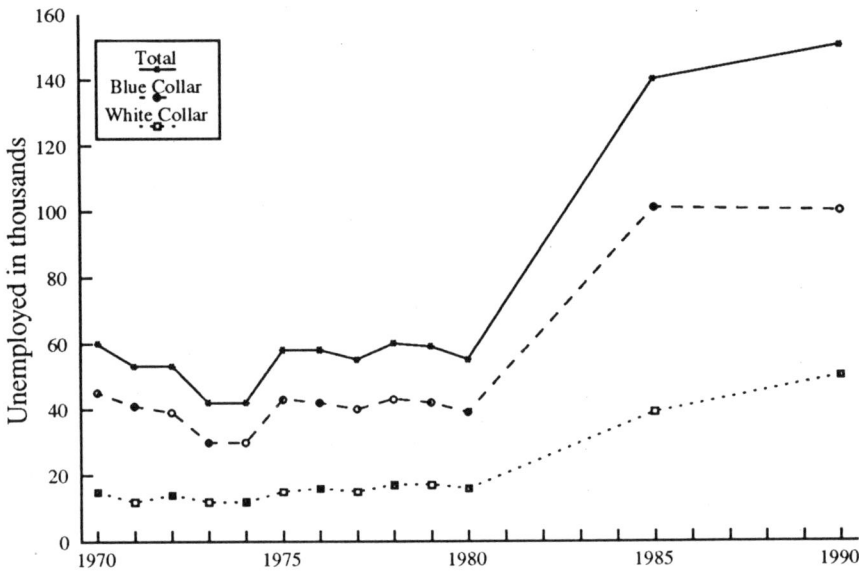

Source: BM für soziale Verwaltung

APPENDIX 7: Work Satisfaction by Occupational Status

% highly satisfied	occupational status
80	agricultural self employed -- large property
	non-agricultural self employed, large enterprise
70	managerial white collar
	highly qualified white collar
60	white collar
	other self employed, medium enterprise
	non-agricultural self employed
	self employed, small enterprise
50	lower white collar
	skilled workers
40	blue collar workers
	family helps in agriculture
	agricultural self emploed
	agricultural self employed -- medium property
	semi skilled workers
	farm laborers
30	unskilled laborers
	agricultural self employed -- small property

Source: Microcensus 1978, from BM f. soziale Verwaltung 1982, 47.

APPENDIX 8: Blue Collar and White Collar Workers 1951-1988

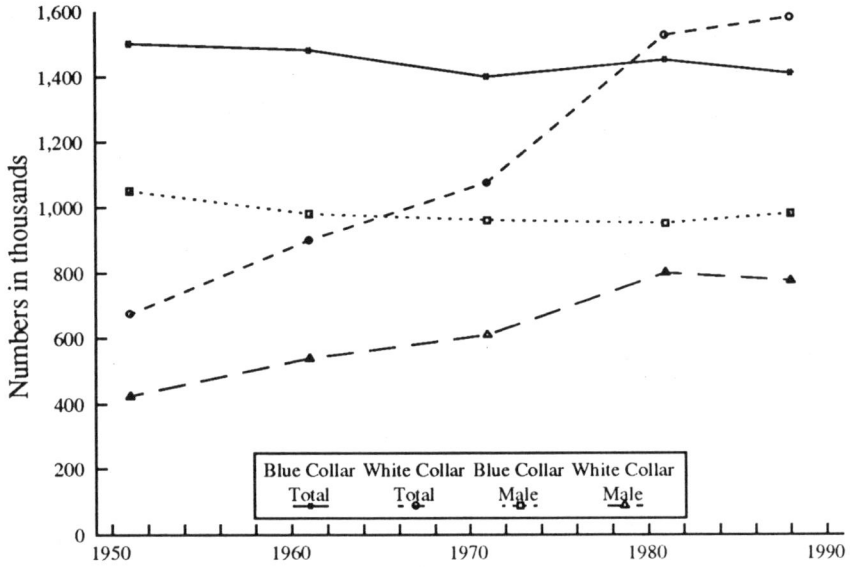

Source: Census data for 1951, 1961, 1971, 1981 and Microcensus 1988 from ÖSTAT, Sozialstatistische Daten 1990, 160 (employed and unemployed).

Austro-Keynesianism Reconsidered

Kurt W. Rothschild

The 1978 Economic Survey of Austria by the OECD (Organization for Economic Cooperation and Development) opened with the following sentence: "The most remarkable feature of the Austrian economy of the last few years has been the simultaneous achievement of a progressive reduction of inflation and continued growth of employment" (5). It expressed the surprised recognition—soon to be shard all over the world--that little Austria, once an economic problem area par excellence, seemed to have charted a course which after 1970 ran counter to the unfavorable experiences in most of the other countries where economic growth had slowed and unemployment had returned as a pressing and growing problem. While after 1970-72 unemployment rose everywhere—and increased dramatically in the 1975 world-wide set-back—Austria was able to maintain a satisfactory growth record and to cut unemployment to the lowest postwar levels. Austria's unemployment rate, which in 1970 had stood (with 2.4 percent) above the average level of 2 percent in nine developed Western European countries (Austria, Belgium, Germany, Italy, Netherlands, Norway, Sweden, United Kingdom) fell to 1.9 percent.[1] Among Western European countries only Sweden, Norway and Switzerland had lower, but not declining unemployment in the 1970s. Moreover, this favorable employment record was achieved without serious inflationary consequences. Austria's inflation rate, which had stood at 4.4 percent in 1970 amounted to 6.4 percent in 1980 compared to 5.8 percent (1970) and 11.3 percent (1980) for the average of the aforementioned nine countries.

This success story of the 1970s and early 1980s which later (in 1979) was christened "Austro-Keynesianism was the result of a variety of factors. Like "Reaganomics," "Austro-Keynesianism" is not a clear-cut, theoretically-defined concept but rather an afterthought systematizing a pragmatic development and its results (with important differences *in content* between the two cases!). Here we have to restrict ourselves to a very brief sketch of the main aspects of Austro-Keynesianism, which will allow us afterwards to judge its significance from today's perspective.

A decisive reason for the divergent developments in the Austrian economy during the 1970s lies in the political sphere. Just at a time when the Western world (with few exceptions) turned conservative—both politically and economically—Austria stepped in the opposite direction. In the 1970 elections, the Socialist party overtook the conservative People's party, replacing the conservative government by a socialist-led coalition government. This government was replaced in 1971 by a purely socialist government after the Socialist party had won an absolute majority. This change of government had a decisive influence on the main directions of economic policy. While in most other countries, the rise in inflation rates and the "monetarist revolution" which preached the advantages and curative powers of "free markets" induced conservative governments to cut back public engagement and intervention for economic growth and full employment which had been typical in the preceding years, the Austrian government and not least its head, Bruno Kreisky, remained faithful to a full employment target, even increasing the emphasis in view of the economic disturbances of the mid-1970s.

While a determined political will to maintain production and employment was an important precondition for the course of events, it could not be decisive by itself. It had to be translated into an effective policy. This was achieved not so much by a clear-cut concept but rather by a more pragmatic policy-mix, though theoretical considerations as well as practical and historical experiences served as important guides. The main elements of this policy mix can be summarized as follows.

First, it was taken for granted that a certain steadiness of final demand is necessary if a cumulative deterioration in production and employment is to be avoided. Since the slow-down in the world economy threatened exports and with them the entire demand basis, public efforts were needed to prevent major set-backs from this side which at the time were considered a purely temporary disturbance in a fundamentally prosperous world development. Thus, a policy of "diving through" was adopted. Public demand was upheld and even increased in spite of falling revenues; budget deficits and a quickly-rising public debt were permitted to develop in the hope that they could easily be reversed in the coming return to world prosperity. In addition, special help was granted to industries and regions whose difficulties could develop into a threat for a wider circle of sectors and regions. These "demand-side" measures were supported by the extension of already existing "supply-side" measures such as special depreciation allowances, tax rebates, interest rate subsidies and the like to provide a prop for investment.

The challenge of growing inflation, which after the 1960s existed in Austria just as much as in other countries, was not met by a deflationary assault with its depressive affects on economic activity, but by a rather original combination of exchange rate and income policies. A "hard currency policy" was adopted that maintained a fixed exchange rate between the Austrian schilling (AS) and the German deutschmark (DM). This policy had two consequences. First, it removed all exchange rate risks vis-à-vis Germany, who is Austria's largest trading partner by far, both on the expert and on the import side. Second, it meant that the schilling—in line with the deutschmark—appreciated vis-à-vis the dollar and other currencies, mitigating world-wide inflationary tendencies. This proved particularly important in the wake of the two oil price shocks in 1973 and 1979.

But this hard currency policy (making Austrian commodities expensive for "weaker" currencies) could have been a threat to Austria's foreign transactions, stimulating imports and hampering exports. This threat was to a considerable extent met by a special Austrian institution, the so-called "Social Partnership," a rather informal body of cooperative contacts between the big and influential organizations of industry (employers' organization, Chamber of Trade), employees (trade unions, Chamber of Labor), and agriculture which had developed in the postwar years to come to terms with the tasks of reconstruction and normalization. Regular contacts in this framework permit a certain degree of steering market developments, and particularly wage-price processes, keeping them within certain bounds and preventing run-away developments. That such "corporatist" structures can be a help in stabilizing economies has been a widespread experience (with Germany, Switzerland, Sweden as typical examples in addition to Austria). This framework enabled Austria to maintain its international competitiveness in spit of the hard-currency policy. Wages and prices were on the whole sufficiently constrained by compromise and consensus to support the viability of the currency policy and its anti-inflationary effects.

We can now indicate in what respects the term "Austro-Keynesianism" is justified and what it signifies. A prominent Keynesian aspect was the obvious insistence on the role of effective demand and its stabilization (as far as possible) even at the cost of rising budget deficits and a certain degree of inflation. Another Keynesian or Post-Keynesian element was the attempt to contain inflation by some sort of income policy rather that through a policy of deflation and high interest rates. Finally, the stimulating effects of this declared public policy of maintaining high employment on business confidence and investment were also in the spirit of Keynesian ideas about the need to reduce uncertainty and risk.

The specific "Austro-"aspects in Austro-Keynesianism can also be summarized under three headings. First, the policy was not a dogmatic, one-sided Keynesian strategy with all the stress laid on demand maintenance and demand support. "Supply-side" measures, providing direct incentives to business and investment, were intensively used as an additional stimulus. Second, introduction of a hard-currency policy via the DM-connection was a very special approach to apply competitive pressure as a constraint on price. And finally, the historically-grown Social Partnership provided a framework that permitted a special type of income policy and market regulation.

This Austro-Keynesianism mixture that got going after 1970 and evolved during the following decade began to decline after 1980 and has practically disappeared as a special characteristic of Austria. The country has fallen into line with general Western European and world development. While between 1973 and 1979 the real GDP (gross domestic product) per capita had grown by three percent per annum in Austria against two percent in the European part of the OECD, growth rates fell and the difference shrank to two percent in Austria and 1.7 percent (OECD) between 1979 to 1989. Full employment ceased to exist. Though an expanding labor force led to further increases in employment, unemployment reached a level of 5.9 percent in 1992, still somewhat lower than the Western European average (7.9 percent) but far above previously accepted targets.

Several reasons contributed to the fading out of the Austro-Keynesian practice and pragmatism. A basic reason was that one of the main premises on which this practice had relied turned out to be false. The idea that a full employment policy connected with a rise in budget deficits and balance of payment problems (caused by a high import level) should be accepted was based on the expectation that the world-wide stagflation and recession would only be a temporary deviation from the growth path of the preceding years. This expectation was widely held at the time, not only in Austria. When it became clear (particularly in the 1981 recession) that a quick return to false, growth-high employment conditions in the international sphere was unlikely, the idea of "diving through" had to be discarded. A certain adaptation to the new situation was necessary.[2]

One obvious problem was that the sufferance of growing budget deficits had led to steep rise in the government debt. From a mere AS 47 billion (12.5 percent of GDP) in 1970 the debt had risen to AS 261 billion (26.2 percent of GDP) in 1980, with a strong rising tendency that ultimately stabilized a round 48 percent of GDP ten years later. While this is not an abnormal level as compared with other countries, the interest burden which it involves made it necessary to pay more attention to the size of deficits with consequent constraints on fiscal policy in general and on employment policy in particular.

These constraining budget effects were intensified by a change in the political background. After 1982 the Socialist party lost its absolute majority, and though still the strongest party in Parliament, it could only rule in coalition with one of the more conservative parties. This—together with the real difficulties and the international "climate"—led to a marked shift in policy targets. Reducing the budget deficit and containing government expenditure became top priorities pushing the employment target into the background. Keynesian skepticism with regard to automatic tendencies toward employment equilibrium was replaced by the more fashionable belief in the self-healing qualities of free, competitive market processes.

But even if these political changes had not taken place and the old priorities had remained unchanged, modifications in the policy would have been required. Originally designed (as far as we can speak of a "design") as a short-term strategy to avoid large-scale unemployment during a period of passing difficulties, it concentrated largely on demand maintenance wherever production and employment were threatened and on the extension of public and private services. But with the persistence of the external stagnation this policy of employment conservation threatened to become a hindrance to structural change which demanded a decline of some of the older industries and an accelerated creation and growth of new industries and products to fit into a changing world scene. While some change in this direction took place, its speed was rather moderate. A continued employment policy would have required a new Austro-Keynesian policy-mix with greater provision for long-term developments and structural change.[3]

A final factor contributing to the dissolution of Austro-Keynesianism is the general decline in opportunities for autonomous national economic policies in the wake of a growing international economic integration and the liberalization of capital movements. This factor, to which we shall return again later on, weighs particularly heavily in a small, open economy like Austria's where external transactions occupy a prominent place (exports including services: 41 percent of GDP; imports 40 percent).

When we come to an evaluation of the Austro-Keynesianism episode and try to derive some lessons from it, a separation between an Austrian and a more general perspective seems in place. As far as the Austrian perspective is concerned, we must distinguish between the situation as it presented itself in the 1970s and as it presents itself today. We must not forget that the premise on which the Austro-Keynesian strategy was built, namely, that the world-wide break in prosperity and growth would only be a short disturbance in a continuing trend, was a reasonable assumption at the time and was shared by many (though not all) economists and politicians all over the world.[4] Seen from this angle, the policy was certainly a success and was recognized as such by other countries and by international organizations. The "Austrian model" which managed to maintain full employment in the midst of a stagnating world with increasing unemployment and which could achieve this without paying the price of higher inflation was studied as an important experiment in several studies and conferences. The fact that this policy was accompanied by a quick expansion of the public debt and by structural inertia was not sufficiently noted to begin with; but it could also be regarded as a reasonable cost, considering the assumption that these drawbacks could easily be repaired in a coming period of regained world prosperity.

The picture changes when we look at the Austro-Keynesian story form a somewhat later perspective. In the later years of Austro-Keynesianism, say after 1980, reasonable doubts about the short-term nature of the stagnant international tendencies and about a return to the "golden era" conditions of the 1960s could no longer be suppressed. They should have led to a serious analysis and reconsideration of the established policy-mix and to attempts to modify it so as to meet the new situation and its longer-term aspects. This would not have required a renouncement of the full employment target as a top priority; but the policy-mix would have required adaptations and changes. Among the things to be done, it would have been advisable (and possible) to create a more flexible budget policy that would allow budget deficits and budget surpluses to be fitted better to the fluctuating economic situation (and so to achieve the desired demand effects at lower rates of debt accumulation); to supplement and modify the employment-oriented, supply-side supports (low interest rates, subsidies and the like) with structural considerations (including ecological needs); to "soften" the hard-currency policy to be able to meet structural balance of payments problems; and to help the Social Partnership to be better prepared for new problems in a changed environment.

The neglect of this need for reforms and (constant) adaptations led to a certain hardening of the earlier approaches, making the policy less effective in later years and creating the already mentioned problems of a quickly-expanding government debt and of structural disequilibrium which then—together with the shift in political weights from 1983 onwards—led to the end of a clearly distinguishable Austrian-type policy. As in other countries, reductions of deficits, containment of the government dept, price stability and international competitiveness became the leading targets, though employment has continued to play a somewhat more prominent role than in some other countries.

It must, however, be stressed that even an adapted and rejuvenated Austro-Keynesianism would have lost effectiveness in the 1980s in view of the loss of sovereignty in economic policy connected with the complete liberalization of capital movements, international integration, and particularly with Austria's membership in the European Economic Space and her intended membership in the European Community. Already today, but to a far greater extent in the future (in case the ECF achieves its aims of currency and political union) a small open economy will have very few opportunities to follow an economic policy of its own with a target-mix that differs from that of the Community as a whole. Fiscal, monetary, and trade policies, will be closely tied to the general trend of Community action. This does not mean that no national action at all can be taken and that small-country governments will be reduced to mere passive policy-takers; but the range of opportunities will be very modest indeed. Perhaps the people of Denmark will be glad one day that their negative vote to the extensive Maastricht plans secured for them a certain degree of monetary and policy flexibility which offers them a somewhat wider freedom of choice in their economic affairs.

A further valuative view from an Austrian standpoint can be taken when one looks back from 1993 asking whether the country *today* is better or worse of because of the special Austro-Keynesian walk taken in the 1970s and early 1980s. From an empirical point of view this is an idle question: we can never satisfactorily construct the alternative past, the answer to the question, what would have happened *if*. But one can speculate. And there the opinions differ.

Some people regard the past events as a failure because the fixation on the employment target had got the country into the habit of accepting budget deficits that lasted too long and that are responsible for the present interest burden, which—together with the structural distortions of the employment-oriented policies—is responsible for some of the present difficulties (including unemployment). This seems to me too one-sided a picture. While the heritage of a high debt and structural imbalance has to be admitted, it cannot be ascribed totally to the Austro-Keynesian elements in Austria's past. Increases in budget deficits and public debt have occurred in most countries as a consequence of cyclical and long-term disturbances though without turning them to employment-augmenting use. Moreover, with 48 percent of GDP, the present size of the Austrian government debt is neither alarming nor excessive when compared with that of other countries (for example, 39 percent on Germany, 28 percent in France, but 93 percent in Italy and 106 percent in Belgium). And as far as structural problems are concerned, most of them could not have been avoided because of the uncertainties in a rapidly changing world scene. Here, too, Austria's achievements and problems do not seem to differ markedly form the average of Western European countries.

On the other hand, the concern about employment in the Austro-Keynesian period has left a positive heritage that is still felt today. Though unemployment increased rapidly after the policy-change in the early 1980s—*relatively* quicker than the Western European average—the fact that the formation of a hard core of basic unemployment was avoided in the 1970s has left its mark on later developments. As mentioned before, Austria's present unemployment of roughly six percent lies still below a Western European average of about eight percent.

What general lessons can be learned from the Austro-Keynesian episode? In particular, how are these lessons of interest for other countries? One point must be stressed right away. Regardless whether one considers Austro-Keynesianism a success or a failure, it could not be an exact model to be followed (or avoided) by other states. Some of the prerequisites for the finally emerging policy-mix had been historically-grown institutions and attitudes that cannot be easily created or transferred to other countries.[5] Among these one has to mention particularly the existence of highly organized and centralized bodies representing the main socio-economic interest groups (employers, employees, industry, agriculture) and their regular contacts (extending to government participation) in the so-called "Social Partnership." Close and fairly smooth contacts between the Central Bank and the government also belong to this picture. This was a precondition for combining a hard-currency policy with a corresponding wage and price policy (an "income policy") which provided a certain balance between employment, price stability, and international competitiveness.

Though the particular institutional and traditional set-up just mentioned is a specific Austrian phenomenon, a general conclusion that may be derived from it and that is supported by studies covering several advanced industrial countries is that a certain amount of corporatism added to the forces of "free" markets can help to stabilize economic development, employment, and inflation.

But other lessons may also be derived from Austria's experience though they have all to be interpreted with care and are not independent of time, place, and current conditions. While the lack of clear-cut concepts in Austria's policy was certainly a drawback, the use of a pragmatic and non-dogmatic policy-mix had its advantages. By attacking several problems (inflation, unemployment, balance of payments) with a variety of weapons in varying proportions Austria reduced the danger of running into extreme errors and enhanced the possibility of correcting a wrong course. Of course, mixing wrong policies would not be helpful. But considering the uncertainties about future developments and about the exact affects of specific policy instruments an open-minded policy-mix seems to be a recommendable strategy.

Another lesson to be learned is the obvious fact that it is easier and less problematical to deviate for a short time from the general trend of the world economy than to achieve a long-term separation from the trend. Over short periods one can use rather heavy medicines to arrive at special results, even if they cannot be maintained for longer periods. In the longer run, the maintenance of a separate course becomes more difficult and requires modifications of the policy which in its first stages had to achieve a shift to a new basis. The neglect of this fact was certainly one of the main shortcomings of Austro-Keynesianism.

But perhaps the main secret behind the (comparative) success of Austro-Keynesianism that would have to be heeded by would-be successors was the strong political will to foster full employment supported by a broad social consensus. Making employment a high priority target did not just mean the enactment of certain employment-promoting measures but led to an infusion of employment considerations into a wide spectrum of policy actions. This added a distinct employment bias to economic policy as a whole. It is very likely that such a basic determination is at least as important as a sound theoretical and institutional foundation. In this connection it is worth quoting the noted British economist Austin Robinson who—when reviewing in 1945 Lord Beveridges' classical "Full Employment in a Free Society" which recommended a Keynesian policy for postwar Britain—made the following remark:

> They (i.e. the proposed instruments to fight unemployment) are not so very different from, nor so very much greater than those with which we failed to defeat unemployment in the thirties that we can feel absolutely confident of success. But what, *more than anything else*, was lacking was an overwhelming national determination to defeat unemployment. (Italics added. K.R.)

Replacing "1930s" by "1980s and 1990s" might explain part of today's problems.

Yet there is one important difference for Western European countries in general that has made it far more difficult to try to get off the band-wagon of general events. The increased integration of the European economies in the European Economic Space and the European Community with their "four economic freedoms" (mobility of goods, services, capital, labor) and their unification of many rules and targets makes life easier for transnational companies but sets severe limits on special national actions in economic targeting and economic policy. Such limits have already been clearly visible in Mitterand's efforts to follow a separate, employment-oriented French route, and they have contributed to the decline of the Swedish welfare state program. They are likely to grow with the intensification of the integration process.

It is obvious that such limits are particularly severe for small countries where above-average expansionary efforts can fritter away in the open space. An Austro-Keynesian policy in the old style may not be repeatable today. The tail cannot wag economically more potent states. There may still be some force in the "locomotive theory": by their own, though restricted attempts to set developments going, they might be able to have an effect on the integrated area as a whole. But in the end, if and when a European Union with a unified currency and policy evolves, the fate and the policy of the Union as a whole (and last but not least the world development) will alone be decisive—for better or worse.

NOTES

1. The unemployment percentages correspond to the ILO procedure relating unemployment to the *dependent* labor force (wage and salary earners plus unemployed). The OECD figures are lower because they calculate unemployment as a fraction of the *total* labor force (including self-employed persons).

2. "Austria has been fortunate to be able to operate a consensus-oriented policy, thus maintaining a better performance than other countries. However, not surprisingly, given the slow growth of activity in other countries, the difficulties in sustaining full employment and maintaining social consensus have increased" (OECD Economic Survey on Austria 1982, 49).

3. Some steps in this direction were taken in the 1980s through special incentives and credits for research and development and the establishment of future-oriented production.

4. Significantly, an international economic conference held in London in 1967 dealt with the question "Is the Business Cycle Obsolete?" Proceedings edited by Martin Bronfenbrenner (New York: John Wiley, 1969).

5. This is a consideration which applies to many types and aspects of economic policy. A neglect of this fact lies behind many shortcomings and failures of Western advice for the transformation processes of the Eastern European countries.

Bruno Kreisky: Perspectives of Top-Level U.S. Foreign Policy Decision Makers, 1959 - 1983

Oliver Rathkolb

Introduction

It is difficult to trace the political evaluations of Bruno Kreisky by top or middle-level decision makers in the pre-1989 Western world. Most of the primary documents for such research—biographical and political briefing papers for state visits and internal talks—are still classified. The private records of the late chancellor, stored in the Bruno Kreisky Archives Foundation in Vienna, however, contain enough evidence to analyze the mainstream debate on Kreisky's "geopolitical insights." Therefore, this essay will focus primarily on U.S. top-level opinions and will concentrate on two key issues:

1) Détente versus Cold War, human rights and the disarmament debate;
2) The Middle East dispute.

Whereas Kreisky's international reputation is acknowledged in general, a concrete analysis on how top-level decision makers dealt with his proposals and his critiques is still lacking. This article will trace Kreisky's contacts with and evaluations by the top U.S. foreign policy elite since the 1960s, including U.S. presidents John F. Kennedy, Richard Nixon, Gerald F. Ford, Jimmy Carter, Ronald Reagan and some of their Secretary of States such as Henry Kissinger, Cyrus Vance and George Shultz. It will also analyze the scope of Kreisky's influence, the limits of his efforts and the repercussions on the image of Austria.

While top-level decision makers accepted much of Kreisky's counsel, he could not influence major policy changes such as the recognition of the Palestine Liberation Organization (PLO). And though his arguments especially in the 1980s convinced prominent journalists like James Reston, they were not accepted by the majority of Jewish leaders in the United States. But even when they were in conflict with Kreisky, U.S. leaders continued to seek Kreisky's advice. This contradicts the domestic political controversies of the early 1980s when Kreisky was accused of damaging Austria's reputation in the Western world and especially in the U.S. by meeting the PLO Chairman Arafat and the revolutionary leader of Libya, Ghadafi. Many supporters of the Austrian People's Party (ÖVP) have argued that with these meetings, Kreisky sacrificed Austria's permanent neutrality. In the late 1980s this argument reappeared, accusing Kreisky of being responsible for the attacks against the ÖVP presidential candidate and former U.N. Secretary General, Kurt Waldheim, by the World Jewish Congress since this was revenge for Kreisky's support of the PLO and the Arab cause against Israel. The author believes that despite short-term negative media coverage, this situation did not influence the perspective of the foreign policy decision making elite.

Détente versus Cold War and the Disarmament Debate

When Bruno Kreisky became foreign minister in 1959, political analysts of the U.S. Embassy in Vienna portrayed the young politician who had served as undersecretary of state (*Staatssekretär*) since 1953:

"[A] convinced anti-communist... strongly pro-Western in sentiment, he advocates close economic ties with the West, but takes a strict interpretation of Austria`s declared policy of military neutrality.... However, he has frequently declared that military neutrality does not commit the individual in his political opinions nor imply a commitment to ideological neutrality (e.g., neutralism)...."[1]

In contrast to occasional statements by Chancellor Raab and some other Austrian leaders, Kreisky argued that it was not Austria's mission to bridge the East-West divide. At the same time, he believed that it was foolish for the great powers to do nothing to ease world tensions. He has consistently urged the necessity of finding a way through negotiation. A creative thinker, and with the sincere intention of facilitating the basis of East-West negotiations, he has made suggestions for solving such major international issues as disarmament and the Berlin questions, and has attempted, through personal contacts and persuasion, to kindle support for his ideas. Kreisky's evaluation of U.S. foreign policy is not entirely uncritical. While he concedes the nature of the communist threat to the free world and American leadership in combatting it, he was not always sympathetic with American policies to cope with that threat.

Bruno Kreisky took from the very beginning a clear pro-Western position in the Cold War and favored the policy of containment. In 1958-1959 he even initiated a propaganda campaign against the Communist World Youth Festival, which took place in Vienna; through the vice president of *Time Magazine*, C.D. Jackson, he obtained U.S. assistance and CIA money for this peaceful and "open" ideological operation.[2] As a consequence of the specific negotiation experiences with Soviet leaders since the successful Moscow negotiations of April 1955 and the signing of the Austrian State Treaty of May 1955, Kreisky firmly believed in permanent talks with the Khrushchev administration to increase détente and lower the tensions between the superpowers.

Whereas the foreign policy of the then-Austrian chancellor Julius Raab was interpreted by U.S. and especially British diplomats as "neutralist," Kreisky was capable of paying heed to "Western" positions even while striving for a permanent improvement in relations with the Soviet Union. He never aroused suspicions that he was favoring one bloc over another. He was unwilling to accept the intermittent stagnation in the geopolitical contacts between the superpowers.

Kreisky's stringent policy of neutrality, which he pursued as undersecretary and since 1959 as foreign minister, embodied an unambiguous anti-communist orientation on ideological issues coupled with a readiness to promote dialogue between the two power blocs. At the beginning of 1959, while still undersecretary, Kreisky attempted to arrange talks between Willy Brandt, then the Social Democratic mayor of Berlin, and Soviet Premier Nikita Khrushchev. Although Kreisky's optimistic interpretation of Soviet signs favoring negotiations on the Berlin problem did not convince Brandt and the local U.S. consul Gufler, Kreisky continued to inform both Brandt and Chancellor Konrad Adenauer on possible steps to solve the Berlin question.[3] In 1963 President John F. Kennedy valued the "judgment of the Foreign Minister."[4] During the Cuban missile crisis Kreisky's interpretation of Soviet intentions was seriously dealt with in the Executive Committee meetings.[5]

The new activist foreign policy which Kreisky inaugurated as Austria's foreign minister since 1959 was registered by the new Kennedy-Administration although it advocated a far more active policy of détente than the United States was prepared to accept on the superpower level. Kreisky's main idea was to cultivate good relations with the so-called "satellite countries" Czechoslovakia, Hungary, Yugoslavia, Poland and Romania, thereby relaxing Cold War tensions on a small scale without losing sight of the Soviet Union and global détente. He felt that the information which he had gleaned from his own experiences and from talks he held with important world or European leaders (Charles de Gaulle, John F. Kennedy, Nikita Khrushchev, Harold Macmillan, Konrad Adenauer) could, once properly evaluated and suitably disseminated, be of value to both East and West.

Just how valued his opinions were may be seen by the international reactions to the talk Kreisky gave on 2 March, 1960 in Warsaw as well as by the frequency of his lectures in the United States. Former U.S. President Harry S. Truman remarked after hearing Kreisky's talk, "The New Image of America in Europe," in 1963, "That's the best damned speech I've heard since 1945," and phoned President Kennedy to call this man to his attention.

Arthur Schlesinger, Jr. underlined in a memorandum to President Kennedy the reasons for this positive impression, since Kreisky's talk "is, in fact, excellent propaganda for a Democratic foreign policy. Kreisky defends Roosevelt's foreign policy, credits European economic revival to the Marshall Plan, praises the Alliance for Progress and the civil rights effort, etc."[6] Considerable differences of opinion did exist, however, as to the pragmatic approach towards détente in the major areas of friction in the world and the possibilities of at least temporary solutions. Kreisky's efforts toward détente were much more far reaching than the Kennedy and later the Johnson administration were prepared to go in the concrete relationship with the Soviet Union. His vision and his own regional approach, however, were accepted and Kreisky never was seen as a naive politician or a Communist fellow traveller. He was aware of the limits of negotiations: "[W]e must not forget that we are negotiating with Communists; we must not be deceived by the new behavior of their leaders or succumb to any illusions because of it."

In the 1970s after Kreisky has resumed his new position as Chancellor of Austria—during 1966 and early 1970 being out of government as opposition leader—he continued this approach. Meanwhile the atomic arms race which already started under President Eisenhower and the U.S. concept of "massive retaliation" had raised the dangers of an all-out atomic confrontation of the superpowers. In 1974, Kreisky tried to convince President Nixon that the projected Conference on Security and Cooperation in Europe (CSCE) would increase liberalization on both sides. Neither Secretary of State Henry Kissinger, British Prime Minister Harold Wilson nor the Dutch NATO Secretary General Joseph Luns were very impressed.

Kissinger opposed Kreisky's references to the possible Soviet concessions (economic concessions, some free tourism, exchange of information) and referred to the "baskets of security conference" as "eyewash, little substance...something in cultural exchange, but not more."[7]

A few months later during an official visit in the United States the Austrian chancellor again referred to "Austria's desire to see some results coming out of CSCE in Helsinki."[8] Meanwhile, President Nixon had stepped down and Vice President Gerald Ford had taken over. This time, Kissinger seemed to be more optimistic about the outcome of the CSCE in Helsinki and asked for " a consolidated European position on what Soviet concessions we wanted....he asked the Chancellor's support in this effort."[9] In the year of the U.S. Bicentennial, the cordial relationship between the United States and Austria led to Kreisky's idea to propose a public subscription campaign to finance a chair of Austrian studies at a U.S. university. President Ford personally appreciated this gesture very much.[10]

One should note that Kreisky was not only accepted as an informed dialogue partner on East-West affairs on the top executive level, he was also widely respected by leading U.S. politicians. Edward Kennedy pointed out that Kreisky was "one of the most impressive people I've ever met in Europe,"[11] and J.W. Fulbright of the Senate Committee on Foreign Relations remarked "that some of the small countries with long experience, such as Austria and Denmark and Sweden, have produced the wisest leaders in our world today."[12]

Before and during the signing of the Helsinki Act in 1975, Kreisky, although arguing in favor of détente, did not abandon his basic democratic appraisal of the fundamentally authoritarian or dictatorial structure of the communist system and continued to intervene in favor of political prisoners like Alexander Solzhenitsyn, Andrej Sakharov and others.

Whereas especially the Nixon and Ford administrations appreciated Austria's active role in the CSCE-negotiations in Helsinki (1973) and Geneva (1973/1975) concerning the "3rd Basket" (containing declarations of intention with regard to exchange of information and culture and to increase human contacts), the Carter administration was not interested in intensifying the East-West-cooperation on this level.[13] From its outset, Kreisky tried to put Carter's human rights campaign into perspective. In 1977 he publicly declared that "he found the Carter administration's emphasis on human-rights issues 'very impressive.' But he expressed concern that the campaign might damage less publicized activities designed to help individuals in authoritarian societies: "There are two kinds of issues—the highly visible and audible, which are important, but also those daily contacts, diplomatic and by other means, which don't ever get publicized."[14]

When Reagan came into office, Kreisky and other leaders of the Socialist International tried to arrange a meeting with President Reagan through Vice President Bush, but both the State Department and the National Security Council refused any direct contacts with this group.[15] An analysis of the conservative think-tank Heritage Foundation, which heavily influenced the concrete political thinking of the Reagan administration, already in October 1981 heavily criticized Brandt's disarmament policies and his contacts with liberation movements in Latin America; it intimated that the international social democratic movement was working into the hands of communism.[16] With regard to Kreisky, a reference from an article in the *Kommunist* from 1976—dispensing compliments to several SI leaders—was cited as "one of the leaders of the Socialist International, who has been evidencing his anti-communism more loudly than anyone else."[17]

Despite Kreisky's obvious and long-standing anti-communism the Reagan administration seemed annoyed about Kreisky's attacks on 14 January 1982, when he spoke about "hypocrisy" with regard to the recent U.S. sympathies for the trade union movement in Poland after General Jaruszelski had established a military dictatorship. Whereas Kreisky believed in Jaruszelski's motives to restore the civil rights in Poland and warned against the end of the policy of détente[18], Reagan's political views were contrary to Kreisky's; the Reagan administration seemed to believe in a possible "revision" of Yalta. When asked about the reasons for his obvious criticism, Kreisky repeated his critical views and pointed out his references on communism, which contain deep and fundamental criticism compared with the often-held views of "dull" western anti-communism.[19] In February 1982 Kreisky accused the U.S. president of favoring dictatorships in Turkey and Latin America and asked for an independent policy with regard to Poland.[20] Kreisky pleaded for a military balance between the superpowers, criticized U.S. rearmament and asked for continued détente. For a U.S. audience Kreisky explained his pragmatic views on the handling of the Polish situation and his deep ideological differences with the new administration in economic policies.[21]

After Kreisky had left office, he surprisingly found himself in a relatively positive dialogue with Reagan on the question of a chance for a new and global détente[22]: "On the establishment of the new administration under President Reagan, it seems to me that the United States started with an ideological foreign policy. The verbal ideological warfare culminated in the declaration of President Reagan that the Soviet Union was the 'evil empire'. Now President Reagan has completely changed his tone. I hope he will continue to do so in the future."[23] This new line in Kreisky's relationship with regard to Reagan was the result of two developments:

1. Someone in Reagan's top decision-making elite wanted to use the communication channel with Kreisky on the disarmament and détente question—even after he had retired from the Austrian government. On 5 May 1983 President Reagan sent a letter to the former Austrian chancellor commenting positively on the role of the neutral and non-aligned countries during the successful conclusion of the Madrid CSCE Review Conference.[24] In return, Kreisky urged Reagan to prolong these East-West-negotiations even if results could not be reached within the "deadline" set by Reagan for the Geneva talks because of the danger for the "relationship of a major part of Europe's young generation to democracy" and "because of decisive and profound importance to the relations between our democracies, the European and the American one." Kreisky feared that Reagan's "deadline ...might involve the danger of turning it into a 'dead line' other than the one implied by Anglo-Saxon usage."[25] Reagan answered on 12 September that he would defend the "NATO dual-track decision" to deploy new intermediate range weapons in Europe, but emphasized that he had set "no deadline to negotiations."[26]

2. Although this correspondence was not continued, Kreisky carefully analyzed a change in Reagan's Cold War strategy since the death of the Soviet premier Andropov (9 February 1984).[27] Both in Japan and in Vienna during October and November 1984 the elder statesman had hoped that Reagan would be "prepared to undertake some very substantial confidence-building measures."[28] When Kreisky realized, however, that the Reagan administration was not accessible to his and similar European arguments against the deployment of new nuclear missiles in Europe, he came out openly criticizing it. After a first public attack against Reagan's Strategic Defense Initiative Program (SDI or "Star Wars") in front of the Socialist Group of the European Parliament in Strutthof on 7 May 1985, he protested in a personal letter against the refusal of the U.S president to meet the President of the Socialist International Willy Brandt on his visit to Europe.[29] In a major lecture for the "Bertelsmann Forum" on 17 September 1985 Kreisky for the first time favored Gorbachev, who could break the ice in the superpower relationship.[30] Despite the rejection of Kreisky's ideas by the Reagan administration, he succeeded at least in preserving not only his image but also the International Institute for

Applied Systems Analysis (IIASA). Founded in 1972-1973 the "IIASA did much to ensure that this experiment in East-West scientific cooperation would evolve into a successful, consequential international research center."[31] In a direct correspondence with Reagan, Kreisky fought for the preservation of this institution when the United States Government wanted to cancel its financial support for it after 1982 because of the fear of unauthorized technology transfer from the West to the East.[32]

The Middle East Dispute

Kreisky himself gave three reasons why he had become involved in the Middle East dispute: this involvement often put him in the international spotlight, with all the advantages and disadvantages entailed in such a conflict where the strong "emotions that have accompanied the Middle East conflict...have not infrequently been the occasion of misinterpretations."[33]

First, Kreisky consistently took up the causes of minorities; this applied, as the circumstances demanded, to South Tyroleans in Italy as well as to Slovenes in Carinthia. Kreisky thus considered himself a sympathizer of minorities in general, and of the Palestinians in particular. As such, Kreisky was indeed "partisan" and realized that he could not always serve as a bridge builder. Second, he supported the right of Israel to exist as a state, but also believed that Israel's only "chance for survival...[lay] in a peaceful environment."[34] Third, he was among the first to recognize—even before the so-called 1973 oil shock—that neither European industries nor, to a certain extent, geopolitical stability could be divorced from Arabian oil.

Since the late 1950s, Kreisky had followed developments in the Middle East closely as undersecretary of state and after 1959 as foreign minister. His first contacts with representatives of the Arab world were within the framework of the United Nations and in connection with the Algerian struggle for independence. Then as well, Kreisky took the side of those who at that time had received no international support; at times Kreisky was willing to take issue with the French diplomatic line. Among the Arab politicians and diplomats with whom he first had intensive contact were Habib Ben Ali Bourguiba from Tunisia and the Egyptian Foreign Minister Machmoud Fawzi and Hassan Mohammed el-Tohami. In March 1964 he met President Nasser in Heliopolis for political talks.

Kreisky continued his interest in the Middle East question although in 1966 he left government and one year later became the opposition leader as chairman of the Austrian Social Democratic party. After his electoral success in 1970 and especially 1971, when he gained an absolute majority, he again intensified his Middle Eastern connections. The first international headlines in September 1973, however, were extremely negative as a result of Kreisky's handling of the "Schönau Transit Camp Affair." Two Palestinian terrorists had threatened to kill four hostages—three Jews and an Austrian customs official, if the transit facilities in the old castle "Schönau" near Vienna for Soviet Jews going to Israel were not closed down. Despite stinging foreign rebukes to Austria for yielding to this blackmail Kreisky stayed firm and closed the Schönau camp.[35]

Even when President Nixon intervened in a news conference, Kreisky stayed his course. Nixon had argued that

"the Austrians are in a very difficult position here....I...met the prime minister, Mr. Kreisky, and everybody who knows his background knows that he is naturally not anti-Semitic, but Austria is in the eye of a hurricane and Austria, therefore, being a relative[ly] small country and relatively weak, militarily, etc., is making a very, what I am sure for Mr. Kreisky, painful decision in this respect. I recall for example that at the time of the Hungarian revolution, Austria opened its arms very generously to thousands of refugees and I know that is the Austrian tradition and custom....I would hope that the prime minister reconsiders his decision, even though I know he has even lately reiterated it, reconsider it for this fundamental reason that goes far beyond his country and even ours, and that is that we simply cannot have governments, small or large, give in to international blackmail by terrorist groups...but naturally I was not meaning to put my friend, Mr. Kreisky, in the position of trying to dictate to him what it should be."[36]

A few weeks later Kreisky himself explained his concern in a letter to Nixon and made quite clear that he had rejected the "terrorists' demand for a halt to transit" as such, but he felt that Schönau which was administered by the Jewish Agency had become even before the terrorist attack a security risk.[37] Nixon appreciated Kreisky's efforts "to establish a new transit assistance facility," but disagreed with the concession to close down Schönau Castle because this "can only encourage further violence."[38]

Despite this difference of opinion on handling terrorist demands, Nixon continued to discuss the Middle Eastern question with Kreisky during a stop in Salzburg on his way to Moscow on 11 June 1974.[39] Meanwhile Kreisky had gained considerable inside information after he succeeded in persuading a majority of the Socialist International to set up a fact-finding mission for the Middle East. In the course of this trip during 9 - 16 March

1974, he had met with President Sadat, the PLO Chairman Yasser Arafat, President Assad of Syria, and the Israeli Prime Minister Golda Meir.[40] During the Salzburg meeting of 1974, Kreisky tried to underline the importance of President Sadat for the peace process in the Middle East and pleaded for the national rights of the Palestinians ("If people want to be Palestinians let them be Palestinians"), stressing that "Sadat will have difficulties without a Palestinian solution."[41] Nixon came close to Kreisky's views showing "sympathy" for the Palestinians: "Jordanians don't want them neither Israelis or Saudis. Who are Palestinians? How can it be done? Must be worked at slowly without pushing it off the cliff. Jerusalem too cannot be discussed openly. Patient diplomacy is in the interest of U.S., Austria and the Middle Eastern countries, but the American Jewish leaders have got to realize that this is also in their interest."[42]

Whereas Nixon planned gradually to change the old approach in U.S.-Israeli relations, President Ford seemed reluctant to carry out Nixon's political visions for the Middle East, and Kissinger, who seemed to agree with some of Kreisky's ideas, placed the responsibility for the failure of peace efforts on the Israeli government ("Israel has missed the train").[43] Nevertheless, Ford continued to strengthen the channels of communication with President Sadat, whom he met for the first time on 1 June 1975 in Salzburg—Kreisky acting as intermediary and host.[44] Meanwhile Kreisky's reputation was growing. At a memorial service for Bruno Kreisky at the U.N. Church Center in New York Henry Kissinger referred to "his leadership" when "Austria—at the edge of the Iron Curtain—grew into a haven for refugees and a transit stop for Jews emigrating from the Soviet Union."[45] Over 200,000 Jews left the Soviet Union via Austria.[46]

It is interesting to note that in 1975 the "International Rescue Committee," a "prominent philanthropic association of Jewish intellectuals,"[47] even honored "Kreisky for his outstanding contributions to the cause of refugees and human freedom"—a symbolic compensation for the attacks against Kreisky, when he closed down the Schönau-camp for Jewish emigrés from the Soviet Union. Both the State Department and the National Security Council recommended against the president or vice president participating in this event personally. They feared, like Kissinger, that this "presidential" role could be "misunderstood by the Soviets inasmuch as most of the refugees aided by Austria—Jews and others alike—have come from Eastern Europe and the Soviet Union, and also because of the recent contretemps related to the emigration of Soviet Jews (who are processed through Vienna)."[48] This internal reluctance on high decision-making levels shows the sensitivity of the problem of Jewish emigration via Vienna and strengthens Kreisky's merits in this area. Even Kreisky's crisis management and negotiating with terrorists after the attack against the OPEC in December 1975 was accepted by the Ford administration.

During a visit to the U.S. in March 1977, when Kreisky officially presented the University of Minnesota with the official Austrian Bicentennial gift, a chair of Austrian studies, he met the top people of the Carter administration: President Jimmy Carter, Secretary of State Cyrus Vance and the National Security Adviser Zbigniew Brzezinski. The Austrian chancellor used this opportunity to discuss the "situation in the Middle East, where he said the United States was providing too many weapons and not enough advice."[49] During the time of Kreisky's visit, Mattityahv Peled, a former Israeli general of the 1967 war and chairman of the Israel Council for Israeli-Palestinian Peace, discussed the question of the recognition of the PLO by the United States. He mentioned the Austrian Chancellor as transmitter of a statement by the PLO to accept the Security Council Resolution 242 "once the reference in that resolution to the 'refugees' is replaced by clear recognition of the Palestinian nation as party to the conflict."[50]

In 1978 again Kreisky was able to bring the concerns of the Palestinians to the White House. On 21 December 1978 the Austrian chancellor passed on two reports of conversations from Beirut with influential advisers in the PLO, Abu Jaafar and Abu Iyad (Salah Khalaf) to President Jimmy Carter. There seemed to be evidence that strong circles in the PLO would accept the Sadat-Begin-negotiations to the extent that the PLO would get a Palestinian State on the West Bank and in Ghaza ("In case that a status of autonomy were granted for these areas, it may be safely assumed that the PLO will make full use of all political changes involved, and that, despite the formal statements in the negative."[51]) The PLO seems to have come in the internal debate close to the Egyptian point of view, quite contrary to the vehement official anti-Sadat statements.

President Carter responded positively to Kreisky's report: "I hope that you will continue to keep me informed of your assessment of trends in the Palestinian thinking. As you know, the next phase of the Middle East peace negotiations should deal with matters of direct concern to Palestinians, and it will be particularly valuable to me to receive your counsel on how best to encourage a constructive Palestinian role in the peace process."[52]

Chancellor Kreisky tried to persuade Carter to enlarge his peace efforts and include a Palestinian solution in the follow-up of the Camp David

Agreement of September 1978. A few hours after his visits to Egypt and Israel the U.S. president sent a special oral message to Kreisky to keep him informed—because he realized that the Egypt-Israel peace talks did not "offer full and immediate solutions for all the problems of the Middle East, particularly for the Palestinians.[53]

In June 1979 Kreisky even arranged a secret meeting between the U.S. Ambassador in Vienna, Milton A. Wolf, and a confidant of Arafat's, Issam Sartawi. These talks seemed to be backed by the U.S. President compared with the repercussions against the U.N. ambassador Andrew Young, who critized the traditional U.S. Middle East policy and had contacts with PLO representatives.[54] In the summer 1979 Kreisky's continued efforts to influence a change in the U.S. position towards the PLO seemed to be successful, when Secretary of State Cyrus Vance indicated that "the United States is strongly opposed to the illegal settlement on the West Bank." At the same time, and this certainly constituted the crux of the Middle Eastern policy of the Carter Administration, the President was "strongly supportive of continuing maximum emigration of Jews from the Soviet Union."[55] Carter's engagement for human rights was overruling the existing criticism towards Begin's policy concerning the Palestinians.

During these months, Kreisky thought that the United States might be prepared to recognize the PLO, especially during the Iran hostage crisis. On 8 November 1979, the New York attorney Leon Charney, who had close relations to the White House, called the secretary of the Austrian chancellor, Margit Schmidt, and asked for the advice of the chancellor how to handle the crisis. Although Kreisky called Charney the next day and declared that he had no personal contacts to Ayathollah Khomeini, he was prepared to talk about this problem in Vienna.[56] Both President Carter, Secretary of State Vance and Assistant Secretary of State Harold Saunders, who headed the American Iran Task Force, agreed that Charney and Robert J. Lipshutz, White House counsel to President Carter, should fly to Vienna, where they arrived three days later.[57] Kreisky observed "that, if anyone in the world could persuade Khomeini to release the hostages, that person was Yasir Arafat, leader of the Palestine Liberation Organization, and that the United States should do business with Arafat!"[58] Obviously Kreisky wanted the Carter administration "to take a demonstrable action openly and directly with the PLO which could be de-facto recognition of the PLO," but at the same time Arafat needed to be told that "this was not a quid-pro-quo to get Arafat's active intervention with Khomeini".[59]

In the meantime, Charney flew to Israel to discuss this proposal with his friend Ezer Weizman, then Israeli defense minister; Harold Saunders discussed the proposal with the top people in the White House and State Department. Although the Israelis did not see a chance to free the hostages by military action, they vigorously opposed using Arafat as intermediary, because this would mean de facto recognition of the PLO. On 14 November Harold Saunders announced the internal decision that the "Austrian connection" would not be used—Arafat having already agreed to fly to Teheran, but to "pursue only the private channel of communication with the PLO, which had been established months earlier, with Israeli concurrence, and not the public channel urged by Kreisky."[60]

President Carter did not risk the severe diplomatic conflicts with Israel and the repercussions of such a debate on U.S. Jewish voters at the eve of an election year. Kreisky pursued efforts to get the PLO recognized by the United States, a procedure which he himself indicated in a speech at the United Nations on 29 October 1979. Kreisky went ahead anyway following a letter by Arafat (5 December 1979), Kreisky officially recognized the representative of the PLO in an official letter of 11 March 1980.[61]

In early 1980, Kreisky was disappointed that the Camp David Agreement could not be extended to direct negotiations with the PLO, and he intensified his public criticism of the Carter administration's Middle East policy.[62] After Reagan's election in November 1980 and after a terror attack in August 1981 against a synagogue in Vienna, Kreisky continued to express his hopes that the United States, with the best chance to mediate, would establish a more balanced relationship with all parties concerned—especially with regard to Israel and the Palestinians.[63]

In Europe, Kreisky has succeeded in increasing interest in the Palestinian question among western European statesmen (the British Foreign Minister Lord Carrington, his French colleague Claude Cheysson and the President of the European Commission Gaston Thorn). Despite deep ideological differences between the conservative Republican Reagan and the Social Democrat Kreisky and numerous bilateral conflicts as a result of Reagan's tough anti-communist policies, Kreisky accepted Reagan's Middle East Initiative of 1 September 1982 as a major change in the U.S. position:

> "Let me now also in this way congratulate you [Reagan] on the historic initiative on the Middle East. I would like to tell you that I am ready to give every possible support to this initiative. In this spirit, I have developed a number of activities and I have, for instance, taken up this matter during a visit to Tunisia over the past weekend, not only with President Bourgiba, Prime Minister Mzali

and Foreign Minister Essebsi but also with high-ranking Palestinian leaders and with the Arab League. In each conversation I have pointed to the historic importance of the American initiative, and I have admonished those who are ready to listen to me to do nothing which could in any way hamper the initiative. It would be, I told them, of crucial importance to achieve a further rallying of U.S. public opinion to this position."[64]

In an oral message Secretary of State Shultz stressed that the Lebanon conflict caused a major policy review on the basis of U.N. Resolution 242 and therefore "required Israeli withdrawal in return for peace," and applied "to the West Bank an Gaza, as well as the Golan Heights."[65] Although the U.S. president indicated that he preferred an association of the Palestinian territories of the West Bank and Gaza with Jordan, in principle the Palestinians should have become the "key" to a solution—a different approach to the Camp David Agreements. In the debates that followed, Kreisky always tried to strengthen both the Reagan plan and the Arab League Charta of Fez, which was published eight days after Reagan announced his plan and asked for a sovereign Palestinian State with Jerusalem as capital: "The positions of negotiations are somewhere in between. But this will take a long time. Until then there will be horrible disappointments."[66]

This development is remarkable given that since Reagan took over the White House the bilateral relations between the United States and Austria in general and Kreisky in particular became relatively tense. The first who tried to break the ice was Senator George McGovern, a former candidate of the Democratic Party for the U.S. presidency. He met Kreisky in July 1982 and was told "that [Kreisky's] feelings were hurt that after Reagan's election, he and Willy Brandt and Olaf Palme ...had written to the Soviet leader and Reagan asking for a meeting to talk about arms control and they never got an answer from Reagan."[67] McGovern wrote to Vice President Bush and Secretary of State Shultz that "it's a great mistake to ignore a man of Chancellor Kreisky's stature."[68] Both called McGovern and assured him that Kreisky would be invited to the White House. Kreisky, however, did not authorize Thomas Klestil, then the Austrian Ambassador in Washington, D.C., who had good personal relations with Reagan's inner circle, to intervene in favor of a meeting with Reagan.[69] The Austrian chancellor referred to the idea of the late U.S. Ambassador Theodore Cummings, who had launched the idea of a meeting as early as August 1981.[70] Cummings, born in Vienna, was a close friend of Reagan's and had worked on the "Jews for Reagan" committee. By August 1981,

Cummings had indicated that he did not agree with the criticism of Austria's Middle East policy but was convinced that peace required a solution of the Palestinian problem and a Palestinian state. Since he was "hand-picked" by Reagan his views on the Middle East had quite an influence on decision-making in the White House.

In the long run, it seems as if National Security Adviser Bill Clark had organized the relaxation of the relationship between Kreisky and Reagan after two years of relative tension. On 30 September 1982 he turned over a letter of Reagan's to Kreisky, dated 28 September, which referred to Kreisky's "efforts in support of the United States peace initiative for the Middle East."[71]

Kreisky continued to back both the Reagan and Fez plans even after he left office in 1983; in an interview in the first half of 1984, he proposed that the Arab countries and the PLO work out the common consensus in these two proposals and take the risk of majority decisions.[72]

Conclusion

As far as détente was concerned, Kreisky's views were always heading toward more direct negotiations with the Soviet leaders to reduce the danger of an all-out atomic war and to assist the cause of human rights in the communist countries. He always stayed a convinced, ideological anti-communist, but did not stop at the policy of containment. Since Khrushchev came to power, he believed that by direct contacts with the Soviet leaders the level of détente could be gradually increased. Neither Kennedy nor Nixon were so optimistic, but Ford accepted Kreisky's views which were partly fulfilled by the Helsinki Conference. As to human rights, Kreisky openly criticized Soviet leaders, but in general favored permanent and silent diplomacy by seeking direct contacts. Never, however, did he act in a consciously opportunistic way. He saw Carter's broad human rights campaign as dangerous because it neither helped the anti-communist opposition nor increased the level of détente. Kreisky was always a very pragmatic politician, but he adhered to certain moral convictions. Another example is the Vietnam War; he did not support it, but he did not criticize it in public debates as his friend, the Swedish social democratic leader Olof Palme did. Kreisky was heavily critized by young people (including his son Peter, who protested against his father) when he met Nixon in Salzburg in May 1972. His interest in détente overruled the then fashionable anti-Vietnam movement. Behind the scenes, he always tried to argue against military intervention in Vietnam.[73]

Since Reagan became U.S. president, Kreisky's arguments about disarmament and détente seemed unacceptable to the new proponents of tough anti-Soviet and anti-communist policies. Whereas Kreisky tried to increase the level of confidence between East and West in Europe even after the establishment of a military dictatorship in Poland, the ideological hardliners within the Reagan administration for the first time in Kreisky's career publicly blasted his approach. Even on the bilateral economic level Austria was critized for its loans and technology transfers to Eastern Europe. Kreisky was personally very disappointed when he met President Reagan in 1983 (comparing him to Truman, Eisenhower, Kennedy, Nixon, Ford and Carter, whom he had met before). But he continued to hope that at least after the first years, concrete disarmament and détente efforts would be carried out. By 1985 Kreisky lost his optimism and began publicly to attack the Reagan "Star Wars" and armament programs, especially when he continued to ignore the Socialist International and its president Willy Brandt as dialogue partner in the disarmament discussion.

Despite these deep ideological confrontations, Kreisky was impressed by the Reagan administration's Middle East approach in 1982. In the second half of this year, all bilateral conflicts could be solved and Kreisky was invited to Washington in 1983. In the long run, he was even accepted as a dialogue partner by the Reagan people and the political argument that Kreisky has damaged Austria's international reputation proved not to be valid. Kreisky was primarily critized for his détente and disarmament approach and especially for his direct bilateral (economic) relations with Eastern Europe and the Soviet Union, not for his Middle East proposals as such.

The pro-Waldheim argument that Kreisky's Middle East policies had caused the attacks of Jewish Organizations against the former Secretary General[74] is exclusively "homemade." It is for domestic party political consumption only. U.S. experts such as George Ball, who himself was an early critic of the traditional pro-Israeli U.S. policy, and the former Presidential candidate George McGovern, do not agree with these ÖVP charges.[75]

Certainly Kreisky's initiatives should not be overestimated. Despite common aims and political values, the Austrian chancellor could not convince President Carter and his advisers to enlarge the Middle East dialogue, start direct talks with the PLO and ask for a Palestinian state, although in 1979 Carter seemed at least to think about using the PLO to solve the Iran hostage crisis. This approach, however, broke down because of strict resistance by the Israeli government. Kreisky's greatest success was the positive presentation of President Sadat and his peaceful aims in solving at least the bilateral Egypt-Israel conflict. In retrospect, Sadat referred to Kreisky as

"an incredible man....Because if people like Kreisky, who is not for the destruction of Israel and who told me so, reign one day over Israel, we'll never have problems of the sort we have today with people like Golda Meir—when she was in power—or with Dayan or Rabin....K. and K. [Kreisky and Kissinger]...are quite a phenomenon—but if they do exist, it means that they must have equivalents elsewhere in the world...including Israel."[76]

The example of Sadat shows the chances of the representative of a small state to influence certain foreign policy trends in the United States, but at the same time proves the impossibility of setting trends as such. Kreisky was not able to convince Carter to explicitly enlarge the Camp David Agreement by including the Palestinian question.

One could end Kreisky's longtime contacts with U.S. presidents, secretaries of state, diplomats and politicians by citing a speech he gave in September 1981 in Bruges (Belgium) trying to channel European anti-Americanism as a consequence of Reagan's Cold War aims. Therein he pleaded for "a creative dialogue" between Europe and the United States.[77] Kreisky was always convinced that the policy of containment and Marshall Plan aid were the "most constructive contributions of the United States to world peace,"[78] Criticizing American foreign policy was part and parcel of Western democratic rights and privileges. Therefore permanent dialogue—even with representatives of opposite ideologies within a western democratic framework—should be possible.

During Kreisky's last official visit to the United States James Reston, the grand old man of U.S. journalism, sang Kreisky's praises. Under the headline "An Old Man's Faith," Reston described his impressions of Kreisky, who always insisted on negotiations—both in the Middle East and on the superpower level. Reston was even more impressed when he had read Kreisky's private correspondence with Yasir Arafat of the PLO, "pleading with him to abandon the tactics of terrorism, and revealing Mr. Arafat's private replies, which were much more sensible than his vicious public pronouncements."[79] He concluded by citing a poem by William Butler Yeats that Kreisky "has beat upon the wall till truth obeyed his call, and has been suggesting here that maybe if President Reagan and Yuri Andropov met, without preconditions, they might be able to do the same. Washington listened to the old man's faith, but wasn't really convinced."[80]

NOTES

1. John W. Fischer to Department of State, 28 August 1959, Record Group 59, National Archives, Washington, D.C., 763.521/8-2859.

2. Compare folder: World Youth Festival Vienna, Dwight D. Eisenhower Library (Abilene, Kansas), C. D. Jackson Papers.

3. Hans Jürgen Küsters, "Adenauer und Brandt in der Berlin-Krise 1958-1963," *Vierteljahreshefte für Zeitgeschichte* (1992), 493-521.

4. Memo of Conversation, 10 October 1963, Country File: USA, Folder: Kennedy, Siftung Bruno Kreisky Archiv, Vienna (hereafter cited SBKA).

5. Michael R. Beschloss, *The Crisis Years. Kennedy and Khrushchev, 1960-1963* (New York: Harper Collins, 1991), 553.

6. Memorandum, Schlesinger to Kennedy, 11 October 1963, Papers of President Kennedy, Press Office Files, Box 111, John F. Kennedy Library, Boston.

7. Hans Thalberg, Handwritten Notes of the Meeting Nixon-Kissinger-Kreisky and German transcript, 11 June 1974, Country File USA, Folder: Nixon, SBKA.

8. Memorandum of Conversation (Kreisky, Androsch, Ford, Kissinger, Scowcroft), 12 November 1974, ibid. Folder: Ford.

9. Ibid.

10. Ford to Kreisky, 21 July 1976, White House Central Files, Name File: Bruno Kreisky, Gerald R. Ford Library, Ann Arbor, Michigan.

11. Interview with George McGovern, Graz, 21 November 1992 (Transcript in the possession of the author); see also the introduction of this volume.

12. Fulbright to Kreisky, 8 October 1973, Promi Correspondence File, SBKA.

13. Briefing Paper, June 1979, Country File: USA, Folder: Briefing Papers, 24, SBKA.

14. *International Herald Tribune*, 16 March 1977.

15. *Die Presse*, 3 June 1982, 1.

16. Arnold M. Silver, "The New Face of the Socialist International" (Paper of the Heritage Foundation, October 1981), research materials, Socialist International, SBKA.

17. Ibid., 15.

18. *Arbeiter-Zeitung*, 15 January 1982, 3.

19. *Notiz*, 25 January 1982, Country File: USA; Folder: USA-General, SBKA.

20. Kreisky-Interview, in *Quick*, 18 February 1982, 106.

21. *Austrian Information* (35/2), 1982, 2.

22. Title of a lecture by Bruno Kreisky for the International Institute for Applied Systems Analysis, 21 November 1984, Bruno Kreisky Speeches, SBKA.

23. Ibid., 9.

24. Reagan to Kreisky, 5 May 1983, Country File: USA, Folder: Reagan, SBKA.

25. Kreisky to Reagan, 10 August 1983, ibid.

26. Reagan to Kreisky, 12 September 1983, ibid.

27. Bruno Kreisky, "In Search of Peace: The Experience of a Statesman," 8 March 1984, 5f. Kreisky Speeches, SBKA.

28. Bruno Kreisky, "Is there a Chance for a New and Global Détente?," 21 November 1984, Kreisky Speeches, SBKA.

29. Kreisky to Reagan, 4 June 1985. Country File: USA, Folder: Reagan, SBKA.

30. Bruno Kreisky, "Entwicklungen bei den Supermächten und die mögliche Rolle Europas," 17 September 1985, Kreisky Speeches, SBKA.

31. Robert McNamara, Bruno Kreisky Lecture Series - Second Distinguished Lecture, Promi Correspondence File, SBKA.

32. Reagan to Kreisky, 20 March 1982, Country File: USA, Folder: Reagan, SBKA.

33. Hans Thalberg, "Die Nahostpolitik," in *Die Ära Kreisky. Schwerpunkte der österreichischen Außenpolitik*, ed. Erich Bielka, Peter Jankowitsch, Hans Thalberg (Wien-München-Zürich: Europa Verlag, 1983), 293.

34. Bruno Kreisky, *Im Strom der Politik. Erfahrungen eines Europäers* (Berlin: Siedler Verlag, 1988), 307.

35. For more details on this and other terrorist attacks (1975: OPEC headquarters; 1981: killing of Heinz Nittel, president of the Austro-Israel Friendship-Society, and in a later attack against the Vienna synagogue murder of three people; 1985: killing of three people—including one attacker—at a strike against the Vienna airport), see John Bunzl, *Gewalt ohne Grenzen. Nahost-Terror und Österreich* (Vienna: Braumüller Verlag, 1991).

36. Telegram, Austroamb. Washington, 3 October 1973, Country File USA, Folder: Nixon, SBKA.

37. Kreisky to Nixon, 25 October 1973, Ibid.

38. Nixon to Kreisky, 15 December 1975, Ibid.

39. For a most recently published overview on U.S. policy towards Israel see George W. Ball, and Douglas B. Ball, *The Passionate Attachment. America's Involvement with Israel, 1947 to the Present* (New York: W. W. Norton & Company, 1992).

40. Thalberg, "Nahostpolitik," 304-307 and Hans Thalberg, *Von der Kunst, Österreicher zu sein. Erinnerungen und Tagebuchnotizen* (Wien: Böhlau, 1984), 459-473.

41. Hans Thalberg, Handwritten Notes of the Meeting Nixon-Kissinger-Kreisky and German Transcript, 11 June 1974, Country File: USA, Folder: Nixon, SBKA.

42. Ibid.

43. Thalberg, *Kunst, Österreicher zu sein*, 458.

44. Gerald Ford, *A Time to Heal* (New York: Berkley Books, 1979), 281.

45. *Austrian Press & Information Service News*, 28 September 1990, 2.

46. Lonnie Johnson, *Introducing Austria* (Wien: Österreichischer Bundesverlag, 1987), 159.

47. Clift to Kissinger, 13 February 1975, White House Central Files, COII Austria, Gerald R. Ford Library, Ann Arbor, Michigan.

48. Ibid.

49. *The New York Times*, 15 March 1977, L 7.

50. Ibid., 12 March 1977, L 23.

51. Kreisky to Carter, 21 December 1978, SBKA, Country File: USA, Folder: Carter, SBKA.

52. Carter to Kreisky, 29 January 1979, ibid.

53. Oral Message Carter to Kreisky, 14 March 1979, ibid.

54. John Michael Luchak, "Amerikanisch-Österreichische Beziehungen von 1955 bis 1985. Neutralität und der Ost-West Konflikt," Ph.D. dissertation, University of Vienna, 1987, 399.

55. Vance to Kreisky, 3 July, 1979, Country File: USA, Folder: Vance, SBKA.

56. Erinnerungsvermerk Margit Schmidt, Country File: USA, Folder: Charney, SBKA; compare also Leon H. Charney, *Special Counsel* (New York: Philosophical Library, 1984), 291-301.

57. Robert J. Lipshutz, "The Hostages - The Austrian Connection," bid, 1.

58. Ibid., 3

59. Ibid., 4.

60. Ibid., 10.

61. John Bunzl, "Zur Nahostpolitik der Sozialistischen Internationale Österreichs unter Bruno Kreisky," *Österreichisches Jahrbuch für Internationale Politik* 5 (1988), 32.

62. Bruno Kreisky, *Das Nahostproblem. Reden, Kommentare, Interviews* (Wien: Europaverlag, 1985), 128, 208, 213f.

63. Bruno Kreisky, "Österreich und der Terror aus dem Nahen Osten," Manuscript, 9 September 1981, SBKA, Middle East File, Folder: Articles and Interviews, 3.

64. Kreisky to Reagan, 12 October 1982, Country Files: USA, Folder Reagan, SBKA.

65. Shultz, Oral Message, ibid.

66. Kreisky, *Nahostproblem*, 186.

67. Interview with George McGovern, Graz, 21 November 1992.

68. Ibid.

69. Lennkh to Klestil, 12 August 1982, Country File: USA, Folder: Klestil, SBKA.

70. Klestil to Kreisky, 3 August 1981, ibid.

71. Reagan to Kreisky, 28 September 1982, ibid.

72. Kreisky, *Nahostproblem*, 230f.

73. Kreisky, *Im Strom der Politik*, 96f.

74. Andreas Khol, "Die Kampagne gegen Waldheim - Internationale und nationale Hintergründe," *Die Kampagne. Kurt Waldheim - Opfer oder Täter. Hintergründe und Szenen eines Falles von Medienjustiz*, ed. Andreas Khol, Theodor Faulhaber, Günther Ofner (München-Berlin: Herbig Verlag, 1987), 184f; 207.

75. Interview with George Ball, Princeton, 2 October 1992, and George McGovern, 21 November 1992

76. Cited after Thalberg, *Nahostpolitik, Ära Kreisky*, ed. Bielka/Jankowitsch/Thalberg, 315f.

77. Ingo Mussi, "Bruno Kreisky und der schöpferische Dialog mit den Vereinigten Staaten," *Ära Kreisky*, ed. Bielka/Jankowitsch/Thalberg, 141.

78. Ibid., 128.

79. *The New York Times*, 6 February 1983, E 17.

80. Ibid.

Duke and Haider:
Right Wing Politics in Comparison

Susan Howell/Anton Pelinka

On two continents, two political figures, David Duke and Jörg Haider, have recently run for political office making strikingly similar appeals to similar segments of their electorates and achieving international notoriety in the process. Both have been accused of being Nazis, extremists, and racists, yet both have consistently received support from middle-class and mainstream voters in their respective countries. One ran for the United States Senate and for Governor of Louisiana; the other was elected Chairman of his political party in Austria and was governor of Carinthia for two years. This essay attempts to identify both the similarities and differences between these two controversial figures.

Differences

The main difference between the two men lies in the high degree of respectability certain parts of Haider's tradition enjoy in Austria. Haider is chairman of a political party, and that party belongs to one of the most traditional European and international "party families"—the Liberal International.[1] Of course, it is important to note that the term "liberal" has a different meaning in Europe from that in America. In the United States, "liberal" signifies a stance left of the political center; in Europe, "liberal" means a centrist (or even slightly center-right) position. The membership of the FPÖ in the Liberal International confers upon Haider a degree of political respectability as chairman of a serious political party. Even after his "proper employment policy" speech in 1991, wherein his tribute to Hitler led to his public censure, his forced resignation as governor of Carinthia, and a suspension of voting rights for his party within the Liberal

International, Haider retained his party chairmanship and the respectability it entailed.

The FPÖ's role as a coalition partner of the SPÖ, the Social Democrats, in the 1980s underlines a second aspect of Haider's respectability. Even considering the fact that Haider's election to this party's chairmanship in 1986 put an end to the SPÖ-FPÖ coalition, his party is still the one that ruled Austria as a minor partner in a center-left coalition. Many who were leading members of the FPÖ before Haider's chairmanship are still in prominent positions within the FPÖ, even after Haider was isolated and labelled as a rightist (or right extremist).[2]

Duke, on the other hand, is a political maverick. The party he is claiming as his political homeland, the Republican, tries to dissociate itself from Duke.[3] Duke stands for a political tradition—the tradition of the Ku Klux Klan, of racial segregation, of white supremacy, of the American Nazi Party. This tradition has never been considered a respectable one within the American political system. Duke is politically isolated by elites even when he is successful.

Duke's political successes fit into the pattern of a political outsider. His election to the Louisiana legislature and his surprisingly strong showing in the 1990 U.S. Senate election and the 1991 Louisiana gubernatorial primary election were successes against political establishments.[4] Duke fights against all the established parties—against his own party, the Republicans, as well as against the Democrats. He not only has the image of a lonesome fighter—he is such a fighter, if his loneliness is defined by the party system. He stands for a U.S. populist tradition—but not for a political party.

The differences between Haider and Duke are rooted in the differences between the respective political systems, especially between the party systems. The American two-party system makes it difficult for any outsider to use the organization and structure of a third (or fourth or fifth) party. The Austrian system, on the other hand, provides such an outsider with certain possiblities—due to the multi-party system and proportional representation.[5] Unconventional forms of politics can be channeled into the party system by third parties. In the United States, one of the two parties must be used for this purpose—at least in the long run. If a candidate cannot fit into the mainstream of Democrats and Republicans, he or she must operate outside of the party system. In Austria (as in almost all continental European coutries), such a non-mainstream approach can be accommodated by already existing traditional third parties, frequently welcomed in coalition governments.

The differences must be seen as historical differences too. Duke and Haider are both linking present resentments with past experiences, but these experiences are rather different. Duke stands for the protest against desegregation, against the impact of human rights on democracy. He stands against the successful mainstream of America's recent past.[6] Haider stands for the protest against de-Nazification and also against basic values of liberal democracy—like the rights of ethnic minorities.[7] But he stands, using this attitude, for a successful Austrian tradition—the past Austrian trend toward authoritarian rule and totalitarian dictatorship. U.S. history is free of such an experience—despite racism, slavery, the Ku Klux Klan and segregation.

The Austrian tradition is deeply influenced by the fact that Austrian democracy is built on the victory of Allied troops, in both 1918 and 1945. Haider's particular position is to a high degree the result of the cleavage "past" (principal conflicts concerning Austria's past) which characterized the Austrian political system and Austrian society.[8] "Past" is the keyword for Austria's role during the years of Nazism. According to Austria's official legal philosophy, expressed by the wording of Austria's Declaration of Independence (27 April 1945), Austria was the victim of Hitler's aggression. But according to the behavior Austrians demonstrated between 1938 and 1945, there was not a significant difference between "German" and "Austrian" behavior. Austrians who were not direct victims of Hitler's racist and totalitarian policies participated in the Nazi regime, in the Nazi war, and in the Nazi war crimes as the Germans did. There was Austrian resistance against the Nazi rule—but there was German resistance, too.

This contradiction between the legal philosophy and the historical realities was the background of the "Waldheim Affair,"[9] which sensitized and polarized even the younger Austrian generation to which Haider belongs. The cleavage "past" includes a generation gap and also an education gap: the better educated among the younger generation in Austria are significantly more aware of such aspects of Nazism as the holocaust and racism. It is exactly this education gap that helps explain the relative lack of support Haider has among university students.

Duke's particular appeal can only be explained by the significance the cleavage "race" still has within the American political system.[10] By using certain keywords and symbols, Duke clearly plays his campaigns along this cleavage. It is not only the fact that he is supported by a "white only" electorate; it is also the public perception of his positions. African-

Americans and many white Americans interpret his policies as an overall attack against civil rights and against political equality.

Of course the cleavage "race" taps certain historical events in America's past, too. Especially in the deep South Duke exploits the old resentments against the victorious North, resentments expressed by the political use of Confederate symbols (like the flag). He expresses an understanding of the past from the viewpoint of the losers— the losers from 1865, the losers of desegregation, the losers of economic progress.

However, it is not the entire South that Duke tries to mobilize; it is only the white South. It is not the backward and poor part of American society Duke tries to speak for—it is the white sector of the less successful element. It is the confrontation of less privileged whites with the more privileged white segment and with the whole non-white society that Duke is exploiting.

Thus, some of the differences between Duke and Haider reflect the differences between a rather complex, culturally diverse society and a rather homogeneous society, between a socially fragmented, large country and a comparatively simple, small country. Duke is the populist outsider from the right in the United States, and Haider is fulfilling the same role in Austria.

Parallels

The aspects Haider and Duke have in common can be summarized as follows:
- Both use the populistic attitude of "we," the outsiders, versus "them," the insiders.
- Both are appealing to values and interests generally considered to be on the extreme right (white supremacy and Pan-German xenophobia).
- Both are playing with fears that socially alienated groups have developed (lower middle class and lower class whites and Austrians).
- Both are successful in attracting less educated blue-collar voters; that is, both are articulating working-class sentiments.
- Both are especially successful in mobilizing young male voters, creating a "movement" of angry young men.

Populistic Attitudes

David Duke attracted voters in Louisiana who felt alienated from and distrustful of government. One of his appeals was that government is not responsive to the needs of the working man and too responsive to the needs of the very poor. It was a populist appeal to the "little man" who felt that government had lost touch with him. This is the group Vice President Agnew called the "silent majority" and political scientist Arthur Miller labeled "cynics of the right."[11] Duke appealed to a fundamental alienation and cynicism about the conduct of public affairs. He tapped that attitude by portraying himself as a political outsider who championed the working man by opposing unfair government policies that aid minorities at their expense.

Furthermore, we cannot underestimate the power of the economic frustration building after seven years of recession in Louisiana. The economic anger exacerbated alienation from government. During economic downturns, white voters are more vulnerable to the appeals of candidates like Duke who refer to the "privileges" or "special favors" given to minorities. The University of New Orleans Governor's race pre-election survey asked a question about whether government is run by "a few big interests looking out for themselves" or "for the benefit of all." Clearly, white voters who felt most left out of the political process were most supportive of Duke (see appendix 1).

Haider, despite his roots in one of the three traditional Austrian camps, uses the term *Altparteien* (old parties) for denouncing the other traditional parties, the Social Democratic SPÖ and the Christian Democratic ÖVP.[12] By using the concept of "them" (the old parties), Haider creates the impression of a confrontation between old and young, decadent and fresh, corrupt and incorruptible. He poses as the knight, fighting the dragon of a system full of spoilsmen defending their personal privileges.

In spite of the responsibilities he and his party had to fulfill in government positions during the 1980s and early 1990s, Haider acts as the leader of a principal, fundamental opposition. From 1983 to 1986, the FPÖ was the junior partner in a coalition led by the SPÖ. Haider never criticized this alliance in principle, and when he became leader of his party in September 1986 he tried to keep the coalition with the Social Democrats. It was the SPÖ that canceled that alliance, not Haider and his FPÖ.[13]

In 1989 Haider became governor (*Landeshauptmann*) in Carinthia through an alliance with the regional branch of the ÖVP. On many levels he established patterns of cooperation with other parties, especially with the ÖVP. He accepted the different positions the FPÖ still occupied as a result of the former alliance with the SPÖ—for instance, the position of the Vice President of the Austrian National Bank (*Österreichische Nationalbank*—comparable with Federal Reserve). Only in 1992, when he started to criticize the level of salaries enjoyed by the managers of the National Bank, Haider also started to criticize the participation of "his" Vice President in the establishment of the bank. This was after six years of silence regarding the position of the FPÖ Vice President.

Extreme Right

David Duke's background and philosphy are replete with ideological connections to National Socialism. In Duke's college years he openly invited an audience at Louisiana State University to call him a Nazi. In recent years, however, he has attempted to dismiss those connections as "youthful indiscretions" while appealing to mainstream conservative voters in the United States. In this manner (some have argued) he fits the Nazi tradition of adapting Nazi ideology to his own culture and tradition.[14]

Perhaps the best example of Nazi ideology in the background of David Duke is his belief in white supremacy. As recently as 1989 Duke affirmed his belief in "racial science" and in the notion that nationality is a matter of genetics, not of culture or shared values.[15] Also recently, he reiterated his belief in genetic determinism and in the intellectual and mathematical superiority of the white race. Crime, according to his racialist theory, is more a result of racial defects than a result of poverty or deprivation. Duke also was an adamant opponent of mixed marriages because they weakened the white genetic pool, and he proposed voluntary sterilization programs for welfare recipients and criminals. Thus, there are undeniable similarities between Duke's ideas about white supremacy and the traditions of National Socialism, although Duke himself repeatedly denies any current connection.

Haider comes from a background deeply involved with Austrian Pan-Germanism. His family and peer groups (high school fraternity, student fraternity, sport organization—*Turnerbund*) embraced this tradition that emphasized a German identity of Austria and the Austrians. While Haider was politically socialized by this tradition, he started his career as a "liberal" in his party, claiming—with others—that the correct position of the FPÖ must be in the center of the political stage, open for coalitions with each of the two other traditional parties.[16] In 1979, he was elected to parliament on the Carinthian FPÖ ticket, and after about 1983 he started to be recognized as the speaker of his party's right wing. In that year he became chairman of the FPÖ's Carinthian party organization. He also became a millionaire after a distant relative (called his uncle) presented him with a large property consisting of a Carinthian valley (*Baerenthal*). This property was at least indirectly Aryanized (taken over from Jewish owners by political pressure) by his uncle—a topic Haider never really cared to discuss.

In Carinthia, Pan-Germanism traditionally focuses on the relationship between the German speaking majority and the Slovene speaking minority. Haider used this ethnic cleavage to become the main speaker for "German" Carinthia.[17] He started to organize internal opposition to his party's leadership on the federal level, criticizing it for being too "soft" on socialism and on the policies favored by the FPÖ's senior partner, the SPÖ. As the leader of an internal opposition directed against the "leftist" coalition, Haider was increasingly perceived as the spokesman of the rightist backlash within a rightist party, while other elements of the party struggled to become a centrist force.

Haider has used certain passwords for appealing to the old Nazis: honoring the "war generation," the "old soldiers," and declaring Carinthia "free," because of its German identity. He has also criticized representatives of his own party who tried to overcome the burden of the Nazi past[18] and tolerated an aggressiveness in his party's papers and other publications, openly advocating Nazi or at least neo-fascist patterns.[19]

In 1991, Haider was censored twice for his extremist attitudes. In June 1991, the majority of the Carinthian Diet (the combined votes of SPÖ and ÖVP) voted in favor of a no-confidence motion. According to the state constitution, Haider had to step down as governor—losing an office held for two years, leading an FPÖ-ÖVP coalition. The reason for this move was Haider's public remark concerning the Nazis' proposed employment policy during a session of the diet. He compared this policy with the policy of the (federal) SPÖ-ÖVP coalition cabinet and called the Nazi policy a "decent" (*ordentliche*) one.[20]

The national uproar was followed by an international one. The European Parliament declared in a resolution that Haider had documented his sympathy with Nazism.[21] The Liberal International, short of expelling the FPÖ from membership, suspended the FPÖ's voting rights for two years. Haider achieved international notoriety.[22]

Fear of Decline

David Duke first achieved notoriety when he was elected to the Louisiana State House of Representatives in 1989. The campaign for that office was successful because he appealed to white suburbanites' fears of economic and social decline. He gave their fears and frustrations a racial target. The campaign was aided by a crime wave in New Orleans, during which a "murder a day" was displayed on the nightly news. Most of the victims and perpetrators were black. Duke's district shared a border with the city limits, and many residents feared that crime would spill over into their neighborhood. Also, this district had a disproportionate number of senior citizens, who in addition to being worried about crime, were strongly opposed to higher property taxes, once advocated by Duke's opponent. Meantime, the economy of Louisiana had collapsed because of the drop in oil prices, and the state unemployment rate was one of the highest in the country. Thus, Duke's base of support was a groundswell of white voter resentment and discontent rooted in the eroding social status of the lower-middle and middle class.

Duke has obviously tapped deep racial resentments among white voters through the use of the symbols of affirmative action and welfare abuse. The same lower-middle and middle-class whites experiencing economic and social decline are overwhelmingly opposed to compensatory social welfare programs and the preferential civil rights policies of the Democratic party. Opposition to these policies reflects several basic beliefs held by many white voters in the U.S. as well as in Louisiana. One of these beliefs is that blacks do not live up to the American work ethic ideals; thus, they do not deserve any special favors. Second, many whites deny that a history of slavery and discrimination contributes to blacks' relative economic deprivation. Finally, they believe that enough has been done to help minorities, and that the welfare system has failed. Given these views, it is a natural extension to blame social inequities on blacks themselves, thereby exonerating society and government.

White voters in Louisiana who held these views "strongly" were the heart of Duke's support (see appendix 2). Two of the questions measuring racial sentiment in the University of New Orleans survey concerned the impact of generations of slavery and whether blacks have gotten less than they deserve. These racial attitudes were the best predictors of Duke support; he received about 60 percent of the vote at the conservative ends of these scales. In Louisiana, much of Duke's popularity can be explained by the fact that about 44 percent of whites hold these strong racial views.

Current national surveys also confirm that many white Americans view blacks as less ambitious and less committed to the work ethic than whites.[23] These racial beliefs are part of the foundation for overwhelming white opposition at the national level to affirmative action and quotas.

Haider did not create, but he exploits, the fears certain social groups have in the face of possible social decline. The best example is the new wave of xenophobia going through Western Europe as a result of the collapse of communist regimes. Haider's latest electoral successes can be explained by his ability to attract voters whose electoral motives are primarily xenophobic. In the Viennese municipal and state elections of November 1991, Haider's FPÖ got 22.5 percent—a sensational outcome—putting the FPÖ in second place in Vienna behind the SPÖ, and, for the first time in history, ahead of the ÖVP. An exit poll indicated the importance the "foreigners" issue had for the whole campaign and especially for the success of the FPÖ. Fifty-five percent of all FPÖ voters declared to have voted "due to the FPÖ's attitude toward foreigners." This item had the second highest acceptance among FPÖ voters, immediately after the more general motive "to reprimand SPÖ and ÖVP." Among voters who had shifted in the direction of the FPÖ, the motive "attitude toward foreigners" was number one among 12 possible motives.[24]

This outcome was the consequence of campaigns in which the FPÖ focused on the question of foreigners. Already in the 1990 general elections, the FPÖ slogan in Vienna was "Vienna must not become Chicago"—a negative image that drew upon fear of crime and racism. In 1991, the FPÖ slogan was "no more immigrants"—immigrants who in almost all cases came from former communist Eastern European countries, including refugees from the post-Yugoslav wars, especially from Bosnia.[25]

An analysis of the social background of Haider's FPÖ electorate shows social and economic weakness. The FPÖ in Vienna, traditionally strong among better educated and better income voters, grew significantly and disproportionately among less educated and low income voters. In the Viennese working-class districts the FPÖ became generally the second largest party behind the SPÖ—changing the FPÖ upper-middle-class image to a lower-middle-class one.

Blue-collar Votes

In 1991 David Duke was the most visible symbol in the U.S. of white backlash against both the civil rights movement and Great Society programs of the 1960s. The civil rights movement enjoyed great popularity in the initial stages. However, as the full implications became known and as the government took an increasingly active role in enforcing equality, support for this social revolution declined dramatically.[26] The decline in support occurred disproportionately among working and lower-middle class whites who faced the greatest competition for jobs, promotions and scholarships and who were also social conservatives. These working- and lower-middle class white voters were the target of successful Republican appeals beginning in 1964. Their switch to Republican presidential voting is the basis for the decline of the Democratic party and the success of Republican presidential candidates since 1968.

David Duke's appeal in Louisiana was to the group of working-class white voters who supported Republican presidential candidates in part because they believed that the Republican party represented conservative racial views. Duke's switch to the Republican Party took advantage of that perception. His support was concentrated among whites without college degrees (see appendix 3); in these groups he probably won 60 percent of the vote in the 1991 governor's runoff election. This figure is particularly stunning since he lost the election by a margin of 61 percent to 39 percent.

Haider was able to rupture the traditional class cleavage that influenced the Austrian party system for one century. The socialist "camp," backed by the overwhelming majority of blue-collar voters, was confronted by the two bourgeois "camps"—the catholic, conservative "camp" (represented by the ÖVP) and the Pan-German "camp" (represented by the FPÖ).[27] Against this pattern, Haider's FPÖ became a second labor party, representing an important segment of the blue-collar electorate. It was again Vienna, the state (and city) where about 20 percent of the Austrian population lives, where Haider's blue-collar success was most evident. The FPÖ received 26 percent of the blue collar vote (skilled and unskilled); and among the skilled workers (*Facharbeiter*), the FPÖ received 35 percent. Among all professional groups, the "skilled workers" proved to be the group most supportive of the FPÖ. (see appendix 4)

According to the traditional party typology, Haider's FPÖ is by far the most successful catch-all party among Austria's traditional three parties. Haider made his party a labor party without losing its bourgeois electorate. With Haider, the FPÖ is both more of a labor party than the ÖVP; and more of a bourgeois party than the SPÖ. Socially, Haider stands for a rather representative sample of the Austrian population.

A Kind of Male Chauvinism?

David Duke experienced a "gender gap" in his support similar to the national gender gap characterizing support for Ronald Reagan. In Duke's case, about ten percent more males supported him than females. The basis for this gender gap is not racial; that is, there is no evidence that males have more racist views than females in Louisiana. However, the genders do differ in their attitudes toward government. Males are more hostile and distrusting of government than females, making them more receptive to Duke's use of phrases such as "the bureaucrats in Washington" and "big government telling people what to do." Also, there is evidence from national surveys that females are more likely than males to favor social programs that support a standard of living such as health care, jobs, and the like. David Duke, in his anti-government posture, railed against government programs as solutions to social problems.

Duke's support was particularly strong among younger white males (see appendix 5), many of whom were angry at the lack of economic opportunities in Louisiana and turned that anger on government and authority in general. Young voters have always been more susceptible to extremist appeals and out-of-the-mainstream candidates, and Duke capitalized on the young white men in Louisiana who felt that government, as they knew it, was not representing them.

Haider's party, like all other West European parties, seems to be following a general trend toward a slight increase in female politicians in the federal, state and municipal parliaments. The "gender gap," on the parliamentary level, is going to be diminished—even within the FPÖ.[28] But on the level of the electorate, the trend is naturally a different one. As a result of different degrees of life expectancy, the Austrian electorate has a female bias. In accordance with this bias, three of Austria's four parties have a biased electorate, too: more than 50 percent of the SPÖ, ÖVP, and Green voters are female. Such is not the case with the FPÖ. Again, the Viennese elections of November 1991 are an example. Consistent with data from other elections, the FPÖ electorate had a male bias; the FPÖ was the only party that had a significantly stronger appeal for male than for female voters (see appendix 6).

This "gender gap" Haider has to face is in addition to the "generation" as well as "education" gaps. Haider's FPÖ is especially successful with younger and less educated, male voters (see appendix 6). The "generation gap" in combination with the "education gap" permits us to analyze Haider's upswing as a first consequence of a phenomenon, rather new for Europe and especially for Austria,[29] of blue-collar, lower class, male, xenophobic authoritarianism.

Conclusion

While there are certainly historical and cultural factors distinguishing David Duke and Jörg Haider, the similarities are striking and probably outweigh the differences. The most compelling similarity is the appeal to a dominant racial/ethnic group's fears as they are confronted with increasing numbers of minorities in close proximity. These fears run the gamut from fear of being overpowered, fear of losing a privileged position, fear of physical threat, fear of economic decline, and simple fear of people different from oneself. Both of these political figures have effectively tapped racism and xenophobia and used them to political advantage.

It is safe to say that Duke and Haider will not be the only spokesmen for these causes in their respective countries. In the 1992 U.S. presidential primaries, Republican Pat Buchanan expressed many of Duke's positions and consistently received about 25 percent of the Republican vote. Duke was not so fortunate. As of this writing he has been forced by financial pressure to sell souvenirs and literature from his campaigns, and his political future is uncertain. Duke blames Buchanan's candidacy for his own failure to attract voters in the primaries.

Haider still plays a glittering role in European right-wing politics. Compared with Le Pen and the French *Front National*, Haider is always able to emphasize his "liberal" role. Compared with liberal parties, like the German FDP, he is much more able to attract right-wing voters. It is exactly this combination of certain centrist and at the same time right-wing appeals, that makes the Haider case so special.

NOTES

1. Friedhelm Frischenschlager and Erich Reiter, *Liberalismus in Europa* (Vienna,, 1984).

2. Hans-Hennning Scharsach, *Haiders Kampf* (Vienna, 1992).

3. For the Duke campaign, see the *Times-Picayune*, reprint from the 20 October to 17 November 1991 issues.

4. *Newsweek*, 18 November 1991, 24-28.

5. For the Austrian Party System, see Anton Pelinka and Fritz Plasser, eds., *The Austrian Party System* (Boulder, 1989).

6. For the development of this mainstream, see Joel Williamson *The Crucible of Race* (New York, 1984).

7. Scharsach, *Haider's Kampf*, 97-141.

8. Anton Pelinka and Erika Weinzierl, eds., *Das große Tabu. Österreichs Umgang mit seimer Vergangenheit* (Vienna, 1987). F. Parkinson, ed., *Conquering the Past. Austrian Nazism Yesterday and Today* (Detroit, 1989).

9. As one example for the numerous publications, concerning Waldheim, see Robert Edwin Herzstein, *Waldheim. The Missing Years* (New York, 1988).

10. Thomas Byrne Edsall and Mary D. Edsall, *Chain Reaction* (New York, 1991).

11. Arthur H. Miller, "Political Issues and Trust in Government: 1964-1970," *American Political Science Review*, 68 (1974): 951-972.

12. Scharsach, *Haider's Kampf*, 215ff.

13. Norbert Steger, "Die sozial-liberale Regierung," in *Meilensteine des Aufstiegs. 35 Jahre Freiheitliche Partei Österreichs* (Vienna, 1991), 61-70.

14. Lance Hill, "Nazi Race Doctrine in the Political Thought of David Duke," in Doug Rose, ed., *The Emergence of David Duke* (Chapel Hill: University of North Carolina Press, 1992), 94-111.

15. Abby Kaplan, Taped interview with David Duke at his legislative headquarters, 21 November 1981, LCARN collection, Amistad Research Center, Tulane University, New Orleans.

16. Brigitte Galanda, *Ein teutsches Land. Die rechte Orientierung des Jörg Haider* (Vienna, 1987), 23ff.

17. Galanda, *Ein teutsches Land*, 78-110.

18. Scharsach, *Haider's Kampf*, 112.

19. See especially the official paper of the Carinthian FPÖ, Galanda, *Ein teutsches Land*, 98-110.

20. Scharsach, *Haider's Kampf*, 126-128.

21. Scharsach, *Haider's Kampf*, 233.

22. Scharsach, *Haider's Kampf*, 231-236.

23. J.A. Davis and Tom W. Smith, *General Social Surveys, 1972-1989* (Chicago: National Opinion Research Center). Susan Howell, *Who voted for Duke? The Polling Report*, 23 December 1991, 1-8.

24. Fritz Plasser and Peter A. Ulram, "Analyse der Wiener Gemeinderatswahlen 1991," *Österreichisches Jahrbuch für Politik 91* (Vienna, 1992) 112.

25. Plasser and Ulram, *Analyse*, 114-117.

26. Thomas Edsall, *Chain Reaction*.

27. For the historical roots of the FPÖ see Max Riedlsperger, *The Lingering Shadow of Nazism: The Austrian Independent Party Movement since 1945* (New York, 1978).

28. For the analysis of "gender" in Austrian politics, see Sieglinde Rosenberger, *Frauenpolitik in Rot-Schwarz-Rot* (Vienna, 1992).

29. Plasser and Ulram, *Analyse*, 110.

APPENDIX 1: Louisiana Governor's Race Vote Intention
by Attitudes Toward Government (Whites Only)

"Would you say that the government is pretty much run by a few big interests looking out for themselves or that it is run for the benefit of all the people?"

	BENEFIT OF ALL	FEW BIG INTERESTS	DK/ REFUSED
Duke	37%	51%	52%
Edwards	51	30	33
DK	12	19	15
N	(99)	(372)	(33)

Source: Governor's Runoff Survey, Survey Research Center, University of New Orleans, 1991.

APPENDIX 2: Louisiana Governor's Race Vote Intention by Racial Attitudes (Whites Only)

"Over the past few years blacks have gotten less than they deserve."

	AGREE STRONGLY	AGREE SOMEWHAT	DISAGREE SOMEWHAT	DISAGREE STRONGLY	DK/ REFUSED
Duke	43%	19%	45%	62%	50%
Edwards	57	61	37	22	25
Dk		20	18	16	25
N	(21)	(88)	(145)	(218)	(32)

"Generations of slavery and discrimination have created conditions that make it difficult for blacks to work their way out of the lower class."

	AGREE STRONGLY	AGREE SOMEWHAT	DISAGREE SOMEWHAT	DISAGREE STRONGLY	DK/ REFUSED
Duke	30%	40%	49%	57%	44%
Edwards	61	45	27	26	24
Dk	9	15	24	17	32
N	(54)	(122)	(75)	(226)	(25)

Source: Governor's Runoff Survey, Survey Research Center, University of New Orleans, 1991.

APPENDIX 3: Louisiana Governor's Race Vote Intention by Education (Whites Only)

	LESS THAN HIGH SCHOOL	HIGH SCHOOL	SOME COLLEGE	COLLEGE DEGREE
Duke	55%	56%	52%	31%
Edwards	30	27	31	50
Dk	15	17	17	19
N	(64)	(178)	(113)	(146)

Source: Governor's Runoff Survey, Survey Research Center, University of New Orleans, 1991.

APPENDIX 4: Viennese Elections, Nov. 10, 1991

	PARTY PREFERENCE AND PROFESSIONAL GROUP			
	SPÖ	FPÖ	ÖVP	Greens
Overall electorate	47.7%	22.6%	18.1%	9.1%
Self employed	21	23	39	7
Public employees (Beamte)	47	15	16	16
"White-collar" employees (Angestellte)	40	25	15	14
"Blue-collar" employees (Arbeiter)	65	26	4	2
Among them:				
Skilled workers (Facharbeiter)	56	35	5	-
Semi- or unskilled workers	73	18	2	3

Source: exit poll, N = 1.100; table put together after Plasser/Ulram, *Analyse*.

APPENDIX 5: Louisiana Governor's Race Vote Intention by Age (Whites Only)

AMONG MALES

	18-29	30 AND OVER
Duke	78%	50%
Edwards	13	33
DK	9	17
N	(23)	(205)

AMONG FEMALES

	18-29	30 AND OVER
Duke	50%	44%
Edwards	39	37
DK	11	19
N	(26)	(249)

Source: Governor's Runoff Survey, Survey Research Center, University of New Orleans, 1991.

APPENDIX 6: Viennese Elections, Nov. 10, 1991

PARTY PREFERENCE AND GENDER, GENERATION, EDUCATION				
	SPÖ	FPÖ	ÖVP	Greens
Overall electorate	47.7%	22.6%	18.1%	9.1%
Men	45	26	12	9
Women	51	17	18	10
- 29 years	33	26	9	20
- 44 years	44	22	14	12
- 59 years	54	19	15	6
- 69 years	59	18	14	4
70 and older	54	18	25	
Without finishing school	72	15	6	2
With finishing school	52	25	12	6
High school graduates	35	20	21	15
University graduates	21	16	29	22

Source: exit poll, N = 1.100; table put together after Plasser/Ulram, *Analyse*.

After the Central European Revolution of 1989: The Contemporary Meaning of Austrian Neutrality

Introduction

Anton Pelinka

In October 1992, at the annual conference of the German Studies Association in Minneapolis, Minnesota, a panel was organized to deal not with German, but with Austrian aspects of contemporary history. Two Austrian diplomats (Emil Brix, Franz Cede) discussed with the historian Josef Leidenfrost and with Günter Nenning. The topic: the Austrian State Treaty and Austria's permanent (or not so permanent) neutrality, linked with the State Treaty not legally, but politically.

It may be seen as a surprise that this topic had been chosen for such a panel. On the surface, State Treaty and neutrality belong to the past—outdated by the dramatic developments that took place in Europe over the last three or four years. The events of 1955 gave Austria a stable role for the Cold War—but there is no Cold War anymore; there is no Communist bloc, the Western alliance tried to balance; there is no need for a small country between the blocs to abstain from any bloc involvement.

But there are other impacts the two major documents of 1955 may still have on the Austria of the 1990s.

Brix mentions in his presentation the indirect meaning State Treaty and neutrality had and have for Austria: the happy abdication from international involvement in general; the satisfaction with the role of an island, which seemed to be a blessed one. But even Cede, from the viewpoint of international law, must concede a diminished political importance—despite the still existing legal significance—the two documents have. In Leidenfrost's words neutrality has become a "fetish" and can be or even must be redefined. But Nenning underlines the weight of domestic and symbolic functions neutrality has in present day's Austria—in spite of all the "elitist" talk of decline or reinterpretation.

The following pages offer the necessary variety of approaches influencing the political discussion of Austria's international position. The discussion, which took place during the meeting of—how very symbolic—the German Studies Association, is published on the following pages. Some aspects have to be added briefly in this introductory note.

The State Treaty was, domestically, a reconciliation without reevaluation. The (former) Nazis, victims of 1945, and their (former) victims of the years between 1938 and 1945, happily agreed on a broad consensus, which included a consensus to forget some of the most important aspects of the Nazi period. Just one day before the State Treaty was signed on 15 May 1955, the Allies agreed to drop the co-responsibility clause from the State Treaty's preamble. Austria and the Austrians should not be reminded anymore what the Moscow Declaration had stipulated. 27 April 1945, the day of the Austrian declaration of independence, was no liberation day for Austrian Nazis. 15 May 1955, was declared to be this very day: *"Österreich ist frei"*—"Austria is free." This was the formula Leopold Figl used on 15 May 1955 for national reconciliation.

Neutrality had form its very beginning both an open agenda—international law and international politics—and a not-so-open agenda. This less outspoken part consisted of domestic elements as well as of symbolic aspects: neutrality as part of an Austrian identity, which no longer should be seen as a German one. For more than three decades, public opinion in Austria perceived Austrian neutrality as a very positive *Leitmotiv* for Austria's international standing. But when, for the first time since 1945, a European war started in 1991, Austria's official attitude was not at all influenced by neutrality. Austria took part, Austria became involved, Austria was very partisan almost from the beginning of post-Yugoslav warfare. Neutrality seems to have lost its *Leitmotiv* function internationally. Has it lost its respective domestic and symbolic function, too?

FURTHER LITERATURE

Paul Luif, *Neutrale in die EG? Die westeuropäische Integration und die neutralen Staaten* (Vienna: Braumüller, 1988).

Alan T. Leonard, ed., *Neutrality: Changing Concepts and Practices* (Lanham, MD: University Press of America, 1988).

Hanspeter Neuhold, ed., *The European Neutrals in the 1990s: New Challenges and Opportunities* (Boulder, CO: Westview, 1992).

Thomas O. Schlesinger, *Austrian Neutrality in Postwar Europe: The Domestic Roots of a Foreign Policy* (Vienna: Braumüller, 1972).

Heinrich Schneider, *Alleingang nach Brüssel. Österreichs EG-Politik* (Bonn: Europa Union, 1990).

The Position of Austria in the Architecture of Europe: The Quest for Identity

Emil Brix

Austria's new position in Europe was determined by a letter, by a treaty and by the removal of barbed wire. In July 1989 the Austrian government sent a letter of application for membership to the European Community. In 1990, the Austrian government welcomed the German unification as a result of the 2+4 treaty. With the fall of the Iron Curtain, Austria, for better or worse, was once again closely involved in all Central European affairs.

But to what degree does the new situation influence the Austrian identity?

For more than thirty years, the Austrian identity was deeply connected with the so-called *annus mirabilis* of Austria's twentieth-century history, the signing of the Austrian State Treaty and the declaration of permanent neutrality in 1955. There was no basic disagreement in Austria that the State Treaty was the cornerstone of Austria's independence and sovereignty, that it was politically and legally the undisputed basis of all international relations, and that in Austria herself it was an all-encompassing symbol of a newly-acquired national identity.

In 1980, a representative opinion poll showed that 41 percent of Austrians regarded the State Treaty as a "decisive" event in the twentieth-century history of Austria. Only 13 percent of Austrians believed that the beginning of the Second Republic in 1945 was of similar relevance. The results of a 1992 opinion poll underlined the symbolic value of the Austrian State Treaty. Sixty percent said that the State Treaty does not restrict our sovereignty; 64 percent were against putting the treaty into question.

At the same time, since the late 1980s all European countries have been confronted with fundamental changes in European and world politics following the downfall of Communism. The French postmodern philosopher Jean François Lyotard summed up this dynamic situation by saying: "A pattern that had kept Europe secure, if immobile, was replaced by a future full of unimagined possibilities."

In this new Europe without bipolarity, the rapid loss of credibility and significance of Austrian neutrality is quite obvious. With the end of the East-West conflict and the beginning of new forms of international conflict (Gulf War, dissolution of Yugoslavia), neutrality soon came to be informally redefined as "solidarity" (Alois Mock). Further steps in redefining and adjusting seem to be only a question of time and political bargaining. Given the political situation of Europe Austria's geographical position, the traditional concept of neutrality can no longer be regarded as a sufficient instrument of security.

But does such an argument also hold true for the State Treaty? In the case of the State Treaty we should not so much concern ourselves with the Treaty as an anachronistic document restricting our sovereignty. We should rather ask whether the Treaty wrongly supports an idea inherent in Austria's perception of itself: that the decision of 1955 was not only an important historical event but also the foremost proof and expression of the existence of an Austrian identity.

I will try to answer whether and to what extent the new situation in Europe also influences the significance of the State Treaty for Austrian politics and for public opinion in Austria.

As with any other international treaty, the relevance of the State Treaty is a legal, a political and psychological one. When the treaty was signed in 1955, it was primarily important as a legal document. Since that time, however, its political and psychological significance has superseded its legal importance. Due to this shift in significance, one can argue that the demolition of the icon is already under way. One could mention that some legal restrictions of the State Treaty were already declared obsolete and redundant by the Austrian Government in November 1990. On the level of international politics, there is no indication that any of the republics of the former Soviet Union will try to deny or even to question Austria's entry into the European Communities. Before 1989, there were clear indications that the Soviet Union would refer to the State Treaty to deny Austria's full integration into Western Europe.

The State Treaty is psychologically important to Austria's self-perception. In this respect, the European changes since 1989 create a renewed interest in all aspects of Austrian history. This interest goes far beyond the year 1955. It concentrates on the elements of peaceful conflict resolutions in the pluralistic Habsburg monarchy, on the cultural achievements of *fin de siècle* Vienna and on the processes of nation building outside of German unification. An analysis of these Austrian characteristics shows that the Austrian State Treaty and neutrality fit easily into Austria's self-image. But such an analysis cannot resolve the basic dilemmas confronting Austria in the shaping of a new Europe. What are these basic dilemmas?

A Desire for Stability

Radical changes in the size, political structure, ethnic configuration and social system of Austria between 1918 and 1955 have left their marks on the Austrian mind: from monarchy to republic; from a large European power to a small country; from a country with at least twelve languages to a German-speaking country; from a country mainly determined by the court, the army and the Catholic Church to a country with a brutal civil war between mass party organizations; from seven years of participation in the Third Reich to the liberation of 1945, which was followed by ten years of tutelage by four allied powers; from military defeat to neutrality. Because of these radical discontinuities in Austrian twentieth-century history, the collective desire for stability is the most obvious part of the Austrian identity. In politics, such a desire corresponds to the Austrian policy of social partnership, to the strong state influence on the economy and on society, and to a tendency to impose democracy from "above." The revolutions of 1989 challenge this desire for stability. As a reaction to basic changes in the immediate neighborhood, the Austrian population clings tenaciously to the State Treaty and to neutrality as elements of stability.

The German Dilemma

Since the end of World War II, there has been little need for Austria to analyze her ambiguous relationship with Germany, because the concept that Austria was Nazi Germany's first victim was a precondition for achieving independence and sovereignty. The State Treaty contains only obligations to abstain from specific forms of cooperation and from an *Anschluß*; it does not say anything about the fact that Austrians participated in the World War on the German side. The State Treaty more or less cleansed the Austrian mind from any responsibility for the participation in the war. With the end of postwar Europe and the unification of Germany, this simple concept of differentiation between the victim and the oppressor is of little relevance for the future relationship between Germany and Austria. German economic dominance in Austria is already regarded as being problematic. These problems cannot be solved by referring to the *Anschlußverbot* in the State Treaty, but only by an Austrian effort to diversify her economic cooperations and to increase contacts with the new East Central European democracies.

The Central European Legacy

The close network of historic and cultural relations with all East Central European countries is a fundamental precondition for all discussions about Austria. In the decades immediately following the Second World War there was little interest in Central European connections. But the Hungarian uprising of 1956 and the Prague Spring of 1968 showed again Austria's *special relationship* with Central Europe which was at that time in foreign policy terms called "good neighbor policy." The 1980s saw a significantly growing interest in the idea of "Central Europe" as a common cultural region between Germany and Russia. With the fall of Communism, history has come back to the Central European region. Austria has to live with all the positive and negative effects of this fact; this provokes new questions about Austria's self-perception. In this fundamental question for the future of Austria, which could not be foreseen in 1955, the State Treaty is of no avail.

The Myth of Uniqueness

1955 gave a new impetus to the old Austrian idea that there is something unique in the Austrian mind, some historically internalized capability to mediate between the east and the west of Europe deriving from the experience of ethnic, religious and political pluralism consistently present in Austrian political and cultural history (for literary expressions see Robert Musil and Thomas Bernhard). Austria's self-image as intermediator (bridge between East and West) proved to be useful during the time of an East-West confrontation, although it increased on the domestic policy level the tendency not to formulate clearly recognizable political positions but to look for a consensus without previously stating the conflict. In the new European situation, such an approach would generate more problems than it could solve. Austrian foreign policy therefore can no longer rely on the dominant principle inherent in the concept of neutrality and the State Treaty—namely to "sit back and wait" for larger powers to formulate their positions and interests.

Even the often-heard argument that it is wise to stick to this principle at least as long as Europe's future security is unclear is only a variation of the Austrian myth of uniqueness, because it gladly accepts Austria's marginality in the main bodies of discussion and decision-making concerning future security concepts.

An Utmost Degree of External Influences

It was the Austrian historian and essayist Friedrich Heer who summed up the problem of an Austrian identity by saying that Austria is a country shaped by an overwhelming degree of external influences. Heer was mainly referring to Austria's century-long role in defending Europe against Turkish aspirations and to the internal weakness of the late Habsburg monarchy, which increased the influence of the German empire. The history of the First Austrian Republic also seems to prove his arguments. Only after the State Treaty and the constitutional law on neutrality did external influences lose their immediate importance for Austria's self-understanding. Neutrality became the key word for this development. In public opinion, foreign policy issues were regarded as of minor importance. As an indirect result of 1955, the Austrian population began to believe that Austria is an "island of the blessed."

Since 1989, Austria has once again felt the power of external influences. Two examples illustrate the situation. In its attempt to join the European Community, Austria must stress that its membership is not so much a strengthening of the "German" factor in the Community as a positive element for further processes of integration of the East Central European countries. A second example also concerns the new democracies in East Central Europe. Most of these new democracies have high expectations for a close economic and political cooperation. Austria's response to these expectations is not purely an economic or foreign policy issue, but will depend on whether the Austrian population agrees to a closer involvement in Central European cooperation.

The foregoing dilemmas are the background for most of the recent attempts in Austria to reassess the significance of the documents of 1955.

Without talking about possible legal changes of the State Treaty and the law on neutrality, there is a growing conviction among all political parties that Austria, for her own sake, has to respond to the new European situation and that the "special" role of the State Treaty for the Austrian identity mighty be detrimental in this process of adjustments.

To understand why it is difficult to come to grips with the outstanding popularity of the Austrian State Treaty by rational analysis of future necessities only, we must look again at some of the main causes for the *symbolic* value attributed to the treaty:

1. The Austrian State Treaty ended the occupation by the armies of

the four Allied powers. Primarily because of the retreat of the Soviet Army, this fact is rightly interpreted as an outstanding political success.

2. Since 1955, the Austrian State Treaty has been the undisputed basis for the nation's independence and sovereignty.

3. During the years following 1955, the economic situation started to improve significantly. Therefore, the Austrian economic success story is strongly identified with the State Treaty and the concept of neutrality.

4. In domestic politics, the Second Republic is a very stable political system. In public opinion, this fact is also attributed to the State Treaty.

5. Most of the present-day political and academic elite was formed in the years between 1945 and 1965. For this "State Treaty Generation" personal experiences with the value of the treaty for Austria play a role in their present-day attitudes towards its significance.

All of these factors, which helped to make the State Treaty popular, are intimately connected with post-war Austrian history. They are not associated with Austria's role in the new architecture of Europe, i.e. EC-membership and close relations with all Central European democracies.

1. In post-Cold-War Europe, Austria has to define her place, as the Austrian political scientist Wolfgang Mantl puts it, by "pondering the anachronisms in our postwar founding documents" without carelessness but with a strong will to integrate into various forms of bilateral and multilateral integration in Europe.

2. This concerns mainly the concept of "neutrality" which is at best a form of hypocrisy detrimental to the Austrian identity, at worst a threat to Austrian security interests. Austria therefore will have to rely on her ability to take part in European integration on all possible levels and not on her ability to reinterpret endlessly the concept of neutrality for domestic policy purposes.

3. The State Treaty has high historic value because it ended the immediate consequences of World War II and readmitted Austria as an equal partner in the community of independent nations. Except for its general clauses on democracy, human rights and especially minority rights, the treaty contains only one element relevant to defining Austria's position in the new political situation of Europe after 1989. This concerns our relationship with Germany.

Therefore, it becomes more and more evident that all political reasoning about the present day significance of the State Treaty must concentrate on its unambiguous exclusion of any "special relationship" with Germany.

But even in this respect—which one might at first sight accept as a convincing and, after German unification, very relevant function—there remains some doubt whether it is plausible and sufficient to base the necessary differentiation between Germany and Austria on a legal document which dates back to the Cold War and which is in many other respects obsolete and redundant. As the most striking example of the failure of such a policy it is worthwhile to remember that the *Anschlußverbot* of the Allied powers after the First World War was of little significance in the late 1930s and did not prevent Nazi Germany from occupying Austria. Therefore, it is dangerous to create a new myth by pretending that the State Treaty may serve as an instrument of security policy in the case of any attempts to question Austrian independence vis-à-vis Germany.

The Austrian State Treaty cannot be regarded as a sufficient instrument in defining Austria's position in any new architecture of Europe. With the changes in European politics since 1989, the significance of the Austrian State Treaty has shifted from a political compromise of international politics towards a national icon that reflects not only post-World-War thinking but also long-term cultural inconsistencies in the Austrian identity.

Neither the State Treaty nor the concept of neutrality may be regarded as mere episodes in the history of Austria; nor may they be regarded as lasting principles of our identity. Austria's identity is constituted by a complex system of long-term traditions and short-term historic events. The Velvet Revolutions of 1989 did prove that the Austrian State Treaty and the concept of neutrality certainly do not belong to the first category.

FURTHER LITERATURE

Austriaca. Cahiers universitaires d'information sur l'Autriche, vol. 32: *L'Autriche et L'Europe* (Rouen, 1991).

Ernst Bruckmüller, *Nation Österreich. Sozialhistorische Aspekte ihrer Entwicklung* (Vienna-Cologen-Graz: Böhlau, 1984).

Friedrich Heer, *Der Kampf und die österreichische Identität* (Vienna-Cologen-Graz: Böhlau, 1984).

Felix Kreissler, *Der Österreicher und seine Nation. Ein Lernprozeß mit Hindernissen* (Vienna-Cologen-Graz: Böhlau, 1984).

Wolfgang Mantl, "Das politische Panorama im Zeitenbruch. Perspektiven des Wandels," in *Die neue Architektur Europas. Reflexionen in einer bedrohten Welt*, ed. Wolfgang Mantl (Vienna-Cologen-Graz: Böhlau, 1991).

Robert Menasse, *Das Land ohne Eigenschaften* (Vienna: Sonderzahl, 1992).

Anton Pelinka, *Zur österreichischen Identität. Zwischen deutscher Vereinigung und Mitteleuropa* (Vienna: Ueberreuter, 1990).

Gerald Stourzh, *Geschichte des Staatsvertrages 1945-1955: Österreichs Weg zur Neutralität* (3rd. ed., Vienna-Cologen-Graz: Styria, 3rd. ed., 1985).

Gerald Stourzh, *Vom Reich zur Republik. Studien zum Österreichbewußtsein im 20. Jahrhundert* (Vienna: Edition Atelier, 1990).

Gerald Stourzh, "Nach der deutschen Einheit: Österreichs Standort in Europa," *Europäische Rundschau* 18 (1990).

The State Treaty and International Law

Franz Cede

I.

Discussing the Austrian State Treaty today is an endeavor where it may be said that fools rush in and angels fear to tread. Putting myself in the shoes of an angel, I must ask to be forgiven for my caution in addressing this sensitive subject. It is important to keep in mind that the Austrian State Treaty represents both a political document and an instrument of international law. It is in the latter context that I shall be approaching our subject matter. The State Treaty has to be considered as a multilateral convention concluded between the four Allied powers (the United States, the Soviet Union, the United Kingdom, France) and Austria. After its entry into force on 27 July, 1955, a number of other states associated themselves with the State Treaty by way of accession. Among these acceding states, Yugoslavia and Czechoslovakia will retain our special interest later. The very nature of the State Treaty as an international legal instrument implies that any meaningful debate on the treaty's destiny today cannot take place without knowledge of international law as it governs treaties between states. Without this knowledge, any proposition that, for example, at this time, the State Treaty has lost its validity or that it is valid in its entirety, becomes like a trap only fools would rush into.

II.

A point, although it may appear repetitive to those who are experts in Austrian studies, needs to be clarified once again. I refrain from naming high-ranking officials, diplomats and politicians alike, still active in various quite important capitals, who keep professing that Austria's international status of neutrality is an integral part of the State Treaty or are even going as far as to characterize Austria as a neutralized country. This, of course is a reminder that even well-informed statesmen nay not always be on firm legal grounds. The confusion about the legal basis of Austrian neutrality, although irritating to Austrian jurists, is understandable and may be explained by the fact that, indeed, during the negotiations that led to the State Treaty Austria's readiness to accept the international status of neutrality provided the political key to the final conclusion of the treaty. However, legally speaking the State Treaty and Austria's neutrality are two strictly separate things. Whereas the State Treaty is an instrument of international law, Austria's neutrality is based on Austrian domestic legislation enacted by the Austrian Parliament on 26 October, 1955. Nevertheless, it seems useful to recall the linkage between the State Treaty and Austria's neutrality. In the final stages of the negotiations on the State Treaty, the Austrian government delegation made a political pledge, enshrined in the Moscow Memorandum of 15 April, 1955, that Austrian would adopt the international status of neutrality along the lines of Swiss neutrality. This pledge was then transformed into reality by the federal law on the permanent neutrality of Austria.

III.

What is the essence of the Austrian State Treaty? First and foremost the treaty reestablishes Austria as a fully sovereign, independent and democratic state (Art. 1). This core provision is also reflected in the title of the State Treaty. The State Treaty concluded the legal consequences on World War II in relation to Austria as was done in the peace treaties of 1947 between the World War II Allied powers on the one hand, and Italy, Romania, Bulgaria, Hungary and Finland on the other hand. For Austria, the recovery of sovereignty meant above all the end of the occupation regime. In the short time at my disposal, it would be impossible to offer a comprehensive presentation of all provisions of the State Treaty. Allow me therefore to draw your attention first to some of them which continue to dominate public debates:

Art. 3: the four Allied powers committed themselves to providing additional safeguards to ensure Austria's independence and sovereignty by including eventually appropriate provisions in the peace treaty to be concluded with Germany. If you consider the 2+4 treaty of 12 September, 1990, between the Four World War II Allied powers and the "two Germanies" you will notice the conspicuous omission of provisions in that document ensuring Austria's independence as stipulated in Art. 3 of the Austrian State Treaty.

Art. 4 of the State Treaty: the prohibition of the *Anschluß* prohibits any measures likely, directly or indirectly, to promote political or economic union with Germany. This prohibition of an *Anschluß* with Germany was often cited, in particular by the former Soviet Union, as an impediment of Austria's aspirations to become a member in the European Community.

Art. 6 obliges Austria to secure to all persons under Austrian jurisdiction the enjoyment of human rights and of the fundamental freedoms.

Art. 7 governs the rights of Slovene and Croat minorities in Austria. Art. 7 stipulates expressly the obligation by Austria to make sure the Slovene and Croat minorities in Carinthia, Burgenland and Styria enjoy the same rights on equal terms as all other Austrian nationals. In addition, these minorities are entitled to elementary instruction in their languages, to the use of these languages before certain authorities and to topographical inscription in these languages.

Art. 8 establishes that Austria shall have a democratic government based on elections by secret ballot and shall guarantee to all citizens free, equal and universal suffrage.

Chapter II (military and air clauses) contains certain restrictions on the equipment of the Austrian armed forces with special types of weapons, such as self-propelled torpedoes or rockets (Art. 13), as well as provisions aimed at preventing German rearmament (Art. 15, 16). We shall come back to these military clauses in a moment.

Art. 20 deals with the withdrawal of Allied forces from Austria and the termination of the occupation regime. Part IV of the treaty disposes of claims arising out of the war and settles the complex question of the so-called "German assets" in Austria. Basically this issue concerned Austria and the Soviet Union, which had confiscated in her occupation zone all property falling under the term of "German assets."

In Art. 21 the Allied signatory powers renounced to the imposition of reparation payments by Austria arising out of the existence of a state of war in Europe after 1 September, 1939.

The issue of German assets in Austria is dealt with in Art. 22. For those not familiar with this question, it was one of the most difficult to resolve in the negotiations on the Treaty with the Soviet Union. I should like to give a brief explanation. Referring to general principles of international law, the Allied powers raised claims against Germany under the title of reparation for damages caused by the German *Reich* and her allies in WW II. At the Potsdam conference on 2 August, 1945, the victorious Allied powers decided to settle these claims by confiscating property and assets of German nationals in Germany and abroad. Pursuant to these decisions,

German assets were also confiscated in Austria and put under the control of the four occupying powers. The transfer of "German assets" to the four powers in Austria, however, turned out to be extremely onerous for war-ravaged Austria. It meant that also those industrial properties fell under the term "German assets" which had been forcibly taken away by the Third *Reich* from their Austrian owners during the *Anschluß* period. In the definitive settlement of this matter in the State Treaty, the United Kingdom, the United States and France agreed to transfer to Austria without compensation all property, rights and interests held or claimed by them as former German assets. The Western powers had in fact renounced these claims already prior to the conclusion on the State Treaty. The Soviet Union which, on the other hand, had kept major assets in the Eastern part of Austria, that is in the Soviet occupation zone, finally agreed to hand substantial compensation payment would be made by Austria in return.

Part of this complex financial package that included the transfer of former German assets to Austria free of compensation by the tree Western powers was the withdrawal of any claims by Austria under the title of war reparation against Germany (Art. 23 para. 3). In returning the so-called German assets to Austria, the Western powers wished to make sure that these assets which changed from German to Austrian owners would not again be retransferred to Germany (Art. 22 para. 13).

Among the remaining articles of the treaty that deserve special consideration, I wish to draw your attention to the final clauses. According to Art. 35, any dispute concerning the interpretation or execution of the Treaty which is not settled by direct diplomatic negotiations shall be referred to the heads of missions of the four powers in Vienna. If they are unable to resolve such a dispute within two months it shall, unless mutually otherwise agreed, be referred to a "Commission." This Commission, to be characterized as an Arbitral Tribunal, is composed of one representative of each party to the dispute and a third member selected by mutual agreement of the two parties from nationals of a third country. Should the two countries fail to agree within a month, upon the appointment of the third member, the Secretary-General of the United Nations may be requested by either party to make the appointment.

This provision was often considered an undue limitation of Austria's sovereignty, as it confers on the heads of missions of the four signatory powers a crucial role in interpreting the obligations under the terms of the treaty in case of disputes. With the disappearance of the Soviet Union as a subject of international law at the end of 1991, the question also arose whether the dispute settlement mechanism of the treaty is still fully operational. This aspect will be further addressed in relation to the issues of state succession in Europe and their bearing on the treaty.

IV.

After this cursory examination of some key provisions of the State Treaty, it is fitting to ask how this instrument of international law has met the test of time. In particular, we shall try to assess the impact of the new international situation as compared to the one prevailing in 1955 when the Austrian State Treaty was signed. From a legal perspective, it can be stated that treaties as well as states have their history and that the obligations under an international treaty may be changing. I refer to the principle of the *Clausula rebus sic stantibus* that makes it possible to review treaty obligations under radically changed circumstances. By the same token, it is a universally accepted rule of treaty law that the Contracting Parties are free to alter, by mutual consent, their practice in the implementation of certain treaty provisions. It is also possible that the factual basis for a particular treaty provision has disappeared and, therefore, the provision itself becomes obsolete. A good example for such a provision that, in my opinion, must be considered obsolete today is the so-called enemy clause in the United Nations Charter (Art. 107) that allows for the continued validity of action in relation to any state which during the Second World War has been an enemy of any signatory of the Charter. At present, as reunited Germany and Japan are fully respected members of the international community and of the United Nations, Art. 107 of the Charter seems like a dead leaf on a tree.

Bearing in mind these considerations, it becomes clear that the State Treaty concluded thirty-seven years ago in a radically different political environment is no exception to the rule that legal obligations are not immutable. The State Treaty cannot be examined today in an abstract fashion without due regard given to the present political dimensions of international relations. A purely formalistic assessment isolating the text of the treaty from the present parameters of world politics would be tantamount to putting this document under a sterilizer.

V.

The most spectacular act of recognition that some provisions of the State Treaty are no longer valid took place in 1990 when Austria, following the Finnish example and after discreet consultations with the four powers, declared most of the military and air clauses of the Treaty obsolete. In the relevant communication of the Austrian Federal Government to the four powers reference was made to the 2+4 treaty on a final settlement concerning Germany and the radical political changes that had occurred in Europe. The four powers accepted this declaration either in giving their express consent or by tacitly agreeing thereto.

VI.

Another recent development that affected the State Treaty has to do with the dismemberment of the Soviet Union, of former Yugoslavia and the breakup of Czechoslovakia. Whereas the Soviet Union was one of the most prominent of the four powers, Yugoslavia and Czechoslovakia, both Austria's neighbors, became later parties to the treaty by way of accession.

Let us first discuss the case of the Soviet Union and the impact of her disappearance on the State Treaty. In the opinion of the Federal Ministry for Foreign Affairs, the dissolution of the Soviet Union has the legal effect that the Soviet Union as a subject of international law disappeared. The claim by the Russian Federation put forward after the end of the Soviet Union to be the juridical continuation of the deceased Union included the move by Russia to step into the Soviet position as far as treaty relations are concerned. Russia, therefore, purports to be legally identical with the Soviet Union; it would seem to be a consequence that Russia then would be a party to the State Treaty. In our view, this claim must be dismissed. With the disappearance of the Soviet Union as a subject of international law, a clean slate was made in the treaty relations between Austria and the successors of the former Soviet Union. No confirmation of the rights and obligations of a contracting party to the State Treaty by Russia can therefore be accepted. The very fact that Russia took over the membership rights of the Soviet Union within the United Nations and other international organizations with the consent of the members of the Commonwealth of Independent States does not, according to our view, change the principle that there is no automatic continuity in the bonds of treaty relations in this case of state succession. The CIS members did not accept Russia's claim to continue bilateral treaties. Whereas the differences on the legal positions on this matter persist between the Russian Federation and Austria, its practical relevance is negligible since the State Treaty's remaining obligations are being honored by Austria anyway.

In the same way we consider the impact of the breakup of Yugoslavia and of Czechoslovakia on the State Treaty. The disappearance of these states as subjects of international law also clearly implies the end of their existence as contracting parties to the treaty.

Can the successor states of these deceased subjects of international law then become new parties to the State Treaty?

This question meets not only an academic interest as it has been raised, for instance, with some insistence by Slovenia, a new neighboring state of Austria, made up of the northern-most component republic of former Yugoslavia. Slovenia keeps, quite legitimately, an eye on the Slovene speaking minority in Carinthia and is most interested to see that Art. 7 of the State Treaty that assures certain rights to this minority is made an obligation of international law vis-à-vis Slovenia.

The legal answer to this question is, simply, no. There is no way that Slovenia as a new member in the international community of states can become a party to the State Treaty. This clearly follows from the very text of Art. 37 that excludes the accession to the Treaty of States other than those which as a member of the United Nations were at war with Germany on 8 May, 1945. This being said, every assurance can be given to our friends in Slovenia that Austria honors Art. 7 of the State Treaty, which continues to be fully in force.

VII.

In the light of the recent international developments, public opinion in Austria, not always well-informed or unbiased, was constantly fed by a discussion on the destiny of the State Treaty under the present conditions. In this debate a controversy erupted between those whom I like to call the "revisionists" and the "conservatives." Among the revisionists the more radical voices went as far as demanding that the State Treaty be thrown altogether into the dustbin of history. On the other end of the spectrum, the conservatives defended the sanctity and legal validity of the State Treaty considering the treaty, as the title of our seminar implies, a "national icon" that must not be touched by any means.

The public debate heated up with interventions by political leaders from the major parties. The State Treaty was again put in the same basket as Austria's neutrality, both being portrayed as the pillars of Austria's sovereignty and independence after the war. Things did not become easier when jurists stepped in offering their views on the legal fate of the State Treaty under the current international conditions.

The sometimes emotional statements by politicians showed that interestingly enough the conservatives were to be found in the ranks of the Social Democratic Party (SPÖ) whereas leading representatives of the People's Party (ÖVP), not to speak of the right-wing Freedom Party (FPÖ), took revisionist positions.

Putting aside the various statements of politicians, the views presented by legal experts on the present status of the treaty can be categorized as follows:

One school of thought professed the conviction that, *grosso modo*, the obligations of the State Treaty had already been fulfilled or had lost their legal force through the radical changes of circumstances between 1955 and the present. The declaration by the Austrian Federal Government of 1990, mentioned earlier, that the military and air clauses of the treaty are obsolete supports this view. Some legal experts went even further by stating that the State Treaty in its entirety is no longer valid. In reviewing the articles of the State Treaty, they arrive at the conclusion that most provisions are either obsolete or no longer applicable. To make their point, they were also referring to the 2+4 treaty that conferred upon unified Germany full sovereignty over her internal and external affairs. In their argument, Austria, characterized by the four wartime allies in the 1943 Moscow Declaration as the first victim of Hitler is Germany, cannot be bound by restrictions of her sovereignty which in the case of Germany, the former main enemy of the Allies, were lifted altogether. To stress their point, the legal revisionists of the State Treaty are considering the disappearance of the Soviet Union, of Yugoslavia and soon of Czechoslovakia as contracting states of the State Treaty even further as evidence of the erosion of this instrument of international law. Those provisions of the treaty that cover matters such as democratic institutions, and the rights of minorities, the argument goes, have already been and continue to be part of the Austrian Constitution. When discussing the prohibition of the *Anschluß* (Art. 4), they point to the sovereign wish of the Austrian people to live in an independent state that today makes this provision superfluous.

The second group of jurists, on the other hand, more or less identical with the "conservatives" as far as the treaty is concerned, are advancing these reasons that speak in favor of a continued validity of the treaty. Their classical proposition is based on the principle of *pacta sunt servanda* and of the need for good faith in the behavior of states in their international relations. With some exceptions concerning provisions which they agree have become obsolete, these lawyers are pleading in favor of the treaty. They are not impressed by the revisionists' arguments trying to nullify more or less the validity of the State Treaty in the light of recent political and legal developments, such as, the legal documents (2+4 treaty) concerning the reunification of Germany. In their opinion the State Treaty has not at all lost its character as a binding norm of international treaty law. The very fact that some provisions, like the above-mentioned article on democratic institutions are being interpreted as undue restrictions imposed on the sovereignty of Austria as a longstanding democratic country, does not keep them from holding these stipulations for Austria as binding international obligations. The disappearance of some contracting states as subjects of international law does not in their view change the continued binding character of the treaty which, after all, was also concluded with other countries that still do exist.

VIII.

At this point, you may wish to know what to make of all this. In my view the State Treaty as an instrument of international law is still valid and must not be discarded because it contains a number of provisions which were not made for a one-time performance, as for example the delivery of goods and services, but are meant to establish a long-term obligation. It is an international instrument that has not lost all its legal significance even in the light of the recent developments. This general statement has to be qualified, however. It would be unrealistic to approach the treaty today without due regard being given to the international political environment. In such a perspective it appears that, in fact, the treaty has lost its relevance in many respects. I share the view that the cases of state succession in Europe do affect the treaty in the sense that major contracting parties disappeared and the successor states of former contracting parties cannot become parties to the treaty. Summing up, the State Treaty, from a legal perspective too, has lost its quality as a national icon. No rule of international law can justly be evaluated without taking due account of the underlying political and juridical parameters at the time of their examination.

FURTHER LITERATURE

"Erläuternde Bemerkungen zum Staatsvertrag," *Stenographisches Protokoll des Nationalrates*, VII. GP.

Gerhard Hafner, "'L'Obsolence' des Certaines Dispositions du Traité d'Etat Autrichien de 1955, *Annuaire Français de Droit International* vol. 38 (Paris: Editions du CNRS, 1991).

Hanspeter Neuhold et al., eds., *Österreichisches Handbuch des Völkerrechts* (2nd. ed., Vienna: Manz, 1991).

Gerald Stourzh, *Geschichte des Staatsvertrages 1945-1955: Österreichs Weg zur Neutralität* (3rd ed., Graz-Vienna-Cologne, 1985).

The 'Anschlußing' of Austria

Günter Nenning

I.

It is true that the Austrian State Treaty as a juridical corpus is a corpse. But the moving force of history is myth and not law, much less international law. As a myth, the Austrian State Treaty is very much alive. Opinion polls show that the Austrians want their government to adhere to the provisions of the State Treaty scrupulously. But what, if anything, do the Austrians mean by this? Of the signatories, the Soviet Union has disappeared and the Western powers are no longer interested in the existence of an independent neutral Austria. In fact, the opposite is true: they want Austria incorporated into the West. Austrian politicians and their experts argue in vain that the Austrian State Treaty no longer has a base in reality.

II.

The State Treaty, to the Austrians, is a symbol of their desire to live on a sort of island, not to be submerged by oceans of any kind: in the past, neither by Communism nor by the West, today not by the European Community (EC) nor by the new unified Germany. This desire is the reason why the State Treaty and neutrality, both outdated by history, get a positive response of up to 90 percent in all opinion polls pertaining to these matters. By saying yes to the State Treaty and to neutrality, Austrians do not mean the old-fashioned juridical and historical contexts. Very intelligently, they lift both the State Treaty and neutrality out of the past and elevate them to a crucial contemporary significance. For the majority of Austrians, adhering to the State Treaty and neutrality means nothing less than adhering to the independence of their country.

If we follow this shift in significance, talking of the State Treaty and neutrality simply means talking of Austria's independence, of the wish of her people not to be absorbed and annexed. In the language of 1938, this simply means—no *Anschluß* to the EC and no *Anschluß* to Germany.

III.

Most of the political class in Austria pretends not to understand the people's wishes. They design juridical pretexts and speak of the changed situation in what is post-postwar Europe, or post-post-postwar Europe. How right they are! But what has not changed is the people's desire to disassociate themselves from foreign involvements. The political class knows that and ignores it. Why? The simplest explanation seems that the *Anschluß*, hidden but real, has gone so far that the political class of Austria is no longer able to act on its own. This seems like a strange parallel to the last days of the pre-*Anschluß* period in 1938.

IV.

On the actual question of *Anschluß* to the EC the people in Austria, like the people in the rest of Western Europe, are split. The results oscillate from poll to poll, but the split remains around 50 percent. The debate on the political union of Europe so far has produced a solid disunion within European nations.

V.

The State Treaty was Austria's chance to attain independence, or rather to attain such realistic measure of independence as is possible for a little country stretched between Western and Eastern power politics. Through most of her history, Austria tried to safeguard her survival by balancing between East and West, if "safety" can ever be attained in so precarious a geopolitical location.

Today, Austria is reduced to a strange balancing between existent power in the West and non-existent power in the East, with the equally strange result that her independence is more endangered today than it had been in the time of the East-West balance of terror.

The West is represented by the powerful mega-economics of the EC and the new Germany. The East is represented by a big black hole. All the power lies in the West; in the East there is none. The very base of Austrian independence, the East-West balance, is no longer existent.

The rug is being pulled out from under the Austrians' feet. The country is slipping toward wholesale *Anschluß* to the West. Austria's economy is "Europeanized," which is a nicer word for "Germanized." What Hitler did with brutal force is now done by impeccably democratic, that is, economic means.

VI.

The nineteenth-century dramatist Friedrich Hebbel wrote the epigram: "Austria is a little stage on which the bigger world has its dress rehearsals." The eating up of little Austria by a European ogre which is, if you scratch off the paint, a German ogre, may prove to be the model for eating up other vital parts, much bigger ones, of the motley old continent.

In the years following 1938, Hitler's *Anschluß* of Austria was the beginning of *"Anschluß-ing"* the whole of Europe. For safety's sake we should now look back to the fascist roots of the "common European house." It is a phrase used by neo-Communist Gorbachev and invented by Hitler in a speech back in 1936. Of course, old fascism is a dead duck, but new Germany is very much alive. She is as democratic as ever before, and she is dangerous as never before.

On the other hand, if Austria is putting up resistance, this time, against the *Anschluß*—this may serve as a model in the right direction: not towards a centralized Europe with no democratic institutions, but toward a Europe of all European nations, each proudly independent, and cooperative in all matters of necessity.

The EC is being restricted to nations dependent on the economy of the new Germany. A non-EC Europe, comprising all European nations, the good ones and the naughty ones, may imply much better checks and balances. *Deloropa,* the platonic super-state, is being buried with indecent rapidity. A resurrection, out of the EC tomb, and a transubstantiation into a Europe of all Europeans, confederate but delightfully different, is both fantasy and possibility.

VII.

In this New World order, deceptively resembling the Old World disorder—only much more disorderly than in times of the good old Cold War—where is security gone, and when does it come back? Nevermore!? Ours will be, for decades to come, a rebirth of chaos. Let us preserve some optimism; let us call it creative chaos: out of it may come God knows what.

A European super-state does not offer security, because it will not come into existence. A Europe of all European nations does exist already solidly non-united, with all sorts of insecurity involved. But this is all the security,

Austria or any other country will get. The rest is illusion. Austria's security is not to be found in NATO or other four-or three-letter acronyms. In case of serious trouble Austria may resemble a newly added province of non-existent Yugoslavia, and Vienna a kind of super-Sarajevo.

Austria just has not enough oil to be protected like the Kuwaiti sheiks.

Someday, the Russian bear will come out of hibernation. Then, the very same Austrian politicians that are now on pilgrimage to Brussels on their knees and elbows will move backward on their knees and elbows to Moscow. They will feast the Muscovite beast on stale State Treaty cake and chant the hymn of perpetual neutrality.

The security of Austria was, is and will be a combination of insecurities. Today and tomorrow, Austria will be secure by balancing the insecurity of being absorbed into Western mega-economics against the insecurity of being absorbed into Eastern chaos.

Austria's insecure security has enigmatically worked for centuries, even a millennium. It is irrational, but empirical. There is no opting out either of history or of geography.

But of course there is an opting out of the notion and the reality of independent Austria—into final *Anschluß*.

FURTHER LITERATURE

Günter Nenning, *Grenzenlos Deutsch: Österreichs Heimkehr in das falsche Reich* (Munich: Knesebeck & Schuler, 1988).

Oliver Rathkolb, Georg Schmid, Gernot Heiss, eds., *Österreich und Deutschland's Größe: Ein schlampiges Verhältnis* (Salzburg: Otto Müller, 1990).

Harald von Rieckhoff and Hanspeter Neuhold, eds., *Unequal Partners: A Comparative Analysis of Relations, between Austria and the Federal Republic of Germany and between Canada and the United States* (Boulder, Col.: Westview Press, 1993).

The State Treaty and Party Politics 1989-1992

Josef Leidenfrost

I.

Austria in late September 1992: The country is still in shock after Denmark's "No to Maastricht" and only slightly relieved after France's "Yes" at a time when the government coalition is trying to convince Austrians how essential it is to join the European Community.

Austria in late September 1992: The country is flooded with political refugees from Bosnia-Herzegovina; the number of so-called "economic refugees" from former East Bloc countries is steadily increasing at a time when all Europe's instruments to prevent conflict and war have failed and when the Iron Curtain was lifted only to be replaced by a "Silver Curtain."

Austria in late September 1992: A brand-new musical called "Elisabeth" is staged at Austria's number one musical theater, a musical on the life and death of Empress Sissy, the wife of Francis Joseph, while newsstands sell books with titles like *Das Land ohne Eigenschaften. Essay zur österreichischen Identität* or *Kann Österreich das Jahr 1994 überleben?*

Three years after the Velvet Revolutions in Central and Eastern Europe, Austria, in its delicate geographical position, and with its long-time historical connections to the whole region, is trying to reorient herself but is losing her orientation at the same time. If there has been a leitmotif throughout the history of this country during the past 45 years, it has been the quest for complete independence from the occupation forces until 1955 and a sit-and-watch-position ever since. State treaty and neutrality have been the keywords to Austria's position in Europe and in the world during the past decades. But these concepts seem to be outdated, as becomes increasingly apparent.

Nowadays, things are changing rapidly. In question at present are the Austrian State Treaty, signed in May 1955 by the four world powers and Austria after ten years of occupation, and the law on Austrian neutrality, approved by the Austrian parliament in October 1955. One needs to dwell therefore on the changing status of the State Treaty and neutrality in the recent European situation. I will focus on its internal review and on the fact of its becoming a topic of domestic politics as much as of foreign policy.

Austrian foreign policy during the early 1990s has not been (if it ever was) exclusively formulated at the *Ballhausplatz*. With the revolutionary changes around Austria in the East as well as in the West, foreign policy has become a dynamic process with no single center of gravity left at all but with many gravitational centers all around, at home and abroad.

II.

One of the gravitational centers for Austrian foreign policy in Europe is the European Community with its headquarters in Brussels. After the slight *Eurosclerosis* in the late 1970s and early 1980s, the European Community gained momentum again when Greece, Spain and Portugal became members of what will soon be the biggest political union in the world. Partly because of this massive process towards unification of the Western European continent, and partly because Austrian foreign policy was looking for new and positive issues after the unpleasant *Bedenkjahr* 1988 and the prolonged Waldheim crisis, the Austrian Minister of Foreign Affairs, Alois Mock, launched a debate in mid-1988 on Austria's position vis-à-vis the European Community and the feasibility of an Austrian membership. Austria's neutrality soon surfaced as a key topic in this debate and in domestic politics. During the preparation of the well-known letter of application for membership in the Community, a passage on keeping Austria's international status neutral was included, coming after a long debate between the ruling Socialists and Conservatives. It also prompted some harsh comments not only from Moscow but also from Brussels at the time and remains disputed until today.

III.

Another gravitational center is located just across Austria's borders: the "New East." Day-to-day politics during that same summer of 1989 were confronted with thousands of East Germans crossing the border between Hungary and Austria where the Iron Curtain had been pierced. *Eine Abstimmung über den Kommunismus mit den Füssen* (voting about Communism with their feet), as this mass migration soon came to be called, began. Tens of thousands more fled Honecker's *Arbeiter- und Bauernstaat* through Czechoslovakia, Hungary, and Austria into the other Germany, and by doing so unleashed the process of German reunification. During the following weeks and months demonstrations in streets became almost daily routine all over Central and Eastern Europe. First in East German cities, then in Czechoslovakia, former communist regimes in these countries were ousted. Some forty-five years of dictatorship collapsed almost overnight. The European continent is not separated by political boundaries anymore.

Besides the free flow of persons and of ideas throughout the continent (as postulated already in the Helsinki Accords of 1975), the more immediate result at the local level has been the possibility of old neighbors becoming new friends. People who had been separated from each other by the iron curtain but had lived right "next door" for decades, only a few kilometers away, have met and gotten to know each other. Many local festivals and consecrations of church bells have been celebrated together since then in the once divided regions. A *new age of regionalism* is beginning in Central Europe. This does not seem to be the age of neutrality anymore.

Looking at the current and most unpleasant events in former Yugoslavia, it seems clear that, more than regionalism, nationalism and radicalism are rearing their ugly heads again. And here I return to the consequences of the Velvet Revolution for Austrian foreign policy.

IV.

Our policy is now faced not with a single center of gravity but with several ones. Since politicians always have to be pushed before they react, somebody, like the press or the media, has to help shape public opinion. In August 1989, the conservative Swiss daily *Neue Zürcher Zeitung* soon after "the letter" had been sent to Brussels, ran a headline questioning the credibility of Austria's neutrality speaking of *"Glaubwürdigkeitsdefizite der österreichischen Neutralitätspolitik"* (lack of credibility of the Austrian neutrality policy). In particular, the article raised doubts about the military aspects of Austria's neutrality, about the Austrians trying to remain neutral and therefore self-defending while joining the EC and, by extension, the Western European Defense Union. To the Swiss it looked like the Austrians tried to "square the circle."

Criticism also rose inside Austria, especially after the collapse of Communism in the neighboring Eastern countries during the spring of 1990. One of the earliest examples of questioning neutrality after the

"*Ostöffnung*" (opening of the East) was an article by the Viennese political scientist Heinrich Schneider, published in late April 1990. He was the first one to bluntly state that "we turned our neutrality into a fetish." His main thesis was that all communities need some leading ideas; each nation has its own identity. In Austria neutrality plays an important role, especially as an element in building Austrian self-confidence.

But, argues Schneider, neutrality is a term used in international law only in connection with war; a concept of foreign policy based on the possibility of war is more than questionable. Neutrality is a concept of staying at a distance, of not wanting to get involved in any kind of international conflict. Over the years Austria has tried to change such a hands-off-approach into something more positive, namely a concept serving peace and overcoming the partition of Europe. Even if this was a legitimate stance at the time, the idea behind it no longer corresponded with the reality and the pace of events after the revolutions in the East. Schneider's conclusions:

1. Neutrality has become a fetish of Austrian foreign policy; there might have been reasons for it when it was formulated, but they have since lost their significance.
2. We should therefore redefine neutrality.
3. The mood of the times offers many reasons for redefining it.

However, the spring of 1990 was not yet the time, it seemed, for politicians and officials to redefine neutrality from an Austrian perspective.

In May 1990 the Austrians celebrated the thirty-fifth anniversary of the signing of the State Treaty in the same way they had celebrated the previous anniversaries. Politicians from the ruling coalition parties, such as Foreign Minister Alois Mock, praised the treaty as "an outstanding example of Soviet confidence in Austrian reliability." Moreover, Mock praised the concept of neutrality as "the best option given our geographical location and our size." Chancellor Franz Vranitzky called neutrality "a basic element of Austrian identity."

V.

After Austria's application to join the European community and the Velvet Revolutions in Eastern Europe, a third gravitational center developed during 1990 which also contributed to diminishing the once unique importance of the State Treaty and of neutrality: German reunification. During the diplomatic evaluation of the international status of the reunited Germany, it seemed that German independence in 1990 would be more independent than Austrian independence after 1955.

It took Austria a long time to realize, after a period of shock, how to get rid of the most restrictive clauses of the Austrian State Treaty. In their *"Vertrag über die abschließenden Regelungen im Bezug auf Deutschland"* the newly reunited Germany and the Allied powers acted quickly in their 2+4 talks. The Austrian government unilaterally declared six articles of the Austrian State Treaty, mainly dealing with military restrictions, to be obsolete. These six articles were article twelve, "Prohibition of Service in the Austrian Armed Forces of former Members of Nazi Organizations, and Certain Other Categories of Persons"; article thirteen, "Prohibition of Special Weapons"; article fourteen, "Disposal of War Material of Allied and German Origin"; article fifteen, "Prevention of German Rearmament"; article sixteen, "Prohibition Relating to Civil Aircraft of German and Japanese Design" and one section of article twenty-two dealing with German Assets in Austria.

The debate over the country's position on the State Treaty and the neutrality law had been launched by someone who was neither entitled nor expected to do so: Jörg Haider, the leader of the FPÖ (Freedom Party) and then Governor of Austria's southernmost province of Carinthia. At a speech in Munich he asserted that full sovereignty for Austria would greatly facilitate Austria's joining the Community. Restrictions on that sovereignty, as imposed under the State Treaty, should be revised. With the new order in Eastern Europe the position of Austrian neutrality would also have to be reevaluated.

His speech launched a major uproar through the entire spectrum of Austrian politics, probably because it was made during the campaign for the 1990 parliamentary elections. The initial headlines were hostile. So were statements from politicians from other parties: *"Haiders Äußerungen sind erstens Schwachsinn, zweitens grob fahrlässig und drittens ein außenpolitisches Bubenstück"* (Haider's statements are feeble-minded and reckless), said Andreas Khol, of the Austrian People's Party. Secretary General of the People's Party Helmut Kukacka stated: *"Dieses gefähliche Gebräu von Instinktlosigkeit, Unkenntnis und Leichtfertigkeit ist völlig ungenießbar"* (this dangerous brew of tactlessness, ignorance and carelessness is absolutely distasteful). Comments from Socialists and Greens were along the same lines if only slightly more moderate.

The press reactions to Haider's comments were mixed. Some liberal and leftist newspapers praised the resistance of socialist and conservative politicians against Haider's *"brandgefährliches Gerede"* (dangerous gossip) and *"biedermännische Brandstiftung"* (simple-minded bomb throwing); but some conservative papers applauded Haider's theory that both documents (the State Treaty and the law on neutrality) should be debated and possibly revised. Andreas Unterberger wrote in the venerable old Vienna daily *Die Presse*: *"Es ist durchaus Zeit für eine legitime Prüfung, ob Staatsvertrag und Neutralitätsgesetz in ihrem Wortlaut noch den Bedürfnissen der Gegenwart entsprechen oder ob sie nicht gleichsam vertragliche oder gesetzliche Ikonen sind"* (It is high time to investigate whether the State Treaty and the neutrality laws still reflect contemporary requirements, or whether they are mere contractual and legal icons). In another article Unterberger called both documents myths and wrote: *"Aus dem Mythos ist schon längst eine Last geworden"* (The mythology has become burdensome a long time ago).

Interestingly enough Austria's Foreign Minister Alois Mock issued no negative comments. He rather started talking about *"einen denkbaren Qualitätssprung der Neutralität in Europa"* (a conceivable transformation of neutrality in Europe), before he travelled to the forty-fifth General Assembly of the United Nations in New York in late September 1990.

VI.

He probably chose that moment because another gravitational center in international politics took shape: the Gulf conflict, namely the occupation of Kuwait by Iraq with all its worldwide consequences. Whereas the Western world closed ranks, first by taking economic sanctions and later by setting up combined military forces, some neutral nations in Europe followed their traditional policy of fence sitting. Austria, with her delicate geographical position in the center of Europe, situated between Northern and Southern flanks of NATO, did not have the easy choice of staying out of the increasingly dangerous conflict.

It is true that Foreign Minister Alois Mock stated at the U.N. General Assembly in the fall of 1990 that Austria would grant overfly permits to Allied aircraft if requested to do so by the international community and backed by U.N. resolutions. History seemed to be repeating itself. During the 1958 Lebanon crisis, U.S. military transport planes had flown across Austria with official permission from the Foreign Ministry and in spite of Austrian neutrality.

At the end of 1990 and the beginning of 1991, developments accelerated even further. After "Operation Desert Storm" had begun, the Austrian Government officially declared that *"die Staatengemeinschaft im Rahmen der Vereinten Nationen alle Mittel ausgeschöpft hat, um der völkerrechtswidrigen Aggression gegenüber Kuwait auf friedliche Weise zu begegnen, und daß es sich nunmehr bei dieser Militäraktion nicht um einen Krieg im klassischen Sinn handelt, sondern um eine gemeinsame Aktion der Vereinten Nationen gemäß dem System kollektiver Sicherheit: Die österreichische Neutralität steht nicht im Widerspruch zu dieser internationalen Solidarität und zu den Aufgaben, die Österreich als Mitglied der Staatengemeinschaft zu übernehmen hat."* (The community of nations has tried everything to peacefully deal with the aggression against Kuwait via the U.N. This military action cannot be considered classical warfare but a common U.N. action according to the system of collective security: Austrian neutrality does not contradict international solidarity and the duties Austria will have to accept as a member of the community of nations.)

This became the formula for the Austrian government to permit the railroad transport of 103 rescue tanks from Bavaria to Northern Italy via the Tyrol, to be shipped to the Gulf. The disparity between official reasons of state and popular sentiment became quite obvious when hundreds of Austrians blocked the railtracks at several locations, trying to block the weapons transfer. It is indeed very difficult to discern the linkage between the Austrian approach to the EC on the one hand and support for the Western coalition in the Kuwait crisis on the other hand. Whatever the linkage may have been, it was not compatible with neutrality at all.

VII.

Yet another gravitational center developed at Austria's southern borders in mid-1991. With the break up of Yugoslavia, the emergence of Slovenia and Croatia culminated in their declarations of independence in late June of 1991. When Austria's Vice Chancellor Erhard Busek und Vienna's Mayor Helmut Zilk attended these ceremonies, Austria once again gave up something of her neutrality. By that time, however, politicians of all parties (except the Greens) had publicly called neutrality into question as a valid foreign policy doctrine.

VIII.

Two years after "the letter" had been delivered to EC headquarters, reactions from Brussels suggested that this was a positive trend since the Eurocrats considered Austrian neutrality to be incompatible with a common foreign policy for the European Community. Chipping away at Austrian neutrality experienced a further twist during the presidential election campaign of 1991-1992. The two main candidates were the Socialist Rudolf Streicher, Minister of Transportation and Nationalized Industries, and the Conservative Thomas Klestil, the Secretary General of the Austrian Foreign Ministry. Klestil, of course, had considerable advantage when it came to debating traditional topics of foreign relations such as the State Treaty and neutrality, after all, foreign policy was his very domain. This made it all the more surprising when he came out with some very radical thoughts on the future of the Austrian State Treaty, namely to abandon it as a foreign policy doctrine. A very decisive and remarkable international event had helped him. On 8 December 1991, the Union of Socialist Soviet Republics was officially dissolved in Minsk, at least as subject of international law.

During the election campaign Klestil said more than once that the State Treaty should be put into a tabernacle. His party leader Erhard Busek followed up with the statement that the State Treaty had become obsolete since one of the five signatories, namely the Soviet Union, had vanished from the international stage. Given such radical departures, the Viennese weekly news magazine *Profil* carried a cover story in January 1992 on "the end of the Second Republic."

The politicians, however, were running way ahead of the deeply-rooted traditional mentality of their Austrian voters. A January 1992 public opinion poll showed that forty-five percent of the respondents thought that Austrian neutrality still was as important as it had been in the late 1950s. And sixty percent thought that the State Treaty did not abridge Austrian sovereignty. Sixty-four percent said that the document should not be questioned, let alone be ignored.

With Austria ready to enter the European Community, something has to happen about Austria's future foreign policy orientation. *Profil* has facetiously offered a possible solution—the comeback of the Habsburgs.

FURTHER LITERATURE

Hubertus Czernin, "Das Ende der 2. Republik: Die Krise der Symbole," *Profil*, 13 January 1992, 16-21.

Herbert Krejci, Erich Reiter, Heinrich Schneider, eds., *Neutralität—Mythos und Wirklichkeit* (Vienna: Signum, 1992).

Herbert Lackner and Andreas Weber, "Das Habsburg Comeback," *Profil*, 14 September 1992, 24-28.

Andreas Lernhart, *Österreich und die EG: Neutralität und Mitgliedschaft* (Vienna: Signum, 1989).

Theo Öhlinger, Hans Mayrzedt, Gustav Kucera, *Institutionelle Aspekte der Österreichischen Integrationspolitik* (Vienna: Verlag der Österreichischen Akademie der Wissenschaften, 1976).

Werner A. Perger, "Ein leises Servus: Österreich muß sich entscheiden: Was tun mit der Neutralität," *Die Zeit*, 13 March 1992, 7.

Karl Heinz Ritschel, *Ist Österreich integrationrreif? Wiener Charme ist zu wenig!* (Vienna: Europahaus, 1964).

Andreas Unterberger, "Neutralität: Sinn und Unsinn," *Wiener Journal* (April 1992): 11-12.

"Glaubwürdigkeitsdefizite der österreichischen Neutralitätspolitik: Von der Vernachläßigung zur Zerstörung des Landesverteidigung," *Neue Zürcher Zeitung*, 23 August 1989, 4-6.

Current articles in *Die Presse, Der Standard, Profil, Kleine Zeitung, Salzburger Nachrichten.*

'Imagination is More than Knowledge.'
Bruno Kreisky's Life as Biography*

Peter Malina

Of late, historical biography has again been enjoying an astonishing popularity, both among historians and those interested in history. After a period of scepticism regarding biographical accounts, historical scholarship is beginning to remember Marc Bloch's dictum that the subject of history is not some abstract "past," but the tangible human being; "The good historian", as Bloch worded it in the first chapter of his "Apology of History," "resembles the ogre of legend. Wherever he scents human flesh he knows that his prey is not far away."[1] Telling stories about people has again become a challenge for historical scholarship, which has recently developed a pronounced "appetite for what is concrete"[2] as a reaction to the history of structures.

This trend toward biography, however, has not remained without contradiction among historians. The question is by no means settled yet as to what role should be attributed to "personality" in history,[3] or as to whether historical biography is possible or even necessary as a form of historical presentation.[4] For Jacques LeGoff at any rate, current historiography is in the process of "turning back the wheel of history," and historical biography, in particular, is experiencing a "phenomenal renaissance."[5] For him, the return to biography also heralds the revival of the historiography of great political events and the reduction of history to the story of individual "great men or women" who make history. In the renaissance of biography he sees nothing but a sign of the reemergence of a concept of history that "has learned nothing and forgotten nothing."[6]

The Historical Approach: Biography as a Construction

The fascination of biography undoubtedly derives from its enabling a special form of "empathy" and a kind of surrogate "participation" in another person's life:

"As people are usually interested in nothing more than in other people, such a participation in another person's life, such a tracing of his tracks can be highly appealing. You tend to identify in some way with the person depicted. You can hardly avoid the temptation to put yourself in his place. From a certain point onwards you are so committed that you just cannot learn enough about him. What you would like best would be to prolong his life."[7]

In biography, the complexity of historical events becomes clearer through foreshortening. However, at the same time it is necessary to put the "hero" of the story in the context of the structure of his society:

"The scope his society gave to action, the limits it set to thinking, the horizons, the relationship between political action and long-term processes, between major and minor history, between the sexes, perhaps the special quality of religion, of philosophy, presumably the feature of the structures of motifs and the specific rootedness in the age - all these things and many others are of interest. And their determining force must be made clear within the framework of conditions they form in conjunction with other factors."[8]

The attractiveness of the historical personality and his biography may also derive from the fact that politics are often presented to the public as the result of the activities of individuals. Hence it is legitimate to ask who the bearers of political power are, where they come from, what qualifications they have and what the aims of their political activities are.[9] For this reason, Arno Mohr sees biography as the soundest method of grasping a political personality in an analytical and meaningful way. A biography critical of its sources offers the possibility "to understand the suprapersonal factors, the tendencies and forces of the time through the eyes of a political personality."[10] Moreover, biography affords the historian complete assurance as to his subject: "The limits of his subject are defined for him in advance. His book will begin with the subject's birth, perhaps with some prelude of family background, and will end with the subject's death, again perhaps with an epilogue on the subject's legacy, political, financial or personal."[11]

Biographies are life stories told in retrospect and as such the results of an often laborious reconstruction.[12] Such a "construction" always allows inferences as regards the historical awareness of its "constructors." A life is made up of many stories. To present them as history necessitates making a selection "because the complexity of life cannot be reflectively reconstructed and narrated without making reductions."[13] So when interpreting biographical accounts we must enquire about the "guidelines of the narration," understood as a "subjective structuring of the past life" that at the same time shows its social relations and relationships.[14]

The following will endeavor to present some approaches to Bruno Kreisky's life. Completeness of the literature employed is just as little intended as is a comprehensive treatment of Kreisky's biography. But using the available biographical portraits, we will enquire which approaches to Bruno Kreisky's life have been revealed and which have remained closed.

Descriptions of a Life: "From Marx to Kreisky"

First, there is the remarkable fact that hardly any of Bruno Kreisky's biographers have tackled the fundamental issue as to whether and how it is still possible to write a "great" biography today. It is taken for granted that the course of his life represents a sequence of chronologically ordered periods, the same ones being mentioned time and time again: his political experiences in Austria in the 1920s and 1930s, his enforced exile in Sweden, his return to Austria, his rise within the party hierarchy, his election success in 1970-71 and his appointment as federal chancellor.

Describing Bruno Kreisky's life represents a challenge to the biographer particularly because biographical and individual and historical and suprapersonal areas overlap permanently in his person. Looking at it more closely, we could divide up Bruno Kreisky's life into at least three parts: the normal biography of a person whose life was determined by his childhood, adolescence, adulthood and old age and by the corresponding stages (school/education, marriage/family/children, occupation); the political biography that was significantly shaped by his rise as a politician and his institutional position within the Austrian political system as party leader and chancellor; and finally, the life that was exposed to suprapersonal, social influences and imprints, one that suffered decisively from his expulsion from Austria in 1938 and his reintegration into postwar society in Austria after 1945.

The biographical approach to Bruno Kreisky is an exciting undertaking in as far as it is or should be a question of becoming aware of the different "images" that shape one's own imagination. Because of his public position, Bruno Kreisky was also part of Austrian public life. In caricatures and anecdotes Bruno Kreisky's life became part of the general political consciousness.[15] The fascination exercised by Kreisky was usually the reason given by his biographers for dealing with him. Viktor Reimann states that he wrote his biography of Kreisky because Kreisky's personality "enthralled" him;[16] for him the election success of the SPÖ in 1970 is the "Kreisky Miracle."[17] In the preface to the portrait of the statesman Kreisky he wrote in conjunction with Paul Lendvai, Karl Heinz Ritschel stated that there were only a few politicians in the Austrian Second Republic worth writing a book about;[18] and Elisabeth Horvath sees Kreisky's charisma especially in his personifying a "kind of Austrian destiny, a specifically Austrian character" as "a part of contemporary history."[19]

Surveying the biographies of Bruno Kreisky published to date, one can discern a number of accents. Essayistic biographical accounts predominate, whereas a scholarly assessment of Bruno Kreisky's life as a politician is only slowly beginning. As regards the appraisal of Bruno Kreisky's political and social relevance, the biographies published shortly after his accession to office as chancellor very soon strengthened the impression that with Bruno Kreisky a new era in the history of the Austrian Second Republic had begun. Viktor Reimann published his Kreisky biography as early as 1970 because it fascinated him "to write about a man whose activity represents a political turning point, the results of which cannot be foreseen."[20]

In 1975 Johannes Kunz (Kreisky's press secretary at the time) edited a book that spoke of the "Kreisky Era."[21] As regards foreign policy, there is no doubt for Erich Bielka, Peter Jankowitsch and Hans Thalberg (all colleagues of Kreisky at the Foreign Office) that the accents of Austrian foreign policy in the 1970s were determined by the "Kreisky Era."[22] On the other hand, Elisabeth Horvath (at the time journalist of the *Wochenpresse* in Vienna) a few years later posed the critical question as to whether it was really an "era" or just an "episode."[23] But for her, too, the "Austrian Way"[24] of 1970-1985 also shaped by Kreisky, was the prerequisite for an important change in Austrian society.

Kreisky's image in biographical literature is shaped by the concept of the "statesman" who guided Austria through the age. Paul Lendvai and Karl Heinz Ritschel, as well as Viktor Reimann, paint the "portrait of a statesman"[25]—albeit with different contours in detail. In the various attempts to narrate a life of Bruno Kreisky, references to world history can be encountered again and again. In his book, published in 1979, Walter Raming sketches a lineage from Marx to Kreisky;[26] Walter Pollak spans the arch of his history of Socialism from the Austro-Hungarian Empire to the Kreisky Era.[27]

Despite all the fundamental agreement as to his preeminent position in Austrian politics, Bruno Kreisky has always remained a paradoxical phenomenon for his biographers. He was the "scion of a bourgeois family" who became a Socialist,[28] the "pragmatist" and the "Social Democrat without a dogma,"[29] the "initiator" with "the courage to leave things undone,"[30] and the "wayfarer between spheres."[31] In 1973, Alexander Vodopivec interpreted Kreisky's political activity as a "tightrope walk" between parliamentary democracy and a union-run state[32], and Walter Jambor depicted a scenario of the "terrible" downfall of Austria after the end of Bruno Kreisky in his book published in 1981.[33] For the political scientist Anton Pelinka, the "Kreisky Era" is nothing but a "Social Democratic paradox" when viewed from the year 1988.[34]

Views of the Man and Background Stories:
"The longer you know him, the more enigmatic he becomes"

Because of his public positions, Kreisky's life has become part of Austrian history. Nevertheless, his public activities remain fragmentary without the background of his "private", personal biography. A comprehensive account of his life will only be possible if it accounts for the tension between the "normal biography" and the specific pre-requisites necessary for a life as a "great" person.

In her biography, Elisabeth Horvath has endeavored to grasp the complexity of Bruno Kreisky's political life and to present its "influences and constellations, its currents and facets."[35] The result is a stimulating and readable biography, characterized by a multitude of anecdotes. She presents "politics" as the expression of very personal interests, for example in the person of the former undersecretary of state Veselsky, who was unable to find support for his economic ideas.[36] Her account contains a wealth of information contributing toward a history of the political elites of the Austrian Socialists, whose political decisions were also determined to a not insignificant degree by very personal interests and inclinations: "It was the arrogance, the swearing behind his back, the vulgar, overbearing and aggressive tone which Kreisky, who had never really believed that he would become one of the leaders of the SPÖ, had to find unbearable."[37]

Accustomed as a journalist to measuring visible political successes, Elisabeth Horvath evaluates the political objectives of Kreisky's government according to the tension between what was achieved and what was desired. She thinks that Kreisky was able to integrate the intellectual potential of the 1968 movement in Austrian society, but let it go to waste unused more or less "until it finally stunted, petered out or just blossomed somewhere in the alternative scene."[38] By attracting political personalities who were able to see their concerns realized, Austria created a spirit in the 1970s that set many things in motion. This is her explanation for the success.

Kreisky's influence was only limited, especially because in Elisabeth Horvath's estimation, he largely lacked the dimension of encouraging, stimulating and initiating.[39] She thinks that in feminist issues, too, Kreisky was not the "dynamic pioneer" many women voters perhaps thought him to be, although feminist policy occupied a much more important position during his chancellorship than it had done earlier.[40] She sees a key to understanding Bruno Kreisky's success in his inimitable "feeling for symbolism" and his intuitive gift of "mobilizing people's emotions"[41] and, not least, in his ability to handle the mass media, whereby he was quite capable of creating a special relationship of trust with certain chosen journalists by making them "confidants."[42] In Elisabeth Horvath's view, Kreisky's attempt to institute Socialist concerns with the help of a non-Socialist public and to introduce aims and ideas, for which it was difficult to find support within the party, by publishing them is symptomatic of this.[43]

It is not surprising that Bruno Kreisky's charisma and the rise of the SPÖ to the status of a "state party,", connected with him did not fail to leave an impression, particularly within his party. Stella Klein-Löw wrote her biography "thinking of and about Bruno Kreisky" and added, "it was not easy to write it."[44] As an insider she unfolded her biography partly on the basis of shared historical experiences. "I have witnessed and followed more than fifty years of experienced, endured and influenced party history between freedom and dictatorship, exile and the return to the movement together with a man who slowly assumed an important position in world affairs, and who wanted to realize the political visions of the past in the reality of the present for the sake of a future in peace."[45]

Stella Klein-Löw describes this personal relationship to Bruno Kreisky in a short chapter of her book (*Erlebnisse und Begebenheiten um Bruno Kreisky*): relations with Kreisky's family and his brother Paul, an illegal meeting, news from Sweden and Kreisky's report on the opinion of the Austrians in Sweden about the Allied plans for the future of Austria and contacts with Kreisky's brother Paul in Israel.[46] It is, above all, the (political) creature Bruno Kreisky that interests and fascinates her: "He is not a hero in the dramatic events that call themselves history. He presents himself as and indeed is one of many, someone to whom you can entrust yourself and your destiny. The longer you know him, the more enigmatic he becomes. The better you understand him, the more you realize that much remains that you have only just begun to comprehend."[47]

For Stella Klein-Löw, politics is largely determined by emotions, and she describes Bruno Kreisky's life as a succession of fortunate and unfortunate relationships. This becomes particularly clear in her depiction of the conflict between Kreisky and Androsch, which she describes as being based purely on motives of a private and unpolitical nature. Kreisky "was shaken by Hannes Androsch's attitude; he was distressed by the conviction that he had been wrong in his estimation of his able young friend.... But there was no way back for either of them."[48] She is not principally concerned with a critical stock-taking of Bruno Kreisky's policies; she "would like to reproduce and reflect the feelings and thoughts of countless people" and give them a voice, "so that nothing is lost of what fascinated us about Kreisky."[49]

The Material of History: Sources and Presentations

In recent years Bruno Kreisky and his policies have frequently become the subject of scholarly studies at Austrian universities. Unlike the non-scholarly approaches to Bruno Kreisky, there are here no major biographical works. Instead, there are a number of detailed studies dealing with aspects of Kreisky's political activity: Eva Böck has analyzed the "free school-book policy" as an example of the economic and social policies of Kreisky's government;[50] Gunnar Staubmann has devoted himself to studies of the changing ideological positions in the development of the Austrian Social Democratic Party up to the "Kreisky Era;"[51] Mehdi Fallah-Nodeh has analyzed Austria's relations with Iran from 1970 until 1983;[52] Bruno Kreisky's Middle East policy is the subject of the study by Ernst Weinisch;[53] Gerda Falkner has dealt with Austrian development policy over the same period.[54]

The scholarly analysis of historical phenomena that have just been "present" is still a problem, not least because of the inaccessible or classified material. Hence the studies on the "Kreisky Era" published to date must necessarily be fragmentary. Wherever studies have centered on the public effects of Kreisky's policies (for example, in connection with the free textbook policy or the media), it is quite possible to make do with the published sources—quite apart from the fact that good-quality, although, unfortunately, not always utilized studies already exist on the contexts of Bruno Kreisky's political activities (in the field of Middle East policy, for example). But the quality of the investigation will always depend on the methodological instruments and the theoretical considerations chosen.[55]

The editors of the anthology *Die Ära Kreisky* have endeavored to summarize and characterize the accents of Austrian foreign policy in the 1970s. They did not want to write an "almanac of Austrian foreign policy," but depict the most important elements in Austrian foreign policy after the State Treaty and sketch its development. The authors had actively participated in shaping foreign policy in conjunction with Bruno Kreisky. As Hans Thalberg put it in his preface, "The authors of this publication speak from personal experience, they have all taken part in the developments they describe in one form or another. They accept the restriction of a subjective view as they are of the opinion that the advantages of a firsthand presentation far outweigh its disadvantages, even when strictly observing scholarly objectivity."[56]

All in all, this contribution to Bruno Kreisky's biography represents an outline of Austrian foreign policy with a focus placed on the 1970s. The outline is oriented by the person of Bruno Kreisky, but it also partly considers the historical contexts. With the selection of their articles the editors have endeavored to cover the areas in the foreign policy of Kreisky's government that were particularly important to Kreisky himself. Apart from the problem of integration and neutrality (Rudolf Kirchschläger), these include relations with the two superpowers (Karl Gruber, Ingo Mussi, Heinrich Haymerle), with the neighboring People's Democracies (Erich Bielka) and the United Nations (Kurt Waldheim). Hans Thalberg deals with Kreisky's Middle East policy and Peter Jankowitsch with Austria's relations with the Third World. The book is concluded by Paul Lendvai's reflections on the "Kreisky effect" and the international media.

Written by foreign policy experts, who at the same time took a leading part in the handling of the foreign policy problems they depict, the articles in this anthology naturally also reflect personal experiences and views. In this light, and here one must agree with the author of the preface, Hans Thalberg, the articles themselves must be acknowledged as testimonials of the age and hence as sources for the history of an important chapter in Bruno Kreisky's political activity. In Thalberg's words, "This publication intends to make a contribution to the contemporary history of the Second Republic," even though its authors judge matters from a subjective point of view, because "Is it really necessary for the participants in historical processes to rest in the grave before anyone can dare to portray these processes?"[57]

The memoirs of participants are undoubtedly an indispensable source for history. Nevertheless, for contemporary history it will also be necessary to resort to traditional sources, such as archive material, to clarify details and present longer-term historical processes. This also applies to historical biography. The edition of Bruno Kreisky's writings, speeches and documents from the years 1931-1945, published in 1986, presents historical research for the first time with the opportunity to reconstruct the biography of the young Kreisky on the basis of concrete source material.[58] Kreisky's political beginnings are documented here, as are the Socialist trial in 1936, his imprisonment by the Gestapo and his exile in Sweden. An important part of the source edition is taken up by Kreisky's correspondence and work as a journalist in Sweden from 1938 to 1945. Kreisky's police file in Sweden is a rarity.

The private collection of Bruno Kreisky's papers that is looked after by the Bruno Kreisky Archives Foundation in Vienna formed the basis for the source edition. Additional material came from Austrian and foreign archives. With its meticulous editorial references and the short, but informative introductory commentariess to the individual chapters, this edition has become more than just a collection of documents on Bruno Kreisky's biography. Not least because of the wealth of Kreisky's contacts with other Austrian emigres, which are documented in this book, has it become easier to add to the history of Austrians in exile.

Biography as Autobiography: Between the Ages in the Maelstrom of Politics

In their selection and commentaries the editors of the source edition *Der junge Kreisky* deliberately avoided presenting biographical details from Bruno Kreisky's life as they were to be reserved for the autobiography being written at the time.[59]

In countless interviews and discussions Kreisky constantly referred to details from his political life which were partly published in printed form.[60] The two-volume autobiography published between 1986 and 1988 is now available for a historical analysis of Bruno Kreisky's life.[61] In his memoirs Bruno Kreisky undertakes the attempt to sum up his life as a continuous entity. In the first volume (entitled *Erinnerungen aus fünf Jahrzehnten*) he portrays his life from the "outset", his first days at primary school in September 1917, life in his family, his first contacts with "politics," the events of February 1934, his arrest and escape from Austria in 1938, his exile in Sweden, the return to Austria, his entry to the diplomatic corps and finally his participation in the Austrian State Treaty in 1955.

The second volume (entitled *Im Strom der Politik*) continues with the 1950s and concludes with the period of the SPÖ in opposition, 1966-1969. Kreisky already structures his life under the aspect of his public activities and according to his political rise: his contacts with Germany, America and Russia, the issue of Southern Tyrol and the bridging of the gap between EFTA and EEC, policies towards neighboring countries and Austria's relations with Yugoslavia, Poland, Hungary, Bulgaria, Romania and Czechoslovakia, the problem of the Third World, and Middle East politics. In some chapters Kreisky takes the opportunity to go into questions of principle that elucidate his views on politics and society: the domestic political situation in Austria in the 1950s, his comments on "the level of politics today," his relations with Charles de Gaulle, another "great man" of European politics, thoughts about anti-Semitism, the "racial theories" and the future of the state of Israel, but also his opinions of the Austrian presidents (including: "Waldheim: eine Klarstellung").

These memoirs, written after time-consuming labors and authorized and revised by Kreisky, are the product of a process of recollection, in the course of which Kreisky reconstructed his life as coherent history. According to the comments on the origins of the book ("Anmerkungen zur Entstehungsgeschichte") at the end of the first volume, these autobiographical records are the result of an arduous operation of memory and recall in which reminders and backup questions helped achieve the final result.[62] Like other memoirs, they only describe the past through memory. A life as biography has always contained an element of reflection and is thus an "experienced life," which is understood and presented according to certain criteria.[63]

Not only biographical "data" (that is, biographically articulated "knowledge") are employed in the treatment of multifarious biographical experiences, but also historical knowledge in the sense of a lifetime's accumulated and acquired experience: the varied quality of the information conveyed by society plays a role, as does the concrete disposition on the basis of which information is selected, processed and altered. At any rate the social context of this lifetime's "learning" is also essential.[64] The question as to whether details, contexts or the course of events are "correct" or "wrong" is surely not of prime concern (for the time being), quite apart from the fact that the historical facts were evidently well-researched by the helpers in the background.

Kreisky's lifetime coincided with a period in Austrian history when a "battered life"[65] was the rule. Kreisky's life, too—something his biography and his biographers do not always want to admit—was also exposed to many blows (the shattering of continuities and careers, the loss of identity).[66] This is evident, for example, in Kreisky's treatment of his Jewish identity, an identity that constantly determined his political life, too—let us remember the election campaign of the ÖVP in 1970, the spectacular conflict with Simon Wiesenthal that has already been described in historical literature[67] or Kreisky's attitude towards Israel.

Identity is a "demanding synthetic achievement," the result of a strategy of intersubjective communication in the course of which the individual must constantly adapt to the changing circumstances relevant to him. The prerequisite for it is a permanent process of inner and outer relationships: "Identity ... is formed intersubjectively in the actions of two individuals; in concrete processes of social interaction, in which the claims of individuals compete for mutual recognition."[68] Jewish identity means being able to deal with threats to and discoveries of identity and integrating these experiences in one's own life.[69] In this context, it is certainly not insignificant that the second part of Kreisky's memoirs include a lengthy chapter commenting on anti-Semitism, "racial theories" and the future of the state of Israel, but without reference to Kreisky's own life.[70]

The Problems Connected with a Biography of Kreisky: The Burden of Greatness

Because of his position within Austria's political system and his function as chancellor, Bruno Kreisky's biography is no longer just a "private" one. As his life was largely spent in the public eye, it is also of public interest, and that also means of interest to contemporary history. If we want to view Kreisky's life as "the life-form of a historically individualized species,"[71] to borrow Thomas Luckmann's principle, it will be necessary to enquire into the social conditions and effects of this personal and individual biography.

Despite the many endeavors already published, the story of Bruno Kreisky's life is still fragmentary. A number of fundamental questions are still open for the historical work on a biography of Bruno Kreisky. One of them is undoubtedly how one can deal with the fascination exercised by the "great man" Bruno Kreisky. One of these attempts to approach Kreisky is Konrad R. Müller's album of photographs, which seeks to portray Kreisky the private man: in a "group photograph with Austrian pensioners" in Mallorca, "trying to make repairs" or "at breakfast with his wife Vera" in his house in the Armbrustergasse.[72] The texts by Gerhard Roth and Peter Turrini are intended to complement the photographs. The texts, too, try to approach Kreisky the man through the intimacy of banal, everyday life. They tell of the Kreisky who is completely relaxed at mealtimes, who sees to it that the front door is shut (otherwise the dogs and not just the cats will come into the house in Mallorca in the night), and who makes sure that the oranges, the cake and the liver sausage for the picknic are not forgotten.[73]

Unlike Müller's private pictures, Irene Etzersdorfer has documented the public Kreisky in a volume combining texts and photographs and entitled *Inszenierungen eines Staatsmannes*. From the fund of "archived publicity" she has endeavored to reconstruct a photographic biography of Bruno Kreisky from the days of success to those of crisis.[74] The pictures are a sign of the desire to make the object of public interest accessible, the desire to have been there: "the photographic testimonials made by his contempories about his changes: fame, sovereignty, but also old age, sickness and solitude."[75] In this collection of pictures the "Kreisky Era" has really become history. With her biography of Kreisky, Elisabeth Horvath has made a venture in the same direction, but from a journalistic point of view. Her aim was to present the complexity of this "political" life and the "influences and constellations, currents and facets" affecting it.

Any biography of Bruno Kreisky is surely also an indication of how the Austrian society treats a "great man," of how it comprehends his biography as "its own," and of how it can incorporate this individual history in collective history. It is the "greatness" of Kreisky that induces his biographers to study his person. However, it is this same greatness that prevents a comprehensive assessment of the "Kreisky phenomenon": when focused on the person, political analyses will come to nothing; the "privatization" of politics precludes a social analysis or a critical position going beyond a statement on details of the biography. Depite the many Kreisky biographies already available, others will still have to be written.

NOTES

* The title of this article refers to a quotation from Albert Einstein ("Imagination is more than knowledge"), which was on Kreisky's desk in Mallorca together with a photograph of Albert Einstein (Elisabeth Horvath, *Ära oder Episode. Das Phänomen Bruno Kreiskys*. Vienna, 1989, 29).

1. Marc Bloch, *Apologie der Geschichte oder Der Beruf des Historikers* (Stuttgart: Klett, 1974), 43.

2. Jacques LeGoff, "Wie schreibt man eine Biographie?" in Fernand Braudel et al., *Der Historiker als Menschenfresser: Über den Beruf des Geschichtsschreibers* (Berlin: Wagenbach, 1990), 103.

3. Imanuel Geiss, "Die Rolle der Persönlichkeit in der Geschichte: Zwischen Überbewerten und Verdrängen," in *Persönlichkeit und Struktur in der Geschichte: Historische Bestandsaufnahme und didaktische Implikationen*, ed. Michael Bosch (Düsseldorf: Schwann, 1977), 10-24.

4. Dieter Riesenberger, "Biographie als historiographisches Problem," in *Persönlichkeit und Struktur in der Geschichte*, 25.

5. LeGoff, 103.

6. Ibid., 105; For LeGoff, a scholarly, responsible biography consists of a "Präsentation und Deutung eines individuellen Lebens innerhalb der Geschichte," which does not ignore the results of the methodological and theoretical discussions about a new concept of history, ibid., 107. He states further, "Was ich an der gegenwärtigen Biographienflut so bedauerlich finde, ist, daß viele von ihnen nichts weiter sind als reine und schlichte Wiederholungen der traditionellen, oberflächlichen, anekdotischen Biographie, die nach platten chronologischen Kriterien verfährt, einer überlebten Psychologie huldigt und unfähig ist, die allgemeine historische Bedeutung eines individuellen Lebens aufzuzeigen," ibid., 105.

7. Christian Meier, "Die Faszination des Biographischen," in *Das Interesse an der Geschichte*, ed. Frank Niess (Frankfurt: Campus, 1989), 100: "Da Menschen sich zumeist für nichts so interessieren wie für Menschen, kann solche Teilnahme an einem anderen, einem Fremden, ein solches Nachgehen seiner Wege von hohem Reiz sein. Man pflegt sich in irgendeiner Weise mit dem Dargestellten zu identifizieren. Man kann kaum der Versuchung entgehen, sich weitgehend in ihn hineinzuversetzen. Von irgendeinem Punkt an ist man derart engagiert, daß man gar nicht genug über ihn lernen kann. Am liebsten würde man sein Leben gleichsam verlängern."

8. Ibid., 109: "Die Spielräume, die seine Gesellschaft dem Handeln bot, die Grenzen, die sie seinem Denken setzte, die Horizonte, das Verhältnis zwischen politischem Handeln und langfristigen Prozessen, zwischen großer und kleiner Geschichte, zwischen den Geschlechtern, vielleicht die Eigenart der Religion, der Philosophie, vermutlich die Besonderheit der Motivstrukturen und das spezifische Eingebundensein in die Zeit - dies und vieles andere ist da von Interesse. Und es muß deutlich gemacht werden in seiner bedingenden Kraft, im Rahmen der Verhältnisse, die es mit anderen Faktoren zusammen bildet."

9. Arno Mohr, "Die Rolle der Persönlichkeit in politischen Institutionen: Biographische Ansätze in der Politikwissenschaft," BIOS 1990, 232.

10. Ibid., 234.

11. Alan J. P. Taylor, "The Historian as Biographer," in *Biographie und Geschichtswissenschaft: Aufsätze zur Theorie und Praxis biographischer Arbeit*, ed. Grete Klingenstein, Heinrich Lutz and Gerald Stourzh (Vienna: Verlag für Geschichte und Politik, 1979), 254.

12. Thougths about "biography as a construction" and a concrete example of it can be found in Rudolf G. Ardelt, "Friedrich Adler—aus psychohistorischer Sicht," in *"Andere" Biographien und ihre Quellen: Biographische Zugänge zur Geschichte der Arbeiterbewegung. Ein Tagungsbericht*, ed. Manfred Lechner and Peter Wilding (Vienna: Europa-Verlag, 1992), 17-26.

13. Albrecht Lehmann, *Erzählstruktur und Lebenslauf: Autobiographische Untersuchungen* (Frankfurt: Campus, 1983), 22.

14. Ibid., 21.

15. Johannes Kunz, *Ich bin der Meinung ... Kreisky in Witz und Anekdote* (Vienna: Molden, 1974); *Also sprach Bruno K. Aussprüche*, gesammelt von Christian Röttinger; *Karikaturen v. Rudolf Angerer* (Vienna: Amalthea, 1981); *Bruno 70: Der österreichische Bundeskanzler in der politischen Karikatur. Eine Ausstellung aus Anlaß des siebzigsten Geburtstages von Dr. Bruno Kreisky* (Vienna: Ulysses, 1981).

16. Viktor Reimann, *Bruno Kreisky: Das Porträt eines Staatsmannes* (Vienna: Molden, 1972), 7.

17. Ibid., 17.

18. Karl Heinz Ritschel, "Der Pragmatiker: Sozialdemokrat ohne Dogma," in Paul Lendvai and Karl Heinz Ritschel, *Kreisky: Porträt eines Staatsmannes* (Vienna: Szolnay, 1974), 9.

19. Elisabeth Horvath, *Ära oder Episode? Das Phänomen Bruno Kreisky* (Vienna: Kremayr and Scheriau, 1989), 7.

20. Reimann, 9.

21. Johannes Kunz, ed., *Die Ära Kreisky: Stimmen zu einem Phänomen* (Vienna: Molden, 1975).

22. Erich Bielka, Peter Jankowitsch and Hans Thalberg, eds., *Die Ära Kreisky: Schwerpunkte der österreichischen Außenpolitik* (Vienna: Europa Verlag, 1983).

23. Elisabeth Horvath.

24. Erich Fröschl and Helge Zoitl, eds., *Der österreichische Weg 1970-1985: Fünfzehn Jahre, die Österreich verändert haben. Beiträge zum wissenschaftlichen Symposion des Dr.-Karl-Renner-Instituts, abgehalten vom 27. Februar bis 1. März 1985 in Wien* (Vienna: Europa Verlag, 1986); here (299-311) is also Bruno Kreisky's article "Der österreichische Weg."

25. See Lendvai and Ritschel, and Reimann.

26. Walter Raming, *Von Marx bis Kreisky: Wege und Ziele des Sozialismus 1888-2000. Berichte zur Zeitgeschichte* (Vienna: Reichsbund, Landesverband Niederösterreich, 1979).

27. Walter Pollak, *Sozialismus in Österreich: Von der Donaumonarchie zur Ära Kreisky* (Vienna: Econ Verlag, 1979).

28. Reimann, 17.

29. Karl Heinz Ritschel, "Der Pragmatiker: Sozialdemokrat ohne Dogma," in Lendvai/Ritschel, *Kreisky: Porträt eines Staatsmannes* (Vienna: Zsolnay, 1974), 7-12.

30. Paul Lendvai, "Der Beginner: Mut zum Unvollendeten," in Lendvai/Ritschel, *Kreisky: Porträt eines Staatsmannes* (Vienna: Szolnay, 1974), 127-208.

31. Horvath, 167-184.

32. Alexander Vodopivec, *Die Quadratur des Kreisky. Österreich zwischen parlamentarischer Demokratie und Gewerkschaftsstaat* (Vienna: Molden, 1973).

33. Walter Jambor, *"Das Ende wird furchtbar sein!" Wird das Ende furchtbar sein? Österreicher unter und nach Kreisky* (Vienna: Verlag Herold, 1982).

34. Anton Pelinka, "Die Ära Kreisky: Zur symbiotischen Adaptionsfähigkeit der Sozialdemokratie," in *Auf dem Weg zur Staatspartei: Zu Geschichte und Politik der SPÖ seit 1945*, ed. Peter Pelinka, and Gerhard Steger (Vienna: Verlag für Gesellschaftskritik, 1988), 58.

35. Horvath, 8.

36. Ibid., 90-92.

37. Ibid., 105.

38. Ibid., 44.

39. Ibid., 55.

40. Ibid., 45.

41. Ibid., 49.

42. Ibid., 50; for Kreisky's ability to handle the mass media cf. Roland Burkhart, *Politikerdiskussionen im Fernsehen. Eine Rezeptionsanalyse der TV-Diskussion zwischen Bruno Kreisky und Alois Mock aus Anlaß der Nationalsratswahlen 1983* (Vienna: Literas Verlag, 1983).

43. Ibid., 77.

44. Stella Klein-Löw, *Bruno Kreisky: Ein Porträt in Worten* (Vienna: Verlag Jungbrunnen, 1983), 10.

45. Ibid., 13.

46. Ibid., 130-141.

47. Ibid., 149.

48. Ibid., 91.

49. Ibid., 5.

50. Eva Böck, "Die Schulbuchaktion: Ein Beitrag zur österreichischen Wirtschafts- und Sozialpolitik der 'Ära Kreisky'," Masters thesis, University of Vienna, 1990.

51. Gunnar Staubmann, "Die entwicklungspolitische Standortsuche der österreichischen Sozialdemokratie von ihren Anfängen bis zum Beginn der 'Ära Kreisky': Versuch einer ideengeschichtlichen Analyse," Ph.D. dissertation, University of Graz.

52. Mehdi Fallah-Nodeh, "Die Beziehungen Österreichs zum Iran unter der SPÖ-Alleinregierung 1970-1983," Ph.D. dissertation, University of Vienna, 1986.

53. Ernst Weinisch, "Bruno Kreisky: Politik in Europa und Nahost. Ein Vergleich mit der Gegenwart," Ph.D. dissertation, University of Vienna, 1991.

54. Gerda Falkner, "Politische Beziehungen, Wirtschaftsbeziehungen und Entwicklungshilfe in der österreichischen Außenpolitik gegenüber Lateinamerika 1970-1983," Masters thesis, University of Vienna, 1987.

55. Ernst Weinisch's study is a typical example of the fact that the quality of a scholarly investigation is largely dependent on the author's recognition and assessment of his own initial stance. The "admiration" for a historical personality, about which the author speaks in his preface, is substantiated neither by a critical factual analysis, nor by a reading of the extensive literature on the Middle East problem.

56. *Die Ära Kreisky*, 13.

57. Ibid., 13.

58. Oliver Rathkolb and Irene Etzersdorfer, eds., *Der junge Kreisky: Schriften, Reden, Dokumente* (Vienna: Verlag für Jugend und Volk, 1986).

59. Ibid., 21.

60. For example the following publications by Kreisky: *Die Herausforderung: Politik an der Schwelle des Atomzeitalters* (Düsseldorf: Econ Verlag, 1963); *Aspekte des demokratischen Sozialismus: Aufsätze, Reden, Interviews* (Munich: List, 1974); *Neutralität und Koexistenz: Aufsätze und Reden* (Munich: List, 1975); *Willy Brandt, Bruno Kreisky, Olof Palme, Briefe und Gespräche 1972 bis 1975* (Frankfurt: Europäische Verlagsanstalt, 1975); *Die Zeit in der wir leben: Betrachtungen zur internationalen Politik* (Vienna: Molden, 1978); *Politik braucht Visionen: Aufsätze, Reden und Interviews zu aktuellen weltpolitischen Fragen* (Königstein/Taunus: Athenäum, 1982); *Das Nahostproblem: Reden. Interviews. Kommentare* (Vienna: Europa Verlag, 1985); *Bruno Kreisky, Reden*, vols. 1 and 2 (Vienna: Verlag der Österreichischen Staatsdruckerei, 1981).

61. Bruno Kreisky, *Zwischen den Zeiten: Erinnerungen aus fünf Jahrzehnten* (Berlin: Siedler, 1986); *Im Strom der Politik: Der Memoiren zweiter Teil* (Berlin: Siedler, 1988).

62. Kreisky, *Zwischen den Zeiten*, 483.

63. Gernot Böhme, "Lebensgestalt und Zeitgeschichte," in *BIOS*, 1990, 140.

64. Christoph Reinprecht, *Zurückgekehrt: Identität und Bruch in der Biographie österreichischer Juden* (Vienna: Braumüller, 1992).

65. Böhme, 148.

66. Ibid., 148.

67. Martin van Amerongen, *Kreisky und seine unbewältigte Gegenwart* (Graz: Styria, 1977); see also the Secher essay in this volume.

68. Reinprecht, *Zurückgekehrt*, 9: "Identität ... konstituiert sich inter-subjektiv im Handeln zweier Individuen; in konkreten Prozessen sozialer Interaktion, in der die Selbstansprüche einzelner um wechselseitige Anerkennung konkurrieren."

69. These are the opening thoughts on the issues of Jewish identity in Reinprecht, *Zurückgekehrt*, 3-4.

70. Kreisky, *Im Strom der Politik*, 274-306.

71. Thomas Luckmann, "Persönliche Identität und Lebenslauf: Gesellschaftliche Voraussetzungen," in *Biographie und Geschichtswissenschaft*, 43.

72. *Bruno Kreisky. Fotografiert von Konrad R. Müller. Texte von Gerhard Roth, Peter Turrini* (Berlin: Nicolaische Verlagsbuchhandlung; Forum Verlag, 1981), 17, 18, 66.

73. Ibid., 6-8.

74. Irene Etzersdorfer, *Kreiskys große Liebe: Inszenierungen eines Staatsmannes* (Vienna: Kremayr and Scheriau, 1987).

75. Ibid., 6.

Austrian Jews from Emancipation to Holocaust

John Haag

The last dozen or so years have witnessed an extraordinary outpouring of research into the history of one of modern Europe's most creative urban minorities, the Jews of Vienna. The English-speaking world's recent fascination with Viennese culture can be dated to 1980 and the appearance of Carl Schorske's *Fin de Siecle Vienna*, a book that became that rara avis—a superbly written work of impeccable scholarship that became a best-seller.[1] A collection of seven essays rather than a volume written at one sitting, *Fin de Siecle Vienna* nevertheless was able to introduce its readers to several major themes of Austrian history since 1848: the decline and fall of liberalism in the last decades of the nineteenth century, the creation of a new and increasingly negative political style exemplified in the careers of Georg von Schönerer and Karl Lueger, and the breathtaking creativity of Viennese culture in the years before 1914. Schorske's book was a stimulating attempt to explain how the coming of cultural modernity in late Habsburg Vienna was the result of a complex interaction of abstract ideas and often brutal political realities, and not surprisingly, it was full of information on the role played in these events by Sigmund Freud, Theodor Herzl, Gustav Mahler, Arnold Schoenberg and other Jewish intellectual luminaries. While Schorske's book was in many ways a superb work of intellectual history, its outline of "politics in a new key" did little more than present a bare outline of how the disintegration of liberal ideals made possible a rapid emergence of new political values largely based on fear, hatred and resentment. Neither did Schorske focus on the most ominous development of Viennese mass politics of the 1880s and 1890s, the emergence of a powerful anti-Semitic movement or how the Jewish community responded to it. It was clear that his path-breaking volume was an invitation and a challenge to other scholars to dig more deeply into these problems.

Even before Schorske appeared on the scene, a few hardy pioneers had begun to clear the academic forest for others to settle and plough. The first significant study of political anti-Semitism in Austria was published in 1964 by the Peter Pulzer, Gladstone Professor of Government and Public Administration and Fellow of All Souls College at Oxford University. This groundbreaking analysis of the socioeconomic roots of anti-Semitism in the closing decades of the nineteenth century remains eminently worth reading almost three decades after its appearance. Fortunately, it has been reprinted in a revised edition that includes a new introduction and a bibliographical note listing the great majority of works that have appeared on the subject of Austro-German anti-Semitism in the last quarter century.[2] Pulzer's book appeared to satisfy the scholarly world's interest in this topic for over a decade, and it was not until 1975, with the publication of Andrew Whiteside's superbly researched political biography of Georg von Schönerer, that another serious publication in this area was available to study and debate.[3] In this and other works, Whiteside made a strong case for the Austrian origins of National Socialism, showing how Hitler's ideas had developed in a political and ideological milieu that would one day foster a full-scale mass totalitarian racist movement. We had to wait another decade and a half for the first English-language biography of the other major anti-Semitic political figure of late Habsburg Austria, Karl Lueger. In his 1990 biography of Lueger, Richard Geehr summed up his many years of assiduous investigations in Viennese libraries and archives, showing how despite his genial personality and genuine accomplishments as a municipal reformer, Lueger left behind a legacy of anti-Semitic demagogy whose "moderation" could one day be easily transformed into a murderous biological racism by other, even less principled masters of crowd manipulation.[4]

These studies, while all of great value for an understanding of Austrian anti-Semitism, did little to provide information about the victims of racial hatred, the Jews of Habsburg Austria-Hungary and the post-1918 First Austrian Republic. Not until the 1980s did significant studies of Austrian Jewry appear in print; fortunately, once these studies began appearing, it seemed that floodgates were opened, and within a few years a great number of significant works had become available. The first of these works, by the gifted young American historian Marsha Rozenblit, appeared in 1984. It was the first comprehensive modern study of the Viennese Jewish community in the late Francisco-Josephinian era.[5] In point of fact, few works of any significance had been written about Vienna's Jews in this century, the works of Sigmund Mayer (1917) and Hans Tietze (1933) being among the few of value, and it was obvious that these efforts were long obsolete. Utilizing a wide range of both archival and published sources, Rozenblit shows convincingly how Jews in Vienna from the years 1867 through 1914 became acculturated to Austro-German society, but nevertheless were never completely absorbed or assimilated by the dominant gentile culture. Vienna's Jewish population in these last decades of Habsburg rule became increasingly socially mobile; relatively few, however, converted to Christianity, chose to marry non-Jews or completely shed their Jewish identity. The great majority of these "new Viennese," who had migrated in three waves, first from Bohemia-Moravia, then from Hungary and finally from Galicia, became salaried, white-collar employees in commerce and industry. Contrary to the anti-Semitic stereotypes common in Austria from the 1860s to the Nazi era, most of Jews did not enter the ranks of the super-rich *Besitz- und Bildungsbürgertum*, but instead lived relatively modest existences as salaried employees in the private sector.

In what ways, besides their Jewish ancestry, did Vienna's Jews differ from their Christian neighbors? First, they did not live throughout the city's *Bezirke* but were to be found concentrated in only three districts: Leopoldstadt, Innere Stadt and Alsergrund. In these districts, rich Jews often lived next to middle-class or even poor Jews. Unlike their gentile fellow-Viennese, Jews rarely moved to new districts when their personal wealth increased. Jews also differed markedly from non-Jews when it came to attitudes toward education. By the 1870s it had become dramatically clear that Jewish boys were attending *Gymnasien* at a far higher percentage of the population than the Jewish minority represented in the overall Viennese population. While Jews were roughly 10 percent of the city's population, about 30 percent of boys enrolled in its *Gymnasien* were Jewish. Rozenblit notes that a clear cause for such overrepresentation cannot be easily discovered, since many of the students were poor and thus not part of an attempt to advertise family success, and the chances of social advancement based on educational credentials or the cultivation of personal contacts made in school were remote in view of the accelerating anti-Semitism of Austrian society at the end of the nineteenth century. Whatever the reason, Viennese Jews, including young women in the years before 1914, placed a much greater value on education than the rest of the Viennese population, which looked at all forms of schooling from a narrowly practical perspective of immediate income-enhancement.

Rozenblit's study also provided some fascinating insights into the development of political consciousness among the Jews of Vienna. As modern biological anti-Semitism appeared on the scene strarting in the late 1870s, the intellectual challenge of this new genre of prejudice let to the creation of new forms of self-defense as well as new ideological configurations within the Jewish community. The most important of these was, of course, Zionism, a movement inextricably linked with the journalist and visionary Theodor Herzl. But despite the growth of anti-Semitism, the Zionist response appealed to very few Vienna Jews, most of whom were white-collar employees with minimal interest in politics—Jewish or otherwise. Despite massive efforts to mobilize these middle-class Jews for the Zionist cause in the early years of the movement (six different Zionist organizations were created to appeal to the Jewish office workers of Vienna), the response was disappointing to Herzl and his successors since none of the organizations could boast of a membership of more than about one hundred. Zionist appeals during national elections also fell on deaf ears in Vienna. In the general election of 1907, the overwhelmingly Jewish Leopoldstadt district ignored the emotional appeals of Zionist candidate Isidor Schalit, providing him with only 529 of the 9,398 votes cast. The winner, who survived a dirty campaign orchestrated by the Zionist press, was an assimilated Jew whose political platform was one of German, not Jewish, nationalism.

The Rozenblit study will long remain a major source of information on the social and economic profile of Vienna's Jewish community in its golden decades under Emperor Franz Josef. Dealing as it does with that community as a collective body of average men and women who worked, paid their taxes, raised their families and worshipped on the Sabbath, it by definition did not deal with the exceptional individuals whose artistic and literary creativity helped make Vienna in the years just before and after 1900 a seedbed of the modern Western world. Fortunately, in recent years other young scholars have begun to investigate various facets of the Viennese Jewish intelligentsia. Two major studies in Viennese cultural and intellectual history that appeared in 1989 now provide scholars with much information as well as with several basic themes around which the often overwhelming masses of data can be structured.[6]

Robert Wistrich has summed up several decades of intensive study of Jewish Vienna in a magisterial volume that skillfully weaves the political, religious and cultural strands of the Jewish experience in Vienna from the revolution of 1848 to the final days of World War I into a rich tapestry depicting one of the most creative periods of modern Central European history. In a book that will be stimulating to both scholars and the educated general reading public, Wistrich presents a vast panorama of notables, artists and intellectuals who in one way or another reflected in their creative as well as their personal lives the basic fact of their Jewishness. Wistrich sees the extraordinary intellectual fecundity of *fin-de-siècle* Vienna as a distinctly Jewish moral response to a modern world in chaos, a response by Jews who had in many instances lost their moorings in a clearly defined Hebrew religious tradition. Acculturated Viennese Jews such as the writer Karl Kraus attempted to strip the hypocrisy from their city's social institutions but, eventually defeated, became little more than embittered, cynical prophets of gloom. The optimism initially felt by many Jewish bourgeois intellectuals in the last third of the nineteenth century had by the early years of this century become a mood of dark despair and self-hate, perhaps best exemplified by the philosopher of misogyny Otto Weininger, for whom the only way out of a self-created cage of despair was suicide at age twenty-three. Even Jews who retained after 1918 a sentimental love for the ideals of Old Austria, like the Galician-born Jewish monarchist and religious apostate Joseph Roth, were resigned to the "Austrian sickness" (*morbus Austriacus*) that would soon sweep away all traces of their doomed world. As Wistrich's fine study makes clear, it was the Jews of Vienna who had the most to lose when the firestorm of 1914-1918 destroyed the already shaky edifice of bourgeois, liberal European civilization. This was the world that had emancipated them from their ghetto, but the freedom it granted them was of short duration.

In his suggestive study, Steven Beller presents an impressive case for the idea that the great bulk of Viennese culture during the period was produced by Jews, and that much of what agitated their hearts and souls and thus stimulated their creativity was derived from traditionally Jewish values and ideals. Beller not only substantiates with impressive statistical analyses the important role Jews played in fin-de-siècle Vienna; he also presents the provocative thesis that the Viennese Jewish intelligentsia had a moral creed all its own contrasting drastically with the morally lackadaisical and intellectually lazy dominant Austrian Catholic culture. In Beller's view, the essence of the modern Viennese cultural temperament that emerged in the last years of the nineteenth century was made possible by the appearance of an intensely serious Jewish bourgeoisie. Profoundly influenced by the ideals of the Enlightenment, these assimilated Jews believed that the solid virtues of the Age of Reason could somehow be restored to a society gone soft through moral decay and general frivolousness. In the creative efforts of such relentlessly aggressive *Kulturkritiker* as Karl Kraus, Beller sees a powerful spirit of "radical ethical individualism" that rose above the soft-headedness of the dominant gentile culture of Vienna. The same piercing sense of moral integrity could be found in the intellectual edifices created by other Viennese intellectuals of Jewish background, including the philosopher Ludwig Wittgenstein, whose innovative philosophy of language was suffused with a powerful spirit of "stoicism," the revolutionary musical innovator Arnold Schönberg, and the clinically objective literary observer of a culture in decay, Arthur Schnitzler. In essence, Beller sees the Viennese Jewish intelligentsia leading the forces of a crusading ethical humanism, taking sides against the obscurantist powers that remained powerfully entrenched in Austrian culture.

This is not the place for an extended critique of the Beller and Wistrich volumes, both of which will remain indispensable sources in the debate over the Jewish contribution to the modern Western spirit in Vienna. But a few comments may be of value for those who wish to pursue this theme in their own research. There can be little doubt that Steven Beller argues his points persuasively and even passionately; but when he tries to depict virtually all of modern Viennese culture as being Jewish—Jewish in that its major practitioners came from Jewish backgrounds, and Jewish in that it invariably was a reflection of moral issues central to the Jewish religious tradition—he advances a thesis that is as difficult to defend as it is superficially beguiling. While Vienna's Jews comprised about one-third of that city's educated population in the years before 1914, they by no means represented the entire educated middle class of the Habsburg capital, and it must be remembered that Viennese society remained dominated by an aristocracy and upper bourgeoisie that was, despite some intermarriage and social mingling, essentially non-Jewish. The notion that Jewish intellectuals' concern for an individualistic ethic based on Enlightenment ideals had as its deepest source of inspiration the traditional values of Judaism ignores the deep rejection by these same intellectuals of their own Hebraic background, which many of them saw as an ignorant and hopelessly backward ghetto *Weltanschauung*. Assimilation was an often painful process of denying one's own intellectual and cultural origins, and traditional Judaic values were essentially incompatible with the secular ideals of individualism and intellectual emancipation so strongly held by Vienna's profoundly Germanized Jewish intellectuals.

Not only because it is a much bigger book, but also because it looks at its subject more broadly and more subtly, the Wistrich study repays the considerable effort needed to master its detailed examination of an extraordinarily complex Jewish community. Where Beller sees Jewish intellectuals fearlessly advocating a secular faith based on the human capacity to exercise critical intellect, Wistrich discovers signs of despair, hopelessness and apocalyptic nihilism. These attitudes, Wistrich suggests, did not emerge in social or intellectual isolation, but rather can be seen deriving from the never-resolved problem of how to proceed with acculturation and assimilation into the dominant Christian culture. In this context, it is not surprising that many Jewish artists and intellectuals--struggling with the dual problems of making sense of the maddening complexities of capitalist society and understanding what place assimilated Jewish individuals would have in the new Central European cultural order—were deeply pessimistic. The sense of moral rootlessness and spritual isolation was by no means a unique experience for Jewish intellectuals in the German *Sprachraum*; but more than any other group, Jews suffered the agonies of modernization. As the rational values of liberal humanism began to evaporate in the closing decades of the nineteenth century, assimilated Jewish writers and artists began to find themselves increasingly isolated and exposed to the growing forces of irrational anti-modernism and to Germanic notions of organic communities that were malignantly hostile to the "un-German" ideals of emancipated Jewry.

The studies of Wistrich and Beller concentrate on showing how and why extraordinary energies were released by the Jews of Austria during Europe's great era of bourgeois supremacy. By focusing on Vienna, however, they have chosen to ignore the larger imperial context in which Viennese Jewry flourished. Fortunately, this larger framework has now been examined with great skill and insight by a scholar who has already published excellent work on the history of Hungarian Jews, William McCagg, Jr.[7] In this pioneering work, McCagg presents a well-organized synthesis of Habsburg Jewry from the last expulsion of Jews from Vienna in 1670 to the collapse of the Dual Monarchy in November 1918. By concentrating on a broad survey of the economic and social progress of the Jews of Vienna, Prague, and Budapest from the late eighteenth to early twentieth centuries, McCagg shows in splendid detail how emancipation radically altered not only the Jewish communities themselves but the larger societies in which Jews lived and flourished. The treatment here is almost of necessity the history of economic and cultural elites, given the fact that poor people, even if they represent the majority of a community, rarely leave behind significant written records.

One of the most valuable insights to be found in McCagg's survey is his emphasis on the deep divisions that could be found within Austro-Hungarian Jewry. Not only did the monarchy's Jews find themselves divided along religious lines, ranging from the ultra-Orthodoxy still adhered to by a significant minority (particularly in Galicia) to the Liberal Judaism practiced by the assimilated urban bourgeoisie, but they also were profoundly affected by the nationality struggles of the day. As nationality tensions increased after 1867, Jews often found themselves in the unenviable position of being forced to choose between competing nationalisms. In many instances, the Jews felt compelled to change their cultural identity (in Prague, this meant abandoning German language and culture for that of the emerging Czech majority), a process that for some proved to be traumatic. Besides producing much individual anguish, the upheavals and transformations imposed on a Jewish community already struggling to assimilate rapid changes also acted as a cultural catalyst, fuelling an extraordinary outpouring of artistic productivity.

The almost unbearable tensions experienced by Jewish intellectuals in late Habsburg Austria-Hungary led not only to personal neuroses but also served to foster an extraordinary explosion of creativity. Cultural rootlessness acted as a stimulus to the emergence brilliant conductor and composer Gustav Mahler not only summed up his own insoluble predicament, but also put his finger on the major source of creative tensions energizing his passionate musicality when he described himself as being "thrice homeless: as a Bohemian among Austrians; as an Austrian among Germans; and as a Jew everywhere." McCagg organizes much of his material around the thesis that the economic and cultural transformation of Habsburg Jewry was the result of a massive decades-long process of "national self-demolition." More than any other group in the Dual Monarchy, the Jews fled from their past, hoping to arrive at a secular millenium once the travails of assimilation had ended. But, as McCagg and George Berkley[8] both argue persuasively, the price of what appeared at the time to be full acceptance by the dominant gentile society could be extraordinarily high.

Assimilation often led to feelings of self-denial and self-hatred, much of which was doubtless sublimated, but which could on occasion surface as in the case of Otto Weininger, a brilliant but emotionally tortured Jewish writer who committed suicide in 1903 (Hitler later praised Weininger as the only Jew who drew the logical consequences of his own Jewishness, that is, by taking his own life). Berkley's book was intended for a popular audience, but unfortunately it does its potential readers a grave disservice: not only is it full of minor errors, but it is also too critical of Vienna's pre-

1938 Jewish community being unable to predict or prepare for a catastrophe that would destroy it during the Hitler years. Thus, most Viennese Jews are made to appear like fools who simply could not read the handwriting on the wall. The wise ones, as he sees it, were the small minority of Zionist and Orthodox Jews who repeatedly warned their fellow Jews of the dangers of complacency and denial of Jewishness. This crudely simplistic approach, while doubtlessly giving some readers a sense of moral superiority, ignores the fact that most Austrian Jews knew that they were resented and that they could never fully participate in society, but also quite reasonably believed that in time the lingering vestiges of prejudice would be overcome.

Much more valuable for a serious study of the failure of Austrian Jewish assimilation is an extraordinary volume by Leo Spitzer, a scholar whose own life history has provided him with unusually rich insights into the difficulties of assimilation in the modern world.[9] Born in Bolivia to Jewish parents who had fled persecution in Austria, Spitzer emigrated to the United States at the age of ten. He was thus was subjected to another round of acculturation and assimilation, a process that he candidly admits in the introduction to his book has never succeeded in totally absorbing him. As a naturalized American, Spitzer went on to become a respected expert in African culture and history, but, probably prompted by personal experiences, he was drawn to investigate the question of assimilation of diverse cultures on different continents. The result of this personal quest was the book *Lives in Between*, a bold and brilliant study in comparative history that studies the May family of Sierra Leone, West Africa, the Rebouças family of Brazil, and the Brettauer and Zweig families of Austria. The May family rose from slavery to the extent that one of its members became Mayor of Freetown, Sierra Leone, whereas in Brazil the mulatto Rebouças family moved up the social and economic ladder to produce many successful professionals. In Austria, the Brettauer and Zweig families escaped from the poverty and cultural confinement of the Jewish ghettoes of Eastern Europe to participate in the economic and cultural life of a rich and powerful continental empire, in time producing a number of eminent individuals, including the world-famous author Stefan Zweig.

In all three families, powerful forces of social change were affecting individuals as a result of the revolutionary ideologies of emancipation that first appeared on the world stage in France in 1789. In time, these ideas crossed oceans and radically transformed human aspirations and social structures in Asia, Africa and the Americas. Two basic ideas strike one after reading the Spitzer book: first, that the vivid life histories of families on three continents are united by the fact that their emancipation could only take place within a specific social, economic and ideological context. Only in an era of self-proclaimed emancipation could groups previously excluded from wealth, power and influence be incorporated into the governing center of the system. The second theme of Spitzer's work is that despite their quite extraordinary achievements, in all three instances the descendants of these families remained alienated and significantly excluded from the mainstream of society, retaining powerful feelings of rejection and marginality. Not surprisingly, a high level of personal frustration and unhappiness can be seen in these seemingly successful families of still-outsiders.

By the end of the nineteenth century, barriers to complete assimilation began to be erected throughout the world as racist ideologies emerged. Seen from this broadly comparative perspective, the appearance of Schönerer and Lueger was part of a universal reaction to the emancipatory impulses unleashed in 1789 and redefined in 1848. Intellectuals among the newly freed minorities now felt compelled to create new ideals to deal with a radically changed world in which emancipation had failed; Zionism and negritude were the fruits of this new mood. Under extreme cultural and personal stress, several of these intellectuals—including Stefan Zweig—committed suicide. All students of Austrian history should read this beautifully researched comparative and cross-cultural study of the travails of assimilation in modern times.

Only in the last few years have significant studies of anti-Semitism in twentieth century Austria been attempted. While the theme necessarily pervades many monographs dealing with contemporary Austrian history,[10] specialized investigations have only come about as a result of the opening up of the Austrian State Archives in the early 1970s, and much more importantly, because of the emergence of a new generation of Austrian historians. Free of the inhibitions and fears of their elders, an intellectually critical group of men and women have been conducting a thoroughgoing (and sometimes painful) analysis of a part of Austria's recent past that was as much consciously suppressed as it was naturally forgotten.[11] The intellectual electricity generated in Austria served to energize foreign, particulary American and British historians, who have in recent years competed amiably with their Austrian colleagues to probe the past of a nation, much of whose psychic energy since 1945 has gone into denying responsibility or guilt. The international controversy raised in 1986 over Kurt Waldheim's wartime activities also accelerated a heightened interest in the sensitive topic of Austria and its Jews. Even before the

Waldheim affair, ongoing academic interest in the Austrian variant of European anti-Semitism was starting to produce first-class works of scholarship.

Published in 1987, the collection of thirteen papers that resulted from a colloquium on Austrian anti-Semitism held in Paris in 1985 was a triumph of clear writing and skilled editing.[12] While obviously only a full reading of this book can give one a clear idea of its many insights, a few highlights should nonetheless be mentioned here. In his cogent essay, Bruce Pauley points out how the roots of post-1918 Viennese anti-Semitism were already to be found in the deeply troubled world of the late nineteenth century, which had rejected liberalism not only as a political and economic credo but as a valid outline of humane social conduct as well. Steven Beller, writing about the tensions of culture and social class in Vienna, argues persuasively that by the end of the nineteenth century there had come into existence several Viennas: a dynamic and modern city creating new forms of mass political mobilization, an essentially aristocratic culture echoing themes from the world of the Baroque, and a literary and cultural realm of irrational fantasy and artistic energy often deriving inspiration from scenarios of violence and destruction. As Sigurd Scheichl points out in his essay, the complexities of Viennese anti-Semitic ideology were more often than not a reflection of the puzzling situation that city's Jewish community found itself in, being at the cutting edge of intellectual and cultural life while at the same time almost completely frozen out of the political process. Not surprisingly, as Walter Weitzmann shows in his brief but informative study of the Vienna *Kultusgemeinde*, the growing pressures of resentment and open hatred faced by Vienna's Jews rarely resulted in unity but in fact often heightened internal divisions and tensions. As Viennese Jewry moved toward the challenge of Nazi racism in the 1930s, it was a deeply fragmented community, uncertain of which survival strategies to choose.

A recently published study of the Vienna Jewish *Kultusgemeinde* by Harriet Pass Freidenreich[13] presents in much greater detail the problems sketched by the Weitzmann essay. In this clearly organized and impressively researched monograph, Freidenreich delves deeply into sources scattered from New York to Vienna and Jerusalem to study the *Kultusgemeinde* as a microcosm of Jewish political behavior. Much more effectively than any previous scholar, she sheds light on how Viennese Jews during the interwar decades defined themselves (either as a nation or as a religious community), on how Jews tried to create their own political parties and lobbies to defend their own interests, on the attitudes exhibited toward the already existing political parties they voted for and became active in, and on the extent to which anti-Semitism determined Jewish voting patterns. In point of fact, there was no single, unified group of Jews comprising anything remotely resembling a community. Viennese Jewry in 1918 was, and had for many decades been, an extremely heterogeneous group that ranged from a miniscule elite of ennobled bankers and industrialists, to solidly bourgeois professionals, down to utterly destitute Galician refugees whose Orthodox religion and Yiddish linguistic identity were culturally alien to the majority of assimilated Viennese Jews.

Freidenreich's book focuses primarily on those who consciously identified themselves as Jews, thus placing considerably less emphasis on members of the group of assimilated Jews who officially opted out of the Jewish community but who were certainly still regarded by anti-Semites as Jews. As a comparative study in Jewish ethnopolitics that examines attitudes and behavior on the communal, local and national levels, this is a study that assumes the reader comes to it with substantial background information. Like the Rozenblit study of almost a decade earlier, this too is a dissection of collective behavior; as such it is often dry and monochromatic, virtually ignoring individual personalities as leaders. It is hoped that the author, who has shown her skill and energy in this book, will go beyond the workings of the *Kultusgemeinde* in her next major work and present a panoramic view of the entire Viennese Jewish community, regardless of its degree of religious or national affiliation. But this wish should not be taken as a criticism of the work under review, which is first-rate in every way because of its understated, calm presentation and strong scholarly apparatus. This book conveys a lasting impression of the extraordinarily volatile and acrimonious nature of Jewish communal politics in the interwar period. Vienna's Jews in the years after 1918 were a deeply divided community. The division was not so much along party-political or religious lines but along the fault line of assimilation to Austro-German culture versus adherence to old loyalties found among the *Ostjuden*, the newly arrived and less-assimilated Jews from Galicia. Political behavior also split along these lines, with non-Zionists following styles of political behavior laid down in the Jewish communities of Germany or Hungary. On the other hand, Zionists and others defining themselves as Jewish nationalists pursued quite different political strategies, reminiscent of those practiced in such multi-ethnic states as Czechoslovakia and Poland.

The final book under review is Bruce Pauley's recently published history of Austrian anti-Semitism.[14] The fruit of over a decade of research and writing, this work is in fact a study of political anti-Semitism in Austria since 1918, with the many centuries of essentially confessional Jew-hatred being confined to the first five (out of a total of twenty-one) chapters. Pauley adds to his laurels as an already respected expert in contemporary Austrian history with a book that deserves to appear in a German-language edition, especially in view of the need for a one-volume survey of this subject in an Austria that is still struggling with anti-Semitism in its recent past. Since the overwhelming majority of Austria's Jews lived in Vienna, and since that metropolis has totally dominated Austria since 1918, this book is actually a history of Viennese anti-Semitism, or at least of Austrian anti-Semitism as practiced in Vienna. Looking almost exclusively at Vienna is not only a reasonable approach; it also leaves open the door for another study—that of anti-Semitism in the other cities and towns of Austria, a study that would doubtless be a significant contribution to the vexing problem (found in post-1945 Austria, Germany and Poland) of "anti-Semitism without Jews".

Based on many years of research in Austrian, German, Israeli and American archives, Pauley's book will surely dominate the field for several decades. The book is clearly organized and written. It incorporates virtually every significant facet of the myriad forces that attacked the Jews of Austria in the 1920s and 1930s and stands as a veritable encyclopedia of racial discrimination and ethnic hatred in one nation. Of particular value is the information on such otherwise respectable political leaders as Ignaz Seipel and Leopold Kunschak, who at times worked the political arena as an informal team, with Kunschak making radical anti-Semitic proposals (declaring Jews a separate nationality to segregate them from the "German-Aryan" majority and consequently to limit severly their civil rights), and Seipel then making moderating comments on each Kunschak proposal. Also quite revealing are details on the occasional use of anti-Semitism by the Social Democrats and the extreme sensitivity of that party regarding its Jewish members, a concern that led it at times to develop strategies to avoid its being perceived as a *Judenschutztruppe*. Indeed, at times some Social Democrats made little distinction between the Jews as a group and the capitalist system they wished to overthrow. In one instance, Albert Sever, Social Democratic governor of Lower Austria in 1919, favored the wholesale expulsion of all aliens who had been inflicting harm on the economy—a group that in de facto terms largely consisted of Galician *Ostjuden*. Only the lack of transportation and, more significantly, diplomatic protests from the United States, halted this plan to rid the infant republic of a hated "army of profiteers."

The most praiseworthy sections of Pauley's book are those dealing with the grossly exaggerated racist estimates of the number of *Rassejuden* in Vienna (in 1932, for example, the crypto-Nazi newspaper estimated that there were 375,000 "racial Jews" in the Austrian capital, this number based on a count of Jewish-sounding names in the telephone directory). As is made clear, the low birth rate of Austrian Jewry meant that demographically both Jews and anti-Semites could reasonably expect a rapid decline of the Austrian Jewish population in the foreseeable future. Using a wide range of both official and polemical sources, Pauley has made a significant contribution to our understanding of cultural conflict and ethnic prejudice. He has shown good judgment by quoting extensively from the writings of such Austro-Nazi fanatics as Erich Führer (*nomen est omen!*) and Robert Körber (a notorious student demagogue who has been called the "Austrian Julius Streicher"), men whose extremism was in fact widely shared, particulary among the younger National Socialist "intellectuals" recruited throughout the 1920s and 1930s from the universities and other *Hochschulen* of Vienna, Graz and Innsbruck. Scarcely mentioned, but well worth including in this volume would have been some details on how Nazi propaganda constantly linked pernicious Jewish influences with such alarmingly "un-German" developments as the increasing frequency of divorces and abortions. Nazism was a militantly anti-emancipatory mass movement that tactically allied itself with various conservative elements hostile to social and gender upheaval. Indeed, for most Nazis, the emancipation of women could only be explained in conspiratorial terms, and at the heart of that conspiracy there was always to be found a Judeo-Bolshevik inner core (the murder of Hugo Bettauer immediately leaps to mind).

Pauley's calm, measured tone lends strength to his study, but at the same time tends to understate the hideously twisted, paranoid picture of Nazi anti-Semitic propaganda. Although it would have required considerable extra research, sources from occult circles (many such short-lived journals and newsletters were published in interwar Vienna) would have provided powerfully effective documentation of the fetid atmosphere of loony paranoia that held the Jews responsible for virtually every evidence of decay in the modern world. Raging Nazi hatred for such bourgeois cosmopolitan organizations as Freemasonry and the Esperanto movement, both of which were for Nazi and other *völkisch* ideologues totally Jewish-controlled phenomena, was a major component of the *Weltanschauung* of the radical Right in post-1918 Central Europe and should be documented in any revised edition of this generally commendable study. Only by reading Pauley's book can one begin to understand how, long before it became a horrifying reality, the Holocaust was born in the minds of men and women who lived in a society that believed that some of their neighbors and fellow-citizens were not, and could never become, completely "human" human beings. It is a terrible tale, but one that must be told in its full complexity. No doubt there will be further studies in this area, but the publications of the last decade on this subject have created a solid foundation on which other, more detailed investigations can be placed.

NOTES

1. Carl E. Schorske, *Fin-de-siecle Vienna: Politics and Culture* (New York: Alfred A. Knopf, 1980).

2. Peter Pulzer, *The Rise of Political Antisemitism in Germany & Austria*, revised edition (Cambridge, Mass.: Harvard University Press, 1988).

3. Andrew G. Whiteside, *The Socialism of Fools: Georg Ritter von Schönerer and Austrian Pan-Germanism* (Berkeley: University of California Press, 1975).

4. Richard S. Geehr, *Karl Lueger: Mayor of Fin de Siecle Vienna* (Detroit: Wayne State University Press, 1990).

5. Marsha L. Rozenblit, *The Jews of Vienna, 1867-1914: Assimilation and Identity* (Albany: State University of New York Press, 1984). Austrian Zionism in the late Habsburg era has been exhaustively probed in Adolf Gaisbauer, *Davidstern und Doppeladler: Zionismus und jüdischer Nationalismus in Österreich, 1882-1918* (Vienna: Verlag Böhlau, 1988).

6. Robert S. Wistrich, *The Jews of Vienna in the Age of Franz Joseph* [The Littman Library of Jewish Civilization] (New York: Oxford University Press, 1989); Steven Beller, *Vienna and the Jews, 1867-1938: A Cultural History* (New York: Cambridge University Press, 1989).

7. William O. McCagg, Jr., *A History of Habsburg Jews, 1670-1918* (Bloomington: Indiana University Press, 1989).

8. George E. Berkley, *Vienna and its Jews: The Tragedy of Success, 1880s-1980s* (Cambridge, Mass.: Madison Books, 1989).

9. Leo Spitzer, *Lives in Between: Assimilation and Marginality in Austria, Brazil, West Africa, 1780-1945* [Studies in Comparative World History] (New York: Cambridge University Press, 1989).

10. F. L. Carsten, *Fascist Movements in Austria: From Schönerer to Hitler* [SAGE Studies in 20th Century History, Vol. 7] (London: SAGE Publications, 1977), asserts (page 97) that "However disunited the *völkisch* camp might be and however much its rival leaders might quarrel there was one issue that united them—anti-Semitism." Although flawed by its lack of a theoretical framework, Carsten's study provides vast detail on the pervasive nature of anti-Semitic sentiments within the various Austrian Fascist and Nazi organizations.

11. Among the works of recent Austrian scholarship that concentrate on the destruction of Austrian Jewry during the years 1938-1945, as well as the lingering shadow of anti-Semitism in post-1945, Austria two studies are particularly noteworthy: Gernot Heiss, Siegfried Mattl, Sebastian Meissl, Edith Saurer and Karl Stuhlpfarrer, eds., *Willfährige Wissenschaft: Die Universität Wien 1938-1945* [Österreichische Texte zur Gesellschaftskritik, Vol. 43] (Vienna: Verlag für Gesellschaftskritik, 1989), and Sebastian Meissl, Klaus-Dieter Mulley and Oliver Rathkolb, eds., *Verdrängte Schuld, verfehlte Sühne: Entnazifizierung in Österreich 1945-1955. Symposion des Instituts für Wissenschaft und Kunst, Wien, März 1985* (Munich: R. Oldenbourg Verlag, 1986).

12. Ivar Oxaal, Michael Pollak and Gerhard Botz, eds., *Jews, Antisemitism, and Culture in Vienna* (London: Routledge & Kegan Paul, 1987).

13. Harriet Pass Freidenreich, *Jewish Politics in Vienna, 1918-1938* [The Modern Jewish Experience] (Bloomington: Indiana University Press, 1991).

14. Bruce F. Pauley, *From Prejudice to Persecution: A History of Austrian Anti-Semitism* (Chapel Hill: University of North Carolina Press 1992).

Hans Dachs, Peter Gerlich et al., eds., *Handbuch des politischen Systems Österreichs* (Vienna: Manz, 1991).

Melanie Sully

This lengthy compendium contains important information of the mechanics of the Austrian political system. Divided into several major sections, it begins with an historical survey offering a short "bird's eye" view. This is followed by an examination of constitutional aspects of the political system, including the functioning of the cabinet, courts and central audit authority. The nuts and bolts of these institutions are, for the most part, clinically and precisely presented.

The next section is devoted to political parties and movements. The Communist Party (KPÖ), traditionally one of the most ardently Stalinist in western Europe, receives more space than seems warranted given its weakness in Austria. The emphasis could have been better placed on the predicament of the KPÖ since the collapse of Communism. The 1991 conference, mentioned at the end, could have been more central. The aim of the book is to concentrate on the period since the late 1970s. Many of the authors quite reasonably start with an historical introduction which leaves little space at the end for exploring more topical themes.

The chapter on the Socialist Party provides useful material but stops short of analyzing the present dilemma of the party. A major reform is supposed to be in progress but, as the book points out, it has in effect been shelved for a two year period. The essay fails to tackle many questions. What are the brakes on reform in the party? What's left of the Left? Where is a discussion of the *bête noir* Bruno Aigner, the former "perestroika" group or the "infected pus boils of a flabby party" (Aigner)?

The People's Party is in a similar mess, and the relevant chapter alludes to organization reforms put through in 1991. Here, some graphics would have helped. One of these reforms set up so-called specialized committees similar to "think tanks." Their job and chances of success could have been critically assessed. The essay on the ÖVP fails to convey the "doomsday" mentality that obsesses a party fighting for survival as one of the big names in Austrian politics. More could have been provided on the reform discussion that took place after the 1990 defeat. There are many documents on this forum which was conducted by expert consultants under Professor Malik. Was this a valuable exercise for the party? Could it have helped reverse the party's decline? In the light of recent developments it seems that a further fragmentation of the "bourgeois" *Lager* can be expected.

The chapters on the FPÖ and right wing extremism for the most part present little new material. The fascination in Austria with the "Haider effect" does not come across, and the book went to press before the current spate of neo-Nazi activities. This clearly was bad luck rather than an omission.

Other sections offer an obligatory account of the workings of the social and economic partnership system. The chapter on the Chamber of Labor fails to deal with such scandals as the notorious Rechberger affair which put the chamber in a bad light. Also it would have been interesting to see if Austrians consider their "model" suitable for export to the former Eastern bloc countries. This is not pursued. The remaining sections deal with specific aspects of government policy, foreign affairs and federalism. Despite a chapter on schools and educational reform, the ambitious plans to transform university education receive little attention.

Generally the chapters do not make for compulsive reading, but that obviously was not the aim of the tome. The authors are professional in their approach. There is no mention in the thin index of the word "scandal" let alone the Lucona or Noricum affairs. Students will find the book indispensable for exams and useful as a reference text. It is a worthy successor to the earlier standard book, edited by Heinz Fischer, *Das Politische System Österreichs*. Fischer himself is one of the contributors to this volume, with a chapter on the Austrian parliament. There are few people better placed to take on this task. Twice floor leader and now President in the National Assembly, Fischer has a wealth of experience in the parliamentary arena. He of the few intellectuals in politics. It would have been interesting to have learned about his novel plans to modernize parliament and to make it more "people friendly." Fischer pioneered the innovative "open day" project and opened the doors of parliament to hundreds of inquisitive Austrians. This project's success speaks against the supposed disillusionment with politics. People do want to know more about politics, politicians and their parliament. Politics need not be an abstract process remote from people's lives. This angle could have been featured more prominently in the book as a whole.

Anton Pelinka and Fritz Plasser, eds., *The Austrian Party System* (Boulder-San Francisco-London: Westview Press, 1989).

Max Riedlsperger

The Austrian Party System is edited by two of Austria's most prominent political researchers, and its list of contributors reads like a *Who's Who* of their colleagues. When the original, 800-page German-language version appeared early in 1988, it was received as the definitive compendium of materials on contemporary Austrian politics. That this American edition cannot be so described is not a criticism of the work contained in it, but rather a comment on the extraordinary change that has taken place in and around Austria since its chapters were written.

Within Austria, the reason for this change is the definitive breakdown of the *Lager*, or political camps. In their introductory chapter, "Compared to What?", co-editors Pelinka and Plasser use *Lager* theory (Wandruszka, 1954) to explain the remarkable political concentration and stability of the Austrian political structure. Incorporating this thinking with the compatible concept of *consociational democracy* (Lipjhart, et al.) they then discuss the political culture of the Second Republic, a culture structured by the parties that had emerged as the political embodiments of the three vertically integrated and mutually hostile "camps" created by the social, economic, religious and national cleavages of the nineteenth century. In 1945 however, in marked contrast to the civil war atmosphere between the camps in the inter-war period, the Socialist Party (SPÖ) and the Peoples Party (ÖVP) resolved to cooperate to construct a new, at least structurally democratic, Second Republic. In successive ÖVP-led coalitions that continued until 1966, the two major parties created what has come to be known as a *consociational democracy*. The parties still used ideological and class-based politics to appeal to their followers within the vertically integrated "pillars" while engaging in "social partnership" among the elites in government, the bureaucracy and nationalized industry. The third, national-liberal camp mobilized a heterogeneous political movement beginning in 1949 that settled out as the Freedom Party (FPÖ) in 1956. It was, however, frozen out of any governmental involvement by the major parties, which reviled it for its insistence that Austrians were part of the "German ethnic and cultural community" and for the Nazi past of many of its leaders. In sum then, the party structure had come to replicate that of the German half of the Monarchy and the First Republic. The difference was that the two major parties first cooperated in government and then ruled alone, while the tiny FPÖ hoped to recover the role that its predecessor parties had played as the "balance on the scale" between the two, but in freely voting parliament unbound by rigid coalition pacts.

This "limping two-party system" that prevailed until 1983 was the basis for the stability of the Austrian political system.

The extraordinarily high concentration of party membership and voter participation are emphasized as characteristic of the Austrian party system throughout the book. Unfortunately for its durability, at the time the contributors were writing their chapters, the break-up of the traditional *Lager* was beginning to permit the emergence of a three- or even four-party system; it was also causing a decline in party membership and voter participation. Though some of the authors inserted caveats that change was in the wind, this process was not sufficiently developed for them to fully appreciate its extent.

In the political transformation of recent years, the FPÖ has emerged as the second largest party in the parliaments of Carinthia and Vienna; Green and Alternative lists are drawing more support than did the FPÖ until 1986; and in the presidential elections of 1992, non-voters became the biggest "party" in Vienna. All this has caused some to speak of the birth of a "Third Republic" and has dated much of the content of this book. For example, the electorates of the SPÖ, ÖVP and FPÖ, which had been stable for decades before the base years 1982/1983 used by Gehmacher and Haerpfer for their chapter, have undergone substantial change. Even Ulram's attempt in "Changing Issues" to anticipate the future course of Austrian politics has been outrun by events that have substituted anxiety about the consequences of the breakup of eastern Europe and the Yugoslav civil war for the "new" concerns about the social-welfare state, the environment and growing disillusionment with government that he identified. Because Sully adopted a historical approach for her study of the softening of electoral support for the major parties, her chapter has not been outmoded by the rapid change that has compromised other chapters. Moreover, a new section added for the American edition permits her to speculate on trends set in motion by the reestablishment of the Grand Coalition after a twenty year absence. Gerlach's analysis of "National Consciousness and National Identity" is one of the most interesting chapters in the book, but it deals only minimally with political behavior and not at all with the party system. Here also, new issues such as Austria's potential admission into the EC, German unification, the end of the Cold War and changing views on Austria's neutrality pose momentous questions affecting Austria's self-image that Gerlach could not have anticipated when the chapter was written. Nick draws much-needed attention to the conflict between the long-standing historic identities of most of the states and the strong control exercised by Vienna, a conflict that was enhanced by the high degree of political concentration that prevailed until recently. In this edition he has added a brief discussion of the unbroken string of FPÖ state elections successes since 1986 that now contradicts his observation about extreme continuities at the outset. Müller's groundbreaking essay is an excellent exposition of the range of patronage possibilities in the Austrian party system. Space does not permit a discussion of the remaining chapters.

Overall, this volume is a collection of mostly excellent, even if outdated, essays which unfortunately overlap in many places and which do not collectively provide a cohesive presentation of the topic. The book is highly specialized; contrary to the editors' hopes of making their subject matter "accessible to an international reading public," it will be read primarily by those who can read it or already have read it in German. The title promises a study of the Austrian party system, but only Herbert Dachs' excellent chapter on "Green-Alternative Parties" and the Gehmacher/Haerpfer chapter on the internal structure of the SPÖ, the ÖVP and the FPÖ electorates are at all party-specific. Indeed, the preponderance of the book is devoted to an analysis of voter behavior. Finally, the translation is poor. A literal rendering of German terms leads to awkwardness and sometimes confusion; e.g *Spannungsfeld* (p. 1 and throughout) is literally translated as "field of tension" rather than cleavage; *Bewältigung* becomes the non-existent noun "overcoming" (p. 12); *Landbund* is translated as the totally unrecognizable "Country Party" (p. 3) rather than the usual Agrarian League; *Kritik* (p. 30) is translated as criticism rather than critique or analysis; "*mobile Wähler*," for some strange reason is converted to "flexible voters" who are "solicited" rather than recruited (p. 31), and so it goes.

In the interest of reducing the size of the German original by almost half, the very useful bibliography has been omitted. On the other hand, most of the chapters have excellent bibliographies of their own. Likewise, the appendix documenting federal, state and corporative body elections has been reduced to tables on national parliamentary and federal presidential elections, the 1978 anti-nuclear energy referendum and a list of petitions for parliamentary decisions. The paperback format of the book seems designed to make it accessible for university classes in comparative politics, but students will certainly need guidance in using it, not only because of the clumsy translation, but also because of the sophistication of the analyses presented. Nevertheless, despite all of these problems *The Austrian Party System* is one of the very few books in English where the reader can sample the range of contemporary Austrian political research. It is a valuable contribution to the literature.

Thomas O. Schlesinger, *The United States and the European Neutrals* (Vienna: Braumüller, 1991).

Paul Luif

Thomas O. Schlesinger, one of the few American experts on European neutrality, wrote a classic study on Austrian neutrality in the early 1970s.[1] His new book explores American policy toward the European neutrals at a time of enormous change in Europe's political landscape and examines how the transformation has shaped the foreign policy of the neutrals. Beginning with reflections on American foreign policy, Schlesinger summarizes aspects of American ideology that are relevant to external affairs. He discusses nine themes, among them rationalism, secularism, universalism and the "anti-communist reflex." He analyzes the character of American policy toward the neutrals, the commonalities in American foreign policy toward these states and the implications of neutrality in Europe for American foreign policy in the future.

The countries he considers are Switzerland, Ireland, Finland, Sweden, Yugoslavia and Austria. The inclusion of Yugoslavia is justified because "[n]eutrality is shifting from legal to political ground, and that inevitably removes the distinction between neutrality and nonalignment"(p.118). Since he does not write from a legal perspective, he can count Yugoslavia among the neutrals, although a close analysis of the foreign policy of (former) Yugoslavia would show quite significant differences compared with the "classical neutrals."[2]

Schlesinger is not attempting an in-depth analysis of the foreign policies of the neutrals. He himself admits that the essays on the neutrals highlight only certain themes that have characterized American relations with these states. He succeeds in presenting the important aspects of the U.S.-neutrals relations with one glaring exception: conflicts with the United States on the transfer of high technology to Eastern Europe. These conflicts had important repercussions on the neutrals in the late 1940s and early 1950s as well as at the height of the "second Cold War" in the 1980s.

These episodes reveal the problems of the neutrals and the concept of neutrality in the second half of the 20th century. Schlesinger briefly mentions the Coordinating Committee for Multilateral Exports (COCOM) with regard to Switzerland and Austria but makes no use of the existing literature.[3] The author also fails to take advantage of the existing publications on the conflict between the United States and Sweden concerning the war in Vietnam. Using the *New York Times* as the only source on this topic is simply not sufficient.

The book—like all publications—contains some oversights and mistakes which should have been avoided. I will try to correct here some of the more important errors. On page 39, Schlesinger writes about the "enshrining of [Swiss] neutrality in the constitution." Neutrality is mentioned in the Swiss constitution, but only in the articles which deal with the powers of the federal organs. It is *not* referred to as a basic principle of the constitution. In March 1986, the Swiss rejected UN membership in a referendum not because "there was not a sufficient majority among the cantons for ratification" (p. 44). Instead, a large majority (75.7 percent) of the popular vote and *all* cantons rejected UN membership.

Britain, Ireland and Denmark joined the EC in 1973, not in 1969 (pp. 57, 92). The Single European Act (SEA) came into force on 1 July 1987 and was fully effective by that date, after the Irish voted for its ratification in May 1987. It is wrong to state that the SEA will "become fully effective in 1992" (p. 57).

Concerning Finland, the 1948 Treaty on Friendship, Cooperation and Mutual Assistance with the Soviet Union stated in its preamble the Finnish desire to stay outside the conflicts of the great powers. Schlesinger wrongly attributes the basis of Finland's neutrality to the Finnish Peace Treaty (p. 67). According to Schlesinger, "Finlandization" seems to be an American invention (p. 67). In other publications, Austrian Foreign Minister Gruber usually is "credited" with the discovery of this notion.[4] In 1955, the Soviet Union unilaterally withdrew from the Porkkala naval base (near Helsinki) and not from the Hanko base (p. 69). To state that "Prime Minister Palme resigned in September 1976 for primarily domestic political reasons" (p. 93) when he actually lost an election and had to resign is quite an understatement.

On page 130, Schlesinger asserts correctly that neutrality "is not mentioned in the Austrian State Treaty." But on the next page he writes about the Swiss model for Austrian neutrality "prescribed by the State Treaty." It is not Article 17 but Article 13 of the State Treaty that imposed a ban on missiles and rockets (p.132). South Tyrol is not *part* of the "Alto Adige region" in Italy but Alto Adige *is* the Italian name of the province South Tyrol (p.136).

The longest account of the U.S. neutrals relations is on Austria's relationship with the United States. Schlesinger explains comprehensively the problems with President Waldheim. He rightly states that direct U.S. economic influence in Austria would decrease as Vienna comes closer to the EC. According to him, the essence of Austrian neutrality lies in the relationship with Germany (p.142). The EC connection should reduce unilateral German influence (p.148). This reasoning—up to now not really made in the Austrian EC discussion—could actually be used as an argument for EC membership and the simultaneous reduction or even abandonment of neutrality.

In the concluding chapter, Schlesinger states what seems to be the underlying reason for publishing this book: the "United States should adopt policies toward neutral states that amount to respect and support equal in effect to that accorded valued allies" (p.177). But, as he admits in the final paragraph, as long as the United States remain a major power, neutrality as a foreign policy of European states will continue to be merely tolerated, and not specially appreciated (p.186). The rapid changes in international relations, especially in Europe, have brought—besides a dismemberment of Yugoslavia—an intensive discussion on the uses of neutrality. It seems that all neutrals are ready to abandon neutrality in the long run if an alternative security policy develops in Europe (be it inside the European Community or some other organization). Then the underlying reality of the up-to-now pertinent questions Schlesinger poses in his book will have disappeared.

In a postscript I have to add a word on the sloppy editing and setting of the book. On several occasions the text states "emphasis added" where no emphasis has been added (e.g., p. 58). Footnotes are usually on the same page, but sometimes on the following page. A footnote on the violations of Swedish territorial waters by Soviet submarines during the Gorbachev regime refers to articles in the *New York Times* from October 1965. The Coordinating Committee (see above) is abbreviated CoCom (p. 42) and COCOM (p. 147). The name of the Swedish scholar Sverker Åström is first written correctly but in the next line "Aström" (p. 84), later his name is "Astrom" (p. 101). Nobody is perfect—but at least some of these (and other) mistakes should have been avoided.

NOTES:

1. Thomas O. Schlesinger, *Austrian Neutrality in Postwar Europe: The Domestic Roots of a Foreign Policy* (Vienna-Stuttgart: Braumüller, 1972).

2. See e.g. the differences in the voting behavior of the neutrals and the nonaligned in the United Nations; Paul Luif, "Neutrality and External Relations: The Case of Austria," *Cooperation and Conflict* 21 (1986): 25-41.

3. See e.g. Jürg Martin Gabriel, "Das amerikanische Exportkontroll-System," *Aussenwirtschaft* 44 (1989): 59-74; Paul Luif, "Strategic Embargoes and European Neutrals: The Cases of Austria and Sweden," in *Challenges and Responses in European Security. TAPRI Yearbook 1986*, Vilho Harle, ed. (Aldershot: Avebury, 1987), 174-188; André Schaller, *Schweizer Neutralität im West-Ost-Handel. Das Hotz-Linder-Agreement vom 23. Juli 1951*, (Bern-Stuttgart: Verlag Paul Haupt, 1987); Jan Stankovsky, Hendrik Roodbeen, "Export Controls Outside COCOM," in *After the Revolutions. East-West Trade and Technology Transfer in the 1990s*, Gary K. Bertsch, Heinrich Vogel and Jan Zielonka, eds. (Boulder-San Francisco-Oxford: Westview Press, 1991), 71-91.

4. See George Maude, "The Further Shores of Finlandization," *Cooperation and Conflict* 17 (1982): 3-16.

Gerald Stourzh, *Vom Reich zur Republik: Studien zum Österreichbewußtsein im 20. Jahrhundert* (Vienna: Edition Atelier, 1990).

Michael P. Steinberg

This short essay collection on Austrian perceptions of Austrian identity from 1867 to the present offers a curious amalgam of blindness and insight. The insight combines with generosity, as Professor Stourzh traces the discussions of Austrian identity from a decidedly *kleinösterreichisch* perspective, eschewing any nationalist posturing and hastening to compare the Austrian republic with the multilingual state and society of Switzerland. But the same comparison betrays the book's blindness, as the Swissification of Austria is designed to perpetuate the myth of Austrian innocence in the twentieth century.

In 1859, Joseph von Eötvös wrote in *Die Garantien der Macht und Einheit Österreichs* that "Austria is to be seen as the product of history" (50). In the five short chapters that make this book, Professor Stourzh makes the same allowance. He begins with a discussion of the Austrian nation and state after 1867; he continues with a survey of the historical foundations of the Second Republic and with an account of the "Swiss model" for Austrian national and state self-constitution. Thus, Austria is seen as a product of its more standard historiography. The historiography that Professor Stourzh chooses to analyze emphasizes the multicultural empire of 1867-1918 and the possibility of national and self-fashioning on the Swiss model after 1918. Although a certain mini-federalism à la suisse may be a relevant category for official political discourse in the Second Republic, it is entirely irrelevant for the period 1919-45, and irrelevant to sub-official discourses of Austrian identity even after 1955. We do not learn about the post-1918 conservative Catholic drive to redefine Austrian identity in its clerical and sacrilizing image, and the *Anschluß* and National Socialist period is passed over hastily. The current, ongoing crisis of Austrian identity resulting from the suppressed memory of the period 1938-45 is avoided completely. The revisitations of xenophobia and anti-Semitism in the post-Kreisky Second Republic are sidestepped. Waldheim is not mentioned once. Jörg Haider is mentioned once, with a citation about Austrian identity being state-centered that makes him sound quite civilized.

On the same page that holds the quotation from Joseph von Eötvös, Professor Stourzh attempts to dispel the kind of Luddite criticism he thinks he may receive from readers who will persist in recalling Austrian collaboration with National Socialism. He speaks of the "new wave of fashion" (*die neue Modewelle*) which he describes according to the phrase "the Austrians were (almost) all for the *Anschluß*, Nazis', etc." In a long corresponding footnote, Professor Stourzh argues for the invalidation of the famous 99 percent pro-*Anschluß* figure in the plebiscite of 10 April 1938. The reason: 150,000 Jews and gypsies (8 percent of the previously enfranchised population) didn't vote! The standard argument for the invalidation of the plebiscite is, of course, the assumption of widespread coercion. In replacing that argument with a far less plausible one, Professor Stourzh does much to revalidate the raw evidence of the numbers.

The new wave of historical fashion that must indeed be greeted with alarm is the revisionist one which Nolte and Hillgruber have championed in Germany in the *Historikerstreit* which the Moscow Protocols made unnecessary in Austria, at least until Waldheim. Beyond state affiliation, the ideology of Austrian identity has been a crucible of exclusion. There are a number of Austrian historians who have recognized this. One thinks of the late Friedrich Heer, who in 1981 published an earnest and penetrating book called *Der Kampf um die österreichische Identität*. For Heer, "Austrian identity" was an ideology in demand of transcendence.

One of the most productive contributions of the so-called "new cultural history" is the critical and differentiating perspective it has brought to the history of identities. Its tendency to focus on historical "outsiders"—to cite the title of Hans Mayer's book on nineteenth-century German women, homosexuals, and Jews—may sometimes show signs of routinized intellectual fashion. Nevertheless, in its intellectually most powerful manifestations, such scholarship succeeds in transcending the historiographical repetition of historical exclusionism. Austrian historiography, in Austria and in America, has by and large failed to address this challenge. Much work is to be done, if the modern history of Austria is to have continued value for scholars and students.

The persistent debate over "Austrianness" necessarily focuses on the tragedy of the former Yugoslavia and the waves of refugees it presses on Austria. This situation postdates the book in question, but intensifies its problematic. The potential acuity of the Austrian immigration question certainly approximates that of the ethnic and racialist tension which has already caused intolerable violence in Germany. In a recent article in the *New York Times* (18 November 1992; 4) entitled "Once More, Turbulence for Austrians," and subtitled "Coping with bigots and many refugees," Craig R. Whitney shows how the problem is represented by two different logics. The first logic, that of Chancellor Vranitzky, is the logic of numbers. Whitney writes, "The Chancellor said the refugee problem was far beyond Austria's ability to solve alone." This direct argument is an unpleasant but perhaps a necessary corrective to what must be called the romance of asylum, wherein the welcoming West tacitly colluded with the closed borders of the East. The second logic, loudly deployed by Jörg Haider and his Austrian Freedom Party, is the logic of cultural hatred. Honed on anti-Semitism, this logic is now redeployed to identify southeastern Europeans as "foreigners." "Foreign," now as before, means racially and culturally other, inferior. Political discourse in Austria as in Germany is in desperate need of distinguishing between these two logics. Historians must help, and the first thing they need do is dispense with the ideologies and illusions of exclusionary cultural identity.

Survey of Austrian Politics 1992

Rainer Nick and Sieghard Viertler

The Federal Presidential Elections

The Federal Presidential Elections of 26 April and the runoff ballot of 24 May, respectively, constituted the only nationwide elections in Austria in 1992. These two ballots have documented, for the time being, the climax of a development during which the Austrian electorate has become more and more mobile at an ever increasing pace. Phenomena frequently recognized in recent years—that is, the opening up of traditional milieus, the weakening of party loyalties which, in this intensity, are typically Austrian, an increasing media orientation of the election campaigns, and the like—have, in terms of Austrian conditions, reached a new and hitherto unknown dynamic state.

The actual prelude to the 1992 Federal Presidential Elections was marked by the decision of Kurt Waldheim, federal president at the time, not to run for office again. Contrary to the traditional candidate behavior of Austria's federal presidents, Waldheim declared in a 21 June 1991 television broadcast that he would not campaign for the presidency again because "he wanted to spare Austria any further polarization." Due to his connection with Austria's more recent history and the subsequent "Watch List" decision, Waldheim had become controversial in Austria and relatively isolated internationally.

His renunciation of a further candidacy later led to massive efforts by the two big parties, the SPÖ and ÖVP, to agree on a common candidate. The decisive reason for this was the parties' mutual wish to prevent a renewed heating up of the political climate, as had happened during the 1986 federal presidential elections. After these efforts had definitively failed, four candidates were nominated, one by each of the four parties represented in the Austrian National Council.

According to the expressed wish of Franz Vranitzky, party chairman of the Austrian Social-Democratic party (SPÖ) and federal chancellor, the SPÖ nominated Rudolf Streicher, then minister for Transport and Traffic, as their candidate. At that point Streicher was—because of his international commitment in the question of Austria's problems with truck transit traffic—considered Austria's second most popular politician after Vranitzky and, according to all estimates, the clear favorite for the office. The aim of the SPÖ was to keep Rudolf Streicher as long as possible in his ministerial position in order to utilize all advantages of presenting his achievements.

The Austrian People's party (ÖVP) decided in favor of Thomas Klestil, the secretary-general of the Foreign Office, who at this point was totally unknown. As with the SPÖ, the candidacy was the explicit wish of party chairman Erhard Busek: Klestil was Busek's candidate. Still, in the course of his campaign, Klestil regarded and presented himself not as a party candidate, but instead made conscious efforts to establish himself as an independent counterpole to Austria's parties.

The Austrian Freedom party (FPÖ) nominated a female candidate for the federal presidency, the third president of the National Council, Heide Schmidt.

With the nomination of Robert Jungk, a scientist in the field of peace and conflict research, the Green Alternative party wanted to give a clearly visible signal to counter the increasing influence of right-wing tendencies in the Austrian political climate.

From the beginning, the nomination of four candidates meant that a second ballot would most likely be necessary, since a candidate needs to reach the absolute majority of all votes to be elected federal president. However, while there was a general certainty that Rudolf Streicher would be one of the two candidates in the expected runoff ballot, some commentators on Austrian domestic policy were doubtful whether the initially unknown diplomat Thomas Klestil would really be able to surpass the popular Heide Schmidt.

In the beginning, several demoscopic surveys confirmed these assumptions. While Rudolf Streicher was always placed near the 40 percent mark, for some time Klestil and Schmidt were leading a relatively close race. Schmidt's campaign lost a great deal of its impetus when for a short time FPÖ chairman Jörg Haider withdrew his support from her because she had criticized Andreas Mölzer, the FPÖ spokesman for political ideology (discussed below). Haider considered Schmidt's criticism of Mölzer unacceptable. Haider had personally selected Mölzer for the latter's office, and thus refused to give Schmidt, the FPÖ candidate for the office of federal president, any further support in her campaign until the controversy was settled in a talk between himself and Schmidt.

In general, differences played a subordinate role in the campaign. For instance, except for Robert Jungk all candidates were for Austrian membership in the EC; on other issues (neutrality, security, the contact of politicians to the citizens) the candidates' opinions—with the exception of Robert Jungk, who never had a chance—differed only marginally in most cases. The campaign—led fairly in all stages—was rather a competition regarding the image and role of the future Austrian federal president.

Thus, the competition between the candidates went hand in hand with a discussion of the four individuals as to their understanding of the principles that should govern the presidential office. While Rudolf Streicher's personal definition of the president's role was rather one of a supreme ombudsman for all Austrians, Klestil argued that the role of the president should rather be one of a party-independent, supreme Austrian ambassador in foreign countries representing Austria on an international basis.

In contrast to former Austrian presidential campaigns, the 1992 campaign noticeably shifted in the direction of local and electronic media. Thomas Klestil's campaign was even readjusted in this direction while already in progress: his campaign increasingly stressed "the dialogue with the people," which meant that in the course of numerous organized discussions, he established contact with different citizens in the presence of media representatives and thus presented a credible image of his commitment to solving the Austrians' problems. The initial climax of the campaign was the first TV confrontation—broadcast during television prime time—in which all four top candidates participated.

In the course of his media-oriented self-presentation during the campaign, Thomas Klestil managed to gain ground on Rudolf Streicher because the Austrians' expectations of a future president's role shifted more and more in the direction of Klestil's "first ambassador of Austria in foreign countries." Additionally, Klestil was, in contrast to Streicher, increasingly better able to projecting his absolute will to win via the medium of television. Still, it was surprising that after the first ballot Streicher's lead over Klestil had dwindled to a mere 3.5 percent. While the SPÖ candidate was able to reach 40.7 percent of all votes, contrary to all forecasts, 37.2 percent of all voters balloted for the "newcomer" Klestil. Schmidt reached 16.4 percent and Robert Jungk 5.7 percent. Although in absolute terms, Klestil placed only second in the first ballot, he was—

because the result ran contrary to all expectations—considered the real winner by the media and the public.

During the time before the runoff ballot, Klestil profited more and more from a noticeable bandwagon effect: he reinforced his messages (international contacts, independence from the parties, counterpole to the power of the parties) and to a large extent managed to direct the topic of the future president's role along the line he had advocated from the beginning of the campaign. As a countermove, there were massive attempts on the part of the SPÖ to support Streicher by mobilizing its party apparatus, which, however, followed a mostly traditional organizational logic. Nevertheless, Streicher was pushed onto the defensive by Klestil, who was acting in a modern and media-oriented way. Klestil started to score more and more among the FPÖ voters, who had in the first ballot voted for their candidate, Heide Schmidt, and now had to decide in favor of either Streicher or Klestil.

The landslide victory from 24 May documents the rapid changes in the Austrian electoral landscape: Thomas Klestil, a candidate acting according to the principles of contemporary media-campaigning, presenting the image of a modern and credible, as well as party-independent candidate, was able to score the best result ever reached by a candidate for the federal presidency in Austria. Klestil won almost 57 percent of all votes, whereas Streicher had already in the first ballot reached the maximum of his potential and could only increase the number of his votes by a mere 2.5 percent. On election day, the extremely close race, predicted by many media representatives and the party headquarters, had changed into a totally surprising 15 percent lead for Thomas Klestil.

The significance of Klestil's lead becomes even clearer when analyzed in detail: he was the first candidate ever to win an absolute majority in all states, including "red" Vienna, which had been considered out of reach for ÖVP candidates. Post-election analyses document that Klestil was able to draw on the support of dynamic voters, who have assumed the central function of being opinion leaders. Streicher, on the other hand, was hardly able to attract voters outside of the traditional SPÖ clientele.

While the SPÖ candidate seemed to be lacking energy in the final phase of the campaign, within half a year Klestil managed to rise from an unknown, seemingly reserved newcomer to a likable "I want" candidate, who—most importantly—was able to utilize the power of television. Thus Klestil opened up a new chapter in the history of the Austrian electorate, which has become more flexible and mobile.

The Restructuring of the Government

Presidential candidate Rudolf Streicher left the government at the end of March, and Federal Chancellor Franz Vranitzky used this occasion to appoint two more new people to governmental posts. The responsibilities of Rudolf Streicher, until then minister for Traffic and the Nationalized Industries, were taken over by Viktor Klima, who up to this point had been a member of the board of directors of the ÖMV (Austrian Mineral Oil Agency). In the field of public health, Minister Harald Ettl was replaced by 35-year-old physician Michael Ausserwinkler, the vice-mayor of Klagenfurt. Harald Ettl returned to his previous position as labor union chairman of the union section "Textiles, clothes and leather." The Viennese SPÖ party functionary Brigitte Ederer became the new undersecretary of state for European questions in the federal chancellory. Her predecessor, Peter Jankowitsch, assumed the function of foreign policy speaker of the SPÖ faction in parliament.

These personnel decisions, which were the sole responsibility of Federal Chancellor Vranitzky, were the expression of a recruitment strategy for political top functionaries oriented toward personality and media efficiency.

On 12 November a further change in the federal government took place: after the death of the vice-mayor of Graz, the ÖVP minister for the Environment, Family and Youth, Ruth-Feldgrill-Zankel, returned to the local politics of Graz. She became the new chairwoman of the People's party in her hometown. Her successor in the ministry was Maria Rauch-Kallat, a 43-year-old municipal councilor in Vienna, who had only weeks before run in vain for chairwoman of the People's party in Vienna.

The "Issue of Foreigners" in Austria

In the course of last year, the question of foreigners in Austria—made for the first time a grand issue in the course of the 1991 municipal council elections in Vienna—increasingly became a focal point of discussions in domestic politics. Decisive reasons for the increased relevance of this complex issue, or rather interrelated issues, included the wave of refugees from former Yugoslavia, as well as the upsurge of right-wing radicalism against foreigners in the Federal Republic of Germany. The sensitivity of the public with regard to the immigration movements led to a more restrictive immigration policy. A first sign of this development was that the definition of a "refugee" was drawn more narrowly by distinguishing between economic refugees and "real refugees." Austria's political representatives reacted with a series of new laws to establish a legal basis with respect to asylum seekers and immigration to provide a controlled and guided access to Austria.

The Asylum Law

The new asylum law was passed on 1 June 1992 and is meant to stop misuses of the law pertaining to asylum seekers as well as to speed up the legal procedures involved. For that purpose a separate Federal Agency for Asylum Questions was created as a direct contact agency with branches in the individual states. Decisive innovations include the following provisions:

- ✦ The asylum seeker has to prove his or her identity;
- ✦ The time period within which an application for asylum must be filed has been reduced to one week after the border crossing;
- ✦ Third-country clause: whoever comes to Austria from a safe country cannot apply for asylum in Austria and will be deported;
- ✦ If the application for asylum is turned down, the applicant is deported immediately. Asylum seekers whose application for asylum is rejected may not await the results of possible appellation proceedings in Austria.

The Law of Residence

The key terms of this bill—expected to come into force on 1 July 1993—concern controls and directives regarding the immigration of foreigners to Austria. In this respect, the following concrete measures are foreseen:

- ✦ An annual immigration quota will be determined, regarding both the whole federal area of Austria and the individual states;
- ✦ Residential permits for a restricted period of time will be issued;
- ✦ The requirements of industry will be taken into consideration;
- ✦ The situation regarding residential buildings and the labor market will be taken into account;
- ✦ Applications for residential permits can already be filed at Austrian embassies in the asylum seekers' home countries;
- ✦ Foreigners residing illegally in Austria will be able to apply for residential permits (however, in the original home country).

The Law Regarding Foreigners

This law, which was passed by the National Council in December, is primarily directed at foreigners who reside in Austria without a legal permit. It empowers the police to search the lodgings of foreigners suspected to be illegal residents upon the slightest suspicion. It will become easier to deport illegal residents as well as criminal foreigners. Furthermore, the law foresees arrest until deportation even for minors and severe penalties for people who are paid to smuggle foreigners into the country illegally. To better control the illegal employment of foreigners, there will be more frequent identity checks of foreign workers.

By the end of 1992 it had become clear that the individual measures—especially the asylum law—had resulted in the intended effect, since the influx of foreigners from non-EC countries had decreased considerably.

The climax of the "discussion regarding foreigners" so far has been a popular initiative started by the FPÖ under the leadership of Jörg Haider. After having overcome some intra-party resistance, Jörg Haider tried to mobilize those Austrians who demand a comprehensive immigration stop of foreigners by means of a popular initiative (support of a political cause through signatures of citizens). Even the most intensive efforts were not able to make Jörg Haider drop this act of mobilization and polarization. The announcement and execution of this FPÖ initiative led to extremely violent reactions in the public and—as a counter-reaction—to a solidarity movement against this popular initiative, comprising large groups such as the church and the other parties. For the time being, the activities of those Austrians with a more friendly attitude towards foreigners have culminated all over Austria in "human chains" formed by hundreds of thousands of people bearing torches or candles.

Conflicts within the FPÖ

The spring of 1992 was, in terms of domestic politics, overshadowed by heavy conflicts within the Austrian Freedom Party (FPÖ), which also led several high-ranking FPÖ party functionaries to leave the party or be expelled from it. The reasons for these conflicts can be seen in the fact that ever since Jörg Haider was elected chairman of the party in 1986, the FPÖ's voter potential not only had tripled (presently 15 to 20 percent) but also that this event was accompanied by a clear change of the party's political direction. Chairman Haider, extremely successful in terms of the various elections, started to restructure the party according to his own ideas and put people that he trusted into FPÖ top positions. The resulting tensions frequently led traditional FPÖ representatives who were unwilling to go along with these procedures and with the changes in political philosophy (tendency towards right-wing populism) to leave the party.

In mid-February Andreas Mölzer, head of the FPÖ's educational institution and FPÖ spokesman for political ideology, drew a great deal of attention: in a discussion regarding the immigration movement into Europe Mölzer postulated the existence of a threat of a *Umvolkung* ("re-nationalization") of the *deutsche Volks- und Kulturgemeinschaft* ("German people and the German cultural community"). The term *Umvolkung* stems from Nazi terminology and led to heated discussions regarding Austria's domestic policy. Within the FPÖ, only the deputy chairman and well-known Austrian businessman Mautner Markhof protested against these statements. He thought to detect increasing "right-wing radical tendencies" in his party and, as a consequence, Mautner Markhof, a "model liberal," left the executive committee of the party and resigned as Haider's deputy chairman. After some initial reservation, the FPÖ candidate for the federal presidency also criticized Mölzer, calling him "the wrong person for this function." This step led to the strongest tension within the FPÖ to this point, culminating in a session of the executive committee of the party. A day earlier, a much-noticed meeting had taken place in Klagenfurt between Heide Schmidt, Norbert Gugerbauer, the chairman of the FPÖ faction in parliament, and Jörg Haider.

During the session of the leading board of the party, Haider demanded either total support for his line (including Mölzer) or else the election of a new party chairman. After the session had taken a turbulent course, it ended with a number of surprises: Norbert Gugerbauer, the chairman of the FPÖ faction in parliament, resigned from all of his positions and withdrew from all political functions. Haider laid down his function as vice-governor of Carinthia and assumed the function of chairman of the FPÖ faction in parliament, thus moving to Vienna. As a reaction to this, Mautner Markhof gave up his seat in the National Council.

The next case of an FPÖ functionary leaving the party concerned the conservative president of the Carinthian Diet, Kriemhild Trattnig, who was no longer able to agree to the style of her party in terms of domestic politics. In mid-September, Friedrich Peter, the party founder of the FPÖ, left the party after Jörg Haider had decided to take the FPÖ on an anti EC course. During the whole time in office, Peter had always clearly advocated that Austria intensify its efforts to become integrated into the EC.

Changes in the Austrian States
The First Direct Elections of Mayors in Tirol and Burgenland

After the positive experiences with the direct election of mayors in Carinthia in 1991, the mayors were directly elected in March 1992 in Tirol for the first time. In the elections, the voters had the opportunity of genuine vote splitting: that is to say, a voter could vote for the mayor on one ballot sheet and for a party on another one.

The direct election of the mayors led, contrary to the general trend, to a stabilization of the high voter turnout of 80 percent. In addition, the political process was given a fresh stimulus by newly-emerging political groupings, which in many places made the stance of the established groups harder. In some communities, for instance, the number of votes for a party and those for that party's candidate for the mayor's seat differed by as much as 30 percent.

In October a similar regulation was used in Burgenland to elect municipal parliaments and mayors. The positive results of these elections have led to a discussion of whether this model should be adopted in all Austrian states. This discussion has been intensified by the great popularity of this model among the voters: already several years before the direct method of electing the mayors was adopted, scientific research in the western parts of Austria showed that approximately 80 percent of the population favored this model.

Elections in the City of Salzburg

In the beginning of October, municipal council elections took place in the city of Salzburg. With a voter turnout of only 52.2 percent, which is extremely low for Austria, these local elections resulted in a complete disaster for the SPÖ. The SPÖ lost almost half of its votes and reached only twelve of the former twenty-one seats. The winners of this election were small local groupings, such as the small party of Masopust, a city councilor who had left the FPÖ, and an automobilist party competing for the first time. Both parties won two seats each. Violent tensions within the SPÖ (the former mayor Harald Lettner wanted to become mayor despite the defeat) for the first time led to a constellation where the top ÖVP candidate Josef Dechant was able to become mayor of Salzburg even with the help of some SPÖ representatives that had split from their party. Traditionally Salzburg is considered a trendsetter for new political movements in Austria.

Lower Austria: Pröll as Successor of Ludwig as State Governor

In October Erwin Pröll (ÖVP), up to this point vice-governor and responsible councilor for state finances in the state government, succeeded Siegfried Ludwig as governor of Lower Austria. Pröll had for more than a decade been a member of the state government and was for some time considered the logical successor of Ludwig, who resigned from politics for age reasons. Erwin Pröll, who—despite his participation in the state government for a great number of years—projects the image of an energetic, reform-oriented politician, for the first time succeeded in instituting state-wide ÖVP primary elections in all twenty-one constituencies for recruiting candidates for the state elections.

Discussion about an Electoral Law with More Focus on Individual Personalities

In 1986, the parties of the Grand Coalition agreed to respond to the pronounced urgings of the population to integrate much stronger elements of personality electoral law into the existing law of electoral lists for the National Council. Since changes in electoral law directly affect central power constellations between and also within the parties, the implementation of this decision had to wait for six years.

Most importantly, the new electoral law for the National Council results in more constituencies (forty-three constituencies instead of nine) and a strengthened system of preference votes. The diminished size of the constituencies is supposed to bring about a stronger contact of most representatives with the population of their constituency.

As a consequence of the new electoral law for the National Council, some states have changed or are also changing the electoral laws for the state diets. In this case as well, smaller constituencies will bring about important changes with regard to candidate nomination and candidate selection. In three states (Carinthia, Tirol, and Burgenland) the mayors were already directly elected. This development has been changing the role of the parties and strengthening—very much following the U.S. example—the position of individual candidates. The role of the parties has also been weakened by the more and more frequent introduction of primary elections—in many cases parallel to U.S. examples. This means that the traditionally strong Austrian party organizations might lose their significance to a substantial degree and that the Austrians' tendency toward an electoral behavior focused on personalities is being continued.

Austria and Former Yugoslavia

As a direct neighbor of former Yugoslavia, Austria is in many ways especially affected by the horrendous war in the Balkan region. At the turn of 1991-1992 in Austria, as in other European countries, policy debates occurred: would a fast and far-reaching policy of recognizing the newly-created states stifle the conflicts in former Yugoslavia, or would a more restrained wait-and-see policy better accomplish this goal. The ÖVP under Foreign Minister Mock tended to support the first view, whereas the SPÖ under Federal Chancellor Vranitzky favored a more restrained policy. After other European states had recognized Slovenia and Croatia in early 1992, Austria immediately followed suit.

Due to the continuous fighting in various parts of former Yugoslavia, the wave of refugees intensified during the summer of 1992. Not least because of the Austrian population's readiness to help, was it possible to accommodate more than 50,000 refugees in the shortest possible time. In 1992, numerous activities by the Austrian government, the Caritas organization, the ORF (Austrian Broadcasting Corporation), the Red Cross, and countless private initiatives managed to raise large amounts of money and goods for the people affected by the war in former Yugoslavia. In proportion to its size, the Austrian population has given more help to the suffering people in the Balkan region than any other nation.

Austria and Europe

The question of Austria's role in a future Europe became a central theme in domestic politics. The discussion reached its peak when the EC decided to start negotiations with Austria about its entry into the EC from January 1993 onwards.

The Transit Treaty

In the western Austrian states, the problem of truck transit with the damage done by exhaust emissions and noise constitutes a highly critical issue. Attempts were made to mitigate this damage by a treaty concluded between Austria and the EC after long negotiations. The terms of the transit treaty foresee a 60 percent reduction of exhaust emissions until the year 2003 through the introduction of a so-called ecological point-system (fewer transits, vehicles with a lower level of exhaust emissions). After difficult negotiations a compromise of 1,263 million transit permits per year for EC member states made it possible for the Austrian federal government to approve of the transit treaty.

EEA (European Economic Area)

The ratification of the treaty regarding Austria's participation in a common European market within the framework of the European Economic Area led to a constitutional debate in Austria. The opposition parties have regarded a membership in the EEA as change of the Austrian constitution and therefore have demanded a plebiscite. The experts in the office for constitutional questions in the federal chancellery and government experts did, however, confirm that the treaty conforms to the constitution and advocate a ratification by the parliament. After having been passed by the Federal Council and the National Council, up to 1300 standards of EC law have to be transformed into Austrian law before the treaty can come into force. Because Switzerland has rejected the EEA treaty in a popular referendum, the point of time for the EEA to come into effect has been delayed for a few months.

EC Campaign

In view of Austria's planned membership in the EC, the Austrian federal government commissioned an advertising campaign (EC hotline, poster series, brochures, panel discussions) which was supposed to create a positive climate for the EC and, in general, arouse the public's interest in the European Community. This advertising campaign itself became the focus of political discussion and was severely criticized.

The EC Course of the FPÖ

In the course of last summer, the FPÖ changed its attitude toward Austria's EC membership. While the FPÖ had been the first Austrian party to advocate Austrian integration into a changing Europe, now Haider decided for the FPÖ to assume an anti EC course. His reasons for this change in opinion include the European Community's centralism, lack of readiness for reforms, and deficit in democratic policies. Haider's turn against his own party's tradition triggered extremely violent reactions (popular FPÖ representatives leaving the party). The majority of all political observers judged this move as one more attempt by Haider to win votes at all cost by means of populist strategies of currying favor, an attempt to utilize the widespread fear of modernization accompanying an EC membership for his movement.

SELECT BIBLIOGRAPHY

Andreas Khol, Kurt Öfner and Alfred Stirnemann, eds., *Österreichisches Jahrbuch für Politik 1991* (Vienna: Verlag für Geschichte und Politik, 1992).

Rainer Nick and Anton Pelinka, *Politische Landeskunde der Republik Österreich* (Berlin: Colloquium Verlag, 1989).

Der Standard

Die Presse

Profil

Wochenpresse

Der Österreich Bericht

Biographical Data of Bruno Kreisky

January 22, 1911	Born in Vienna, Austria as second son of Max and Irene Kreisky (née Felix).
1927-1934	Active member of the youth organization of the Social Democratic party. After the outlawing of the social Democratic party in 1934, the illegal "Revolutionary Socialist Youth" is founded under the leadership of Kreisky and Roman Felleis, then Kreisky's best friend.
1935-1936	Imprisoned because of his illegal activities.
1938	After the invasion of Austria by German troops, Kreisky is taken into protective custody and interned a second time. In September 1938 he can escape to Sweden after he has been released under order to leave the country.
1939-1945	Employee on the economic staff of the Stockholm consumer cooperative and part-time journalist.
April 23, 1942	Marries Vera Fürth. They will have two children: Peter Staffan and Suzanne Christine.
1946-1951	Appointed to represent the interests of Austria in Sweden. He is assigned to the Austrian legation in Stockholm.
1951-1953	After his return to Austria in 1951 Kreisky becomes assistant chief of staff in the President's Office and political adviser of President Theodor Körner.
1953-1959	Kreisky is undersecretary in the Foreign Affairs Department of the Austrian Chancellory.
1956-1983	Member of Parliament
1959-1966	Minister of Foreign Affairs

1967-1983   Chairman of the Socialist Party of Austria; honorary Chairman until 1987

1970-1983   Chancellor of Austria

July 29, 1990   Bruno Kreisky dies in Vienna at age 79

Publications (selection):

The Challenge: Politics on the Threshold of the Atomic Age (1963)
Aspects of Democratic Socialism (1974)
Neutrality and Co-existence (1975)
The Times We Live In: Reflections on International Politics (1978)
L'Autriche entre l'Est et l'Ouest (1979)
Between the Times: Memoirs from Five Centuries (1986)
In the Stream of Politics: Memoirs II (1988)
A Program for Full Employment in the 1990s (1989, co-author and editor)
   also speeches (Reden, Vols. I and II, 1981) and articles on international affairs

Decorations and Awards:

Gold Grand Cross of Honor, Austria
Freedom Award (1975)
Jawaharlal Nehru Award for International Understanding (1985)
Martin Luther King Jr. International Peace Award (1989)

List of Authors

Emil Brix is the Austrian consul general in Cracow (Poland) and also the managing director of the "Mitteleuropa-Zentrum Krems" (Lower Austria).

Ambassador *Franz Cede* is the director of the office of international law in the Austrian Federal Ministry for Foreign Affairs.

John Haag is an associate professor of history at the University of Georgia in Athens.

Otmar Höll is visiting professor of political science at the University of Vienna and a research fellow at the Austrian Institute for International Affairs in Laxenburg (Lower Austria).

Susan Howell is a professor of political science and currently chair of the Department of Political Science at the University of New Orleans.

Marina Fischer-Kowalski is an assistant professor heading a department for social ecology at the Institute for Interdisciplinary Research and Continuing Education (IFF) in Vienna.

Josef Leidenfrost is the director of the Foreign Relations Bureau in the Austrian Academic Exchange Service, Ministry of Science, Vienna.

Paul Luif is a research fellow at the Austrian Institute for International Affairs in Laxenburg (Lower Austria) and lectures at the University of Vienna.

Peter Malina is chief librarian at the Institute of Contemporary History at the University of Vienna.

Günter Nenning is a political writer and columnist in Vienna.

Rainer Nick is an assistant professor of political science at the University of Innsbruck.

Oliver Rathkolb is the scientific director of the Bruno Kreisky Archives in Vienna and a research fellow in the Ludwig Boltzmann Institute for History and Science at the Institute of Contemporary History at the University of Vienna.

Kurt W. Rothschild is professor emeritus of economics at the University of Linz.

Max Riedlsperger is a professor of history at the California Polytechnic State University in San Louis Obispo.

Herbert Pierre Secher is a political scientist and professor emeritus at Memphis State University in Memphis, Tennessee, and is a native of Austria who was forced to emigrate with his parents in 1939.

Michael Steinberg is an associate professor of history at Cornell University.

Melanie Sully is a visiting professor of contemporary history and political science at the University of Vienna.

Peter Ulram is the research director of the public opinion institute 'Fessel' in Vienna and lecturer in political science at the University of Vienna.

Sieghard Viertler is a political consultant in Innsbruck.